Signs & Seasons

Understanding the Elements of Classical Astronomy

being a *First Course* in CLASSICAL ASTRONOMY

Originally presented herewith in the Year

2007

of the **Incarnation** of *Our LORD and Saviour* JESUS CHRIST

as such is Commonly Reckoned

Calculated particularly for the Meridians of CHRISTIAN HOMESCHOOLERS *residing in the United States of America, but usable by persons of all* LONGITUDES AND LATITUDES, *especially such persons North of the* EQUATOR.

But surpassing all stupendous inventions, what sublimity of mind was his who dreamed of finding means to communicate his deepest thoughts to any other person, though distant by mighty intervals of space and time?
Of talking with those who are in India; of speaking to those who are not yet born for a thousand or ten thousand years; and with what facility, by the different arrangements of twenty characters upon a page!
— Galileo Galilei, from "Dialogue Concerning the Two Chief World Systems"

Of making many books there is no end; and much study is a weariness of the flesh.
— The Preacher, from Ecclesiastes 12:12

If I'da knowed what a trouble it was to make a book, I wouldn't 'a' tackled it.
— Mark Twain, from "The Adventures of Huckleberry Finn"

By **Jay Ryan**, Astron. Cart., B.C.Sch.

Published by FOURTH DAY PRESS, Cleveland, Ohio, U.S.A.

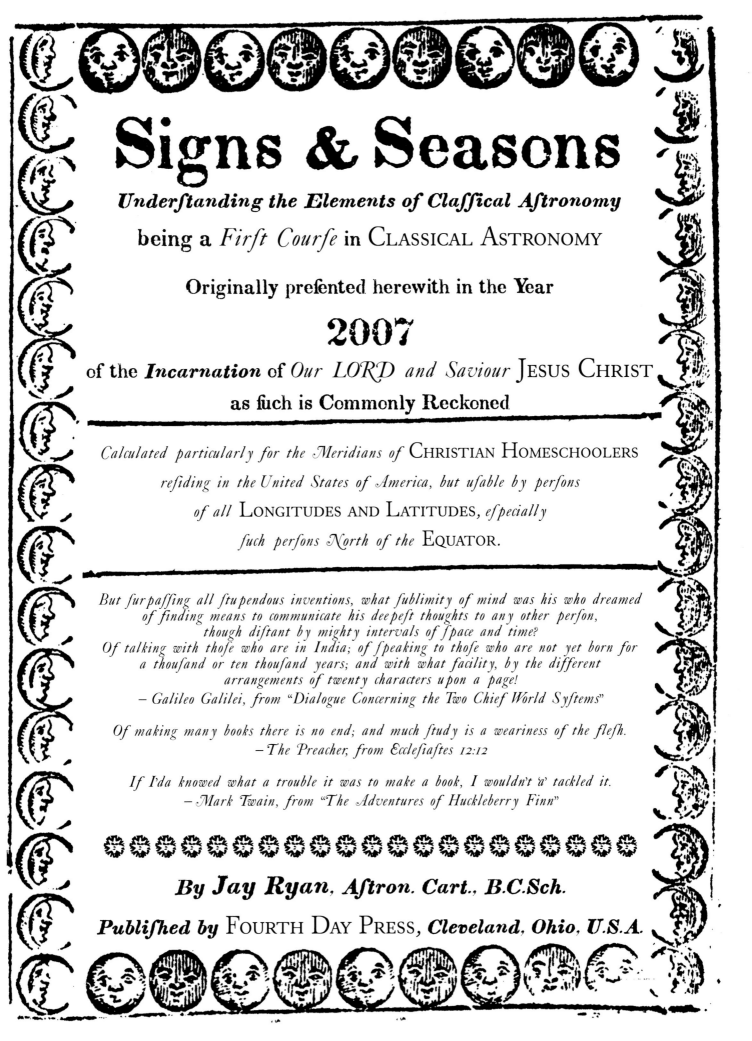

Signs & Seasons
Understanding the Elements of Claffical Aftronomy

© 2007 Jay Ryan
(Minor Revifions - © 2010 Jay Ryan)

Fourth Day Press
Cleveland, Ohio
www.ClassicalAstronomy.com

And God faid, Let there bee lights in the firmament of the heauen, to diuide the day from the night: and let them be for fignes and for feafons, and for dayes and yeeres. And let them be for lights in the firmament of the heauen, to giue light vpon the earth: and it was fo. And God made two great lights: the greater light to rule the day, and the leffer light to rule the night: he made the ftarres alfo. And God fet them in the firmament of the heauen, to giue light vpon the earth: And to rule ouer the day, and ouer the night, and to diuide the light from the darkenefs: and God faw that it was good. And the euening and the morning were the fourth day. – Genefis 1: 14-19

International Standard Book Number: 978-0-9792211-0-1
Library of Congrefs Control Number: 2006910459

✿ Frontifpiece ✿

The Frontifpiece of this book is in the ftyle of the Cover Pages of the Olde American Colonial Almanacks of the 17th and 18th centuries. The "Moone" Border is adapted from Samuel Danforth's 1647 Cambridge Almanack.

Other portions of Signs & Seafons emulate the ftyle of the Colonial Almanacks, particularly in the ufe of italics and Capital Letters to add emphafis.

𝕿𝖆𝖇𝖑𝖊 𝖔𝖋 𝕮𝖔𝖓𝖙𝖊𝖓𝖙𝖘

Introduction *vii*

Prologue   *The Sky Above*   Page 1
The Luminaries; Stars, Fixed and Wandering; Time; The Cycles of the Sun and Moon; The Calendar; The Traditions of Classical Astronomy; Modern Artificial Timekeeping

Chapter 1   *The Light He Called Day*   Page 9
Telling the Time of Day; Divisions of the Day; Dividing the Light from the Darkness; Direction and the Sky; The Horizon; Astronomical Alignments; Movements of the Sky; A Day Over Washington, D.C.

Chapter 2   *The Darkness He Called Night*   Page 29
The Bears; Orion; The Naming of the Stars; The Celestial Sphere; The Rolling of the Sphere; Always Visible, Never Visible; The Circle of the Meridian; The Celestial Equator

Chapter 3   *The Cycle of the Month*   Page 55
The Wandering Moon; Lunar Calendar; The New Moon; The Waxing Crescent; Earthshine; First Quarter; The Gibbous Moon; The Full Moon; The Rising and Setting of the Moon; The Waning Moon

Chapter 4   *The Tabernacle for the Sun*   Page 71
The Ecliptic; The Sun's Motion along the Ecliptic; Astronomy or Astrology?; The Oblique Circle of the Zodiac; Following the Zodiac; The Southern Zodiac; "Signs"; Rounding Out the Circle

Chapter 5   *The Cycle of the Year*   Page 93
The Sun's Passage through the Zodiac; March Hath XXXI Days; April Hath XXX Days; May Hath XXXI Days; June Hath XXX Days; July Hath XXXI Days; August Hath XXXI Days; Summer Heat; September Hath XXX Days; October Hath XXXI Days; Standard Time; November Hath XXX Days; December Hath XXXI Days; January Hath XXXI Days; February Hath XXVIII Days; March Again

Chapter 6 *The Seasonal Skies* Page 119

Rolling through the Seasons; The Winter Sky; The Spring Sky; The Summer Sky; The Autumn Sky; Perseus, Father of the Persians; The Winter Sky Again; The Annual Courses of the Stars; Progression of the Seasonal Skies

Chapter 7 *The Wandering Stars* Page 145

The Classical Planets; The Modern Planets; The Superior Planets; The Inferior Planets; Motions of the Inferior Planets; Motions of the Superior Planets; The Dance of the Planets; The Moon as a Classical Planet; The Seasons of the Moon's Phases

Epilogue *The Calendar* Page 167

The Lunar Calendar; The Solar Calendar; The Roman Calendar; The Julian Calendar; Passover and Easter; Easter – Pagan Origins?; Changing Customs; The Error in the Calendar; Calendar Reform; The LORD's Timekeepers Abandoned

Field Activities Page 185

Activities are provided to accompany each chapter to enable the student of the sky to make systematic observations of the Sun, Moon, stars, and planets. These field activities will assist in creating a field journal that will enable a high school student to establish work hours toward high school credit. These activities can also be used by younger students under parental supervision.

Appendix Page 227

Glossary Page 229

Biographia of Quoted Authors Page 237

Astronomical Tables Page 243

I. Finding Orion; II. Finding the Big Dipper; III. Finding the Zodiac Constellations; IV. First Magnitude Stars; V. The Constellations of Signs & Seasons; VI. Oppositions of the Superior Planets, A.D. 2005-2020; VII. Cycles of Venus, A.D. 2005-2020

Bibliography Page 251

Index Page 255

Dedicatory Preface

ALL GLORY TO GOD AND TO HIS SON CHRIST JESUS, who paints the world with matter and energy onto the four-dimensional canvas of space and time. May this humble and crude work, depicting Your magnificent celestial order, be pleasing to You, O LORD.

Dedicated to my children, David, Richard, Samuel, Veronica and Florence. May you all learn to love and appreciate the LORD's sky as I do.

Also dedicated to all the readers, young and old, who learn from this work. May the LORD richly bless your efforts to discover His starry sky.

Special thanks to my wife Debbie for her years of support, encouragement and patient long-suffering of my astronomy efforts, up to and including this book.

Special thanks also to my mother, Gail, for everything, especially for feeding my curiosity as a boy; also thanks to her sister, my Aunt Gloria, for her considerable inspiration.

Particular thanks to the following people, whose support, encouragement, and practical advice helped make this book possible: Paul and Gena Suarez, Mrs. Jeannie Fulbright, Mrs. Laurie Bluedorn and Mrs. Mary Jo Tate. Thanks also to Mr. Michael McCoy and Dr. Donald B. DeYoung.

Thanks to friends who have kindly reviewed drafts of this book and have offered their helpful opinions: Miss Helena Bluedorn; The Fulbright family; Mr. Michael P. Doherty; The Eliason family; Mrs. Debbie Piper; Mrs. Ruth Shipley; and Mr. & Mrs. Richard C. Kaiser.

Thanks to good friends who have been Wife Counselors over the years: my in-laws, Richard and Barbara Halusker; Dr. Richard J. Barker; Mr. James C. Cook; The Dawson Gang; Mr. John A. Klein; Mr. Paul M. Kubek; Mr. Kevin P. Meath; Mr. John M. Palmer IV; Dr. David R. Parsons; Mr. Lee A. Steffney; Mr. R. Scott Walker; and Mr. Joseph Zgrabik.

Thanks to Professor Owen J. Gingerich for timely encouragement in the early days.

And thanks to the many friends, too numerous to mention, who have offered support to these many-varied astronomy efforts since their beginning in the Year of Our LORD 1990.

Introduction

Astronomy is one of the most important subjects in all human history. It is said to be the oldest science. Down through the ages, many useful things have been learned from studying the sky. The starry sky figures prominently in legend and literature around the world. The Bible has much to say about the Sun, Moon, and stars. Astronomy is more important to our lives than people tend to think. The Sun is a part of astronomy, and what would life be without the Sun? How would we see anything in our world? How would the plants grow for our food? Indeed, without the Sun our world would quickly freeze and die. Clearly, astronomy is as fundamental to our existence as *day and night!*

Classical Astronomy is very different from the more familiar *Modern Astronomy*. Essentially, Classical Astronomy is the *visual observation* of the motions of the celestial bodies – the simple act of studying the cycles of the Sun, Moon, and stars with our unaided eyes. In contrast, Modern Astronomy is largely an activity of professional scientists and is based on measurements taken from telescopes and other artificial instruments. With Classical Astronomy, we can learn useful and practical skills, such as how to tell time and navigate by the sky. With Modern Astronomy, the layman is typically presented with conclusions drawn from scientific research, which don't have much connection to everyday life.

Contemporary astronomy education and popularization are devoted to Modern Astronomy. Textbooks and the media are filled with images from space probes and fancy instruments, and elaborate theories of things that no one can see. Students learn very little about *the clockwork of the heavens,* the mathematical progression of the Sun, Moon, and stars. Though the starry sky is enjoyed by small groups of amateur astronomers and planetarium enthusiasts, it is generally neglected in the classroom and rarely featured in TV shows and magazine articles. Many people look up at night wishing to understand what they see, but instead find a crowd of unknown stars.

Contemporary "Big Ball Astronomy"

Today, with the prevalence of Modern Astronomy, the very word *astronomy* calls up images of *NASA* space flights, the Hubble Space Telescope, and *PBS* programs about "black holes." Some people think astronomy has something to do with *science fiction* – "far-out" ideas about space ships and *UFOs* and bug-eyed aliens from other planets. Still others confuse the science of astronomy with the ancient superstition of *astrology* and imagine that the legitimate study of the celestial sky has something to do with magic and divination. These misconceptions are reinforced by the omissions of the educational establishment and the popular media.

Like many homeschool parents, I had a public school education, and my classrooms didn't treat the subject of astronomy very well. Most of my meager astronomy lessons were concerned with *astro-facts*, disconnected little nuggets of astronomy information such as "The Sun is a big ball of hot gas," "The Earth is 93 million miles from the Sun," and "Mars is a red planet." A typical astronomy lesson teaches how big the planets are, how many moons they have, what they are made of, etc. This is conventional *"big ball astronomy"* education – lessons about "big balls in space," handed down on the authority of mainstream science without any demonstration, observation, or methodology.

At the "advanced" level, "big ball astronomy" education teaches of exotic celestial objects such as pulsars and quasars and theories of the origin, evolution, and destiny of the universe. Conventional astronomy education is filled with topics such as *black holes, the Big Bang,* and *extrasolar planets.* Undoubtedly, most of us have had a similar experience in learning astronomy, since this is the manner in which the subject is typically mishandled in our generation.

Reclaiming Our Lost Astronomical Heritage

At one time, Classical Astronomy was understood by nearly everyone – scholars and common folk alike. Everyone knew how to tell time and find direction by the Sun, Moon, and stars. In ancient and medieval times, Classical Astronomy was recognized as part of the *Quadrivium* of sciences, along with *Geometry, Arithmetic,* and *Harmony.* The Quadrivium, along with the *Trivium* arts – *Grammar, Dialectic,* and *Rhetoric* – defined the *Seven Liberal Arts* of a classical education.

Classical Astronomy represents the *true heritage* of astronomy – a study of the celestial creation, not only for its usefulness, but also for its own natural beauty. Is there anyone who has not been amazed by a blazing sunset? Or seen a wondrous crescent moon hanging in a deep blue twilight? Or been astounded by the sight of bright, twinkling stars in a dark, rural sky? Such celestial sights truly prove that:

The heavens declare the glory of God, and the firmament sheweth his handiwork.
– Psalm 19:1

As we will see in *Signs & Seasons*, Classical Astronomy is an interesting pursuit that can add to our appreciation of the LORD's Creation. In the chapters that follow, we will learn to observe the changing appearances in the sky, from day to night and over the course of the seasons. We will follow the course of the Sun and learn how the length of daylight changes over the passing months. We will trace the path of the Moon and the progression of its phases. We will identify the principal constellations and note their motions across the sky, over the night and with the changing seasons. We will also discover the clues in the sky for finding direction, using the Sun by day and the constellations by night. Significantly, we will find that all of these things can be done with *the eyes alone*, with no special instruments.

The purpose of *Signs & Seasons* is to help the reader become an observer of the celestial bodies and to understand the clockwork of the heavens. The discovery of the sky can be a joy and a thrill. You will wonder why you never noticed these things before. Once you learn to understand the sky, you will never forget it. The sky will become part of your outdoor experience. Observing the *signs and seasons* will become part of your life and will help you appreciate God's Creation.

The Goals of "Signs & Seasons"

Signs & Seasons introduces the celestial basis for timekeeping and navigation from the Sun, Moon, and stars. The book will show that Classical Astronomy was part of the average person's knowledge base throughout history until about the mid-nineteenth century, when the LORD's celestial timekeepers were replaced by clocks and other artificial instruments.

Signs & Seasons lays a proper foundation for Classical Astronomy with a detailed study of the basic cycles of timekeeping:

THE DAY — *observing the variations of day and night*

THE MONTH — *measuring months by the phases of Moon*

THE YEAR — *understanding the signs in the sky that mark the passage of seasons*

Signs & Seasons teaches readers to identify the *stars and constellations* and to pick out the *planets* from among the stars. Since such things have not been properly taught, many people labor under the misconception that the planets are *invisible!* Very few have heard that the planets are not only very easily visible, but are among the brightest "stars" in the sky! In *Signs & Seasons,* these topics are taught *systematically,* in a way that shows the connections to everyday life. Many readers will be surprised at how many topics they had heard about but did not fully understand!

In the back of the book, a special section of *field activities* is provided for conducting extensive field observations and creating and maintaining a *field journal.* In this way, the readers will acquire skill at astronomical observation and recording results. High school students can compile the field journal to obtain high school science credit. However, these activities can be easily adapted by parents of younger children into a unit study for the whole family.

It should be noted that *Signs & Seasons* is heavily illustrated with drawings by the author. Astronomy is a *visual* subject. We can only perceive the sky with our eyes. *Signs & Seasons* uses a *visual* medium — *illustration* — to depict the *visible* appearances of the sky, to prepare readers for what they will observe in the field. While other books simply use illustration for ornamentation, the illustrations herein are a large part of the lesson.

By providing visual lessons and field instructions, *Signs & Seasons* seeks to equip readers to grasp the logic and order — the *understanding* — of the natural celestial system. Readers are exposed to a direct method of scientific observation and learn not simply to accept scientific conclusions on authority. In this way, students can learn to approach Classical Astronomy as a *concrete science* and to distinguish verifiable, repeatable scientific methodology from thin evidence and inferred conclusions, such as the "proofs" typically cited to support evolutionary theory.

A Biblical, Literary Approach to Astronomy

Unlike other astronomy books, *Signs & Seasons* is based on the Biblical purpose for which the *Sun, Moon,* and *stars* were created – *for signs and seasons, days and years* – as it is written in Genesis 1:14. *Signs & Seasons* includes extensive Bible quotes and quotations from classic authors – philosophers, poets, and historians, Christian and secular alike. Students will read the words of Augustine, Cicero, Pliny the Elder, Basil the Great, Macrobius, John Sacrobosco, and Isaac Watts. (A biographical profile of each author is provided in the Appendix.) This will emphasize that practical astronomy was widely understood and practiced in ancient and medieval times, though forgotten today in our high-tech, button-pushing generation.

Indeed, there is hardly any literature written by the ancient Greeks and Romans that did not make extensive reference to Classical Astronomy. It would be very difficult for a modern reader to fully appreciate Dante, Chaucer, Shakespeare, Donne, and Milton (or even Tolkien for that matter!) without an understanding of the clockwork of the starry sky. It is therefore hoped that the extensive quotations in *Signs & Seasons* will help promote a revival of interest in the classics and will inspire students to consult the primary sources for their knowledge.

Many of the quoted authors were men of Christian faith, and their faithful words are quoted here. But some reading this book, enamored with the conventional vanities of our generation, might find it unseemly to read words of Christian faith in a work on the science of astronomy. To that I answer that astronomy has passed through 2000 years of Christendom, and in those centuries, many writers of faith have commented on the starry discipline. One need only read the Colonial Almanacks to see scientific astronomy alongside the Christian faith of the men who founded this American nation. I would submit that one would indeed be *outside the flow of historical astronomy* to insist that a profession of Christian faith is unseemly in this context.

The subject of astronomy is often surrounded by controversy. Some Christians have bound up their understanding of astronomy with astrology, pagan influences, origins, calendar disputes, "The Gospel in the Stars," geocentrism, and flat-earth theories. However, these topics can become lengthy tangents that draw away from the main lesson. Such topics are beyond the scope of *Signs & Seasons*. Rather, we simply seek to explain traditional skycraft from Biblical and classical sources, as it was commonly known from antiquity through the early nineteenth century. Perhaps some of these topics can one day be explored in subsequent volumes, should the LORD bless us with the opportunity.

Conclusion

Excellent recommendations were given in 1900 by astronomer Asaph Hall, the famed discoverer of the moons of Mars:

> *To begin with the elementary Astronomy, it seems to me that it should be taught in the high schools and preparatory schools, as well as in the colleges. Preparatory work in it ought to be accepted for admission to college. By elementary Astronomy I mean those common, every-day facts of the science which can be learned by any intelligent student without mathematical training; for example, why the stars rise and set, the motions of the planets and the moon among the stars, the reasons for the seasons, the names of the principal constellations and why they seem to change with the seasons. These are things that are before our eyes all the time, and every one who is fairly well educated ought to know something about them.*

Over a century later, Professor Hall's advice is still unheeded. But *Signs & Seasons* takes up Professor Hall's challenge, to equip students (and their parents!) to observe and utilize the LORD'S sky. It is hoped that a series will follow *Signs & Seasons* to explore astronomical connections to geometry, geography, navigation, and the physics of the modern era. In this way, perhaps a young generation of Christian students can take up what the secular world has abandoned and reclaim the lost heritage of the LORD'S starry Creation, to the greater glory of God. I remain,

YOUR HUMBLE SERVANT,

JAY RYAN
ASTRON. CART., B.C. SCH.
CLEVELAND, OHIO, USA

Here Beginneth

Signs & Seasons

✿ Anno Domini MMVII ✿

Prologue
The Sky Above

The LORD by wisdom hath founded the earth; by understanding hath he established the heavens. — Proverbs 3:19

We all see the same sky above. The sky is blue by day and starry by night. The sky appears this way from every place on Earth. People of all nations, tribes, and cultures see the same blue sky and the same Sun, Moon, and stars. Everyone who has ever lived in all history has seen the sky in this manner. And yet most people see only blue color and a scattering of stars. They haven't been shown the *understanding* that the LORD has established above our heads.

The Sun, Moon, and stars pass silently overhead, as they have since the Creation. Concealed within their motions are the signs used to tell the time of day and the season of the year, as well as other signs that point to direction so that travelers may find their way, there and back again. We shall see that indeed, the wise Creator has concealed many useful things such as these in the sky above.

The Luminaries

And God made two great lights, the greater light to rule the day, and the lesser light to rule the night: and he made the stars also. —Genesis 1:16

In all the world, has there ever been anyone with sight that has not noticed those great Creations of the Fourth Day, the Sun and the Moon? Together, these bodies are known as the **luminaries**, the celestial bodies created to shine light upon the Earth.

—◦◦◦✳◦◦◦—

The Sun blazes forth its life-giving radiance from on high, giving light and warmth to our world. The Sun's arrival each morning awakens all creatures, signaling to them to shake off the sleep of night and begin a new day. The Sun's rays cause our food to grow, and the Sun's heat drives the winds, which bring the rains. Surely the Sun is the greatest of all the LORD's provisions, for without it we would all soon perish. Of all the things in our lives, what else can be compared to that great luminary, the Sun?

No created object makes a more wonderful or glorious display than the Sun. For, besides illuminating the world with its brightness, how admirably does it foster and invigorate all animals by its heat, and fertilize the earth by its rays, warming the seeds of grain in its lap, and thereby calling forth the verdant blade!... And the LORD, that He might claim the entire glory of these things as His own, was pleased that light should exist, and that the earth should be replenished with all kinds of herbs and fruits before He made the Sun. – John Calvin (circa A.D. 1560)

As darkness falls over the land, that lesser luminary, the Moon, can be seen. The Moon's scarred and mottled face shines feebly, with a glow weak and puny compared to the great light of the Sun. Yet the Moon's lesser light is sufficient to banish the full darkness of night. Passing through a cycle of phases from month to month, the Moon is a marvel in itself.

But the planet of the Moon, being the last of all, most familiar with the earth, and devised by Nature for the remedy of darkness, outgoes the admiration of all the rest. – Pliny the Elder (circa A.D. 50)

Sun and Moon, from "The Crucifixion" by Albrecht Dürer circa A.D. 1500

Stars, Fixed and Wandering

During the deep night, the black sky is covered with **stars**, those twinkling points of light from celestial bodies very far away. A dark, starlit sky, far from the city lights, is surely a breathtaking sight.

And he brought him forth abroad, and said, Look now toward heaven, and tell the stars, if thou be able to number them: and he said unto him, So shall thy seed be. – Genesis 15:5

Anyone can see that there are places in the night sky where stars seem to be grouped together. Long, long ago, even before history was written down in books, ancient people already recognized patterns in these groupings of stars. These groupings were named after familiar objects, people, and living creatures of the earth. These star patterns are the **constellations**.

The patterns of the constellations did not change from season to season or from year to year. It was observed that there were *fixed stars* in the night sky. But even in antiquity, at the dawn of recorded history, it was noticed that there were some "stars" that were *not* fixed, but that moved across the night sky over the span of seasons and years.

The Sky with the Comet of 1618

The ancient Greeks called these moving stars **planets** (πλανετος), which in the Greek language means "wanderers." The luminaries themselves were observed to also move against the constellations, so the Sun and Moon were also regarded as planets.

Time

Time is the agent of change which orders the progression of our lives from youth to old age. Time is observed by everyone, yet understood by no one. Time never stops, yet it permits us to measure its passage. Time passes, hour by hour, minute by minute, days passing into weeks and months into years. Our day-to-day lives are divided and regulated by these cycles of time, and our lives are marked and limited by the measures of time.

Over the centuries of human civilization, very sophisticated techniques of time measurement have been developed. In our modern world, we have precise clocks that measure time to within a billionth of a second. In a fast-paced world like ours, minutes and seconds are important. Our lives are regulated by the clock. Clocks tell us when to wake up and when to go to sleep. We make all our plans and keep all our appointments by the clock.

The "Tetragrammaton", a stylized depiction of God with the four Hebrew letters of "Yahweh," was often shown in the sky in old woodcuts and engravings.

Yet for millennia of human history, during the ages before artificial clocks, our ancestors relied on observations of the Sun, Moon and stars in order to tell time. In a simpler time, the sundial was the most accurate timekeeper available. In a slower-paced world, it was sufficient simply to find the hour of the day from the sky above.

Sun, Moon, and Tetragrammaton
From the frontispiece of the 1611 King James Bible

The Cycles of the Sun and Moon

All of our modern methods of timekeeping have their origins in the cycles of the heavenly bodies. Time has always been reckoned by changes in the periods of light and dark, variations of the Sun and the Moon in the sky above.

And God said, Let there be lights in the firmament of the heaven, to divide the day from the night: and let them be for signs and for seasons, and for days and years. – Genesis 1:14

The Sun rises each morning, crosses the sky, and passes below the horizon at the evening sunset. In this way, our lives are divided into periods of light and darkness, so that **the day** is our basic unit of telling time. This daily cycle of light and dark is perhaps the plainest fact of life on Earth. Indeed, our language is full of references to the daily cycle of the Sun: "one day at a time," "another day another dollar," and "tomorrow is another day."

From day to day, over a span of evenings, it's easy to see that the Moon follows a cycle of changing phases. The Moon is sometimes a skinny crescent and round at other times. The circle of the Moon's face increases and decreases over the span of about four weeks and a day, sometimes two. This cycle of changing phases is **the month** and is used to measure longer periods of time.

Over a period of months, the days grow longer and then shorter. The changing daylight is accompanied by changes in the weather as the air grows warmer, then colder. These changes result in the **seasons**, which follow each other in a recurring circle, returning to the same place after 365 days. The seasons result from the Sun's rolling cycle of **the year**.

These cycles of the Sun and Moon have been a constant feature of human life ever since these luminaries were created.

The three cycles of heavenly light also recur according to this number, the great, the intermediate and the small cycles. The great cycle is the annual one by the Sun, the intermediate is the monthly one by the Moon; and the small is the daily one by the rising and setting of the Sun. – Macrobius (circa A.D. 400)

The Calendar

Human lives are marked by change. People are born and live for a time on this Earth, during which they grow old and die. Nations rise and fall, and mighty empires sweep over the lands, only to crumble to dust. Great changes occur over the course of history, and yet the sky above remains the same.

The Sun, Moon, and stars that we see today are the same ones that shone down on Moses and Pharaoh, Daniel and Nebuchadnezzar, and Jesus and Caesar. The luminaries don't change in ways that the eye can see, though they continue to

From "The Shepherdes Kalender" (A.D. 1506)

roll along through their cycles, marking off our short lives. For this reason, the celestial bodies had historically been used for the reckoning of the **calendar**.

The earliest calendars were made by counting the monthly cycles of the Moon. The ancient Hebrews of the Bible used a calendar based on the cycles of the Moon's phases. The Chaldeans of Mesopotamia also used a lunar calendar. According to Jewish tradition, the patriarch Abraham was a great Chaldean astronomer.

The first calendar based on the annual cycle of the Sun was developed in ancient Egypt. The Egyptians discovered that on a certain morning, every 365 days, a certain star would rise before the Sun, which would always happen just before the annual flood of the Nile River.

The Traditions of Classical Astronomy

The ancient Greek philosophers combined the older astronomy of Egypt and Babylon into the grand mathematical system of *Classical Astronomy*. They developed geometrical methods to measure and predict the motions of the celestial bodies. In fact, *trigonometry*, the study of triangles, was originally developed for work in astronomy. The Greek philosophers Aristotle and Ptolemy established a "geocentric" astronomical system in which the Earth was understood to be at the center of a rotating cosmos.

"The Astronomer" by Albrecht Dürer (circa A.D. 1500)

The Greeks called the Sun *Helios* and the Moon *Selene*. Eventually, the Greek world was conquered by Rome, and the astronomical legacy passed to the Romans. Though they didn't add to Greek astronomy, Rome's innovations were practical. Roman dictator Julius Caesar adopted the Egyptian solar calendar, instituting the *Julian calendar*, essentially the same calendar we still use today!

The Romans were avid students of Greek astronomy and popularized it throughout their empire. Many Romans such as Geminus, Manilus, Pliny, and Macrobius wrote works of astronomy which were widely studied in the early centuries A.D. Most learned Romans such as Cicero were well acquainted with the principles of astronomical science. The Romans called the Sun *Sol* and the Moon *Luna*, names which we still recognize today.

The Sun (Sol) is so named either because he is "solus" (the Latin word for "alone"), so eminent above all the stars; or because he obscures all the stars and appears alone as soon as he rises. Luna, the Moon, is so called from "lucendo" (the Latin word for "shining"). –Cicero (circa 50 B.C.)

The classical astronomy of the ancient Greeks survived for many centuries in Christian Europe, mainly for maintaining the church calendar. In time, this calendrical study resulted in many advances that led to modern science.

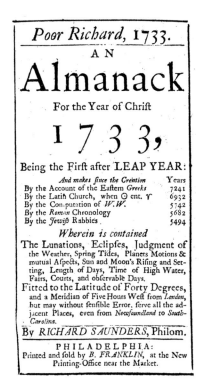

Christian Europe developed the modern **almanack**, a resource that includes tables of the Sun's rising and setting for each day of the year, along with tables of the Moon's positions and the positions of planets and other noteworthy celestial objects. For centuries before the invention of mechanical clocks, the almanack was useful for **skycraft**, the art of finding the time during the day and also at night.

The European almanack tradition was strong throughout the Middle Ages and into the modern era. An almanack was included in the 1611 King James Bible to assist with times for prayer and Bible study. Following the invention of the printing press, almanacks became inexpensive and thus widely available. The almanack found its greatest expression in the early American colonies. The first English publication in America was an almanack, printed at Harvard in 1639.

In time, a "heliocentric" astronomical system was developed in which the Sun was proposed to be the center of the universe instead of the Earth. This theory became popular because it simplified the mathematics used to create an almanack. In time, it was found that the actual motions of the planets were more easily explained and accurately predicted by the Sun-centered theory.

This led to the discovery of *classical physics*, and the laws of nature became better understood. It was learned that the same natural laws that govern the earth were also in control of the timeless timekeepers of the sky. Today, these

The Heliocentric Solar System from "Foster's Almanack" (A.D. 1675)

same laws of physics are used to create the technology of the modern world. The arts of making automobiles, refrigerators, and computers are ultimately drawn from the study of the sky above.

Almanacks were also created to aid the skycraft of sailors in navigating at sea, where the Sun, Moon, and stars are used to find direction. These same celestial methods were used to survey territories and cities of the early American republic. If your town has roads that run east to west and north to south, your town was probably surveyed from the stars!

Modern Artificial Timekeeping

Improvements in navigation led to the perfection of accurate mechanical clocks. By the nineteenth century, these mechanical clocks began to replace the common almanack. Today, our system of time is based on vibrations inside an artificial atomic clock, measured to a billionth of a second. Nowadays, time is no longer measured by the *Two Great Lights*. The gadgets and gizmos of Man now sit in the place of God's celestial order.

Timekeeping has been separated from the Sun, Moon, and stars, and thus astronomy has disappeared from the popular mind. Most of us never even glance up from our busy lives to look at the sky above. Fantasy tales of space travel and bug-eyed aliens have filled the void left by Classical Astronomy. And more people today have heard of "black holes" than understand why the seasons change.

But the luminaries continue in their ancient cycles, whether anyone notices them or not. The Earth is our home – the only planet on which we will ever live – and it is only from the Earth's surface that we can view the Sun and Moon. The Earth and Moon circle the Sun in a cosmic ballet of continuous motion. We all ride along as the Earth's passengers, as our world glides silently in a continuous journey through the days, the months, and the seasons.

The Sun and Moon, like time itself, do not stop, but are always changing, rising and setting, varying their positions in the heavens, until the appointed end of days. There is a marvelous created order to the sky above. We will learn of this order in our story, and of the *understanding* through which the heavens were established. We will see how the *signs and seasons,* and *days and years* that divide and limit our lives are drawn from the Two Great Lights in the sky above.

Chapter 1
The Light He Called Day

The heavens declare the Glory of God, and the firmament sheweth his handiwork... In them hath he set a tabernacle for the Sun, which is as a bridegroom coming out of his chamber, and rejoiceth as a strong man to run a race. – Psalm 19:1, 4-5

Have you ever watched a *sunrise*? Have you ever observed the drama in the sky as night turns into day? The morning stars twinkle in the dark sky as the first rays of dawn graze the horizon. Then the stars disappear one by one with the advance of morning twilight.

The last stars disappear as the sky becomes tinged with shades of pink and orange. The sky grows radiant, and a chorus of birds can be heard, as though to proclaim the arrival of another morning!

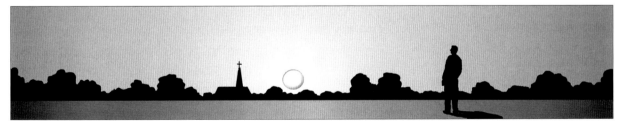

Finally, the Sun appears above the horizon - as the bridegroom from his chamber - a great, bright orb to chase away the shadow of night. The new day dawns as the Sun begins his race across the sky.

We praise You, Lord, for all Your creatures,
Especially for Brother Sun,
Who is the day through whom You give us light.
And he is beautiful and radiant with great splendor,
Of You Most High, he bears Your likeness.

– Francis of Assisi (circa A.D. 1200)

Each morning, the Sun rises and moves across the sky. As time passes, the Sun rises higher and higher into the morning sky. The rising of the Sun has been very predictable – so predictable that people everywhere and through all history have used **the day** as the most basic unit for passage of time.

And God said, Let there be light: and there was light. And God saw the light, that it was good: and God divided the light from the darkness. And God called the light Day, and the darkness he called Night. And the evening and the morning were the first day.

– Genesis 1:3-5

Of course, we all understand that the word *day* has two meanings. It can mean the actual period of the daylight, from dawn until nightfall. But the word *day* can also mean the interval for measuring time, the period from one sunrise to the next sunrise. These two meanings have always been understood since ancient times.

"Day" declares not the stay only of the Sun upon the earth, according to which day is one thing, night another, but also its entire circuit from east even to east, according to which we say, "so many days have passed" (the nights being included when we say "so many days" and their spaces not counted apart).

– Augustine (circa A.D. 400)

Telling the Time of Day

At one time, everyone knew how to "read" the sky. People could roughly tell the time of day just by knowing the Sun's position in the sky. When you live close to the land, you just *know* what time it is. Maybe not to the exact minute, but close enough!

The Sun is *very bright*, much too bright to look at. But we can look at the shadows of objects that block the Sun's bright light. We can know the Sun's position in the sky just by looking at the directions of the shadows on the ground. A lot of astronomy involves shadows, as we will see.

If you watch closely over the course of a sunny day, it's easy to see that the shadows shift to follow the Sun's movement. The shadows of trees, buildings, and people always point in the direction *away* from the Sun, wherever it might be in the sky. The shifting shadows of the Sun can be used to measure the time of day.

The **sundial** was used for thousands of years to tell time. A common sundial consists of a pointer or **gnomon** (pronounced "know-mon") for casting the Sun's shadow and a **dial** with markings along the edge to show different times of the day.

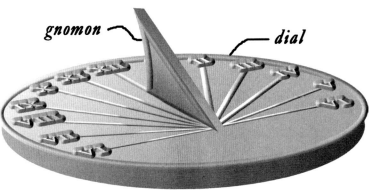

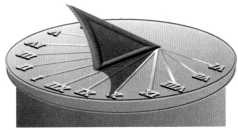

As the Sun moves across the sky, the gnomon shadow follows the Sun and marks off the day's progress on the dial. The earliest historical account of a sundial is the miracle of the *Sundial of Ahaz* recounted in the Bible, dated from the time of King Hezekiah and the Prophet Isaiah, about 700 B.C.

And this shall be a sign unto thee from the LORD, that the LORD will do this thing that he hath spoken: Behold, I will bring again the shadow of the degrees, which is gone down in the sun dial of Ahaz, ten degrees backward. So the Sun returned ten degrees, by which degrees it was gone down.

– Isaiah 38:8

The sundial was first introduced into Greece from Babylonia around 600 B.C. Sundials were very popular in the Roman empire and were used through the early years of the American republic. In an age before modern clocks, sundials were the only devices for measuring the time of day.

A sundial is featured on the "Fugio" cent, the first American coin. The Latin word "fugio" means "I fly," indicating that "time flies".

Divisions of the Day

In order to measure shorter periods of time, the day is divided into smaller intervals, called **hours**. The sundial is marked so that the gnomon shadow points to the hour corresponding to the Sun's position in the sky. Since ancient times, it has been common to measure the day as *twenty-four hours* from one sunrise to the next. We will see later how the number of hours of daylight and nighttime change over the course of the seasons.

The name "hours" has been given to the 24 divisions which make up a day and a night.

– Macrobius (circa A.D. 400)

For centuries, timekeeping was totally dependent on the Sun. By the 1700s, mechanical clocks and watches were used for keeping track of the time. In keeping with the traditions of timekeeping, clocks were designed to resemble the sundial. The clock's face is also called a "dial," and the clock's hands are made to resemble the gnomon shadows. The hands even move "clockwise" to imitate the direction of the sundial shadows with the passing hours.

Those necessary and useful instruments, clocks, watches and dials, owe their origin to the observations of the Heavens.

– Isaac Watts (A.D. 1726)

It is the middle of the day when the Sun reaches its highest point in the sky at the hour we call **noon**. At noon, the Sun has reached the **meridian**, an imaginary line that defines the middle of the sky. The word *meridian* is taken from the Latin word *meridiem*, which literally means "middle of the day."

It is called "meridian" because, wherever a man may be, and at whatever time of year, when the Sun with the movement of the firmament reaches his meridian, it is Noon for him. For like reason, it is called the "circle of midday."

– John Sacrobosco (circa A.D. 1230)

The meridian literally divides the day into morning and afternoon. The ancient Romans called the morning hours **A.M.**, from the Latin words *ante meridiem,* which mean

"before the middle of the day." The afternoon hours were called **P.M.**, from *post meridiem,* literally "after the middle of the day." These are among the many ancient astronomy conventions that survive to this day.

Historically, the Sun's meridian passage occurred at 12:00 P.M. However, in our modern world, we use a system of *standard time.* This basically means that clocks and sundials measure time differently, so that people across hundreds of miles can read the same time on their clocks. **High noon,** when the Sun reaches the meridian, can occur earlier or later than 12:00 P.M., depending on your location. (We'll learn more about this in later chapters.)

Dividing Light from Darkness

After crossing the meridian, the Sun descends into the afternoon sky. The shadows grow long as the Sun draws near the sunset and finally sinks from sight as another day draws to an end.

From the rising of the Sun unto the going down of the same, the LORD's name is to be praised. —Psalm 113:3

After sunset, the sky grows dim in the gathering dusk. Darkness deepens as night falls, and the evening stars come out one by one. But far off, in the direction of the sunset, the Sun still shines over distant lands and seas. If we could see far above our world, we would see that the daylight lands are divided from the dark lands of night.

The Sun's rays shine continuously onto our Earth, but not everywhere at once. Only half the Earth sees the sunshine at any given time, and it is that half that sees **the day**. The other half is in the Earth's shadow, where the Sun's light cannot be seen. That half of the Earth experiences **the night**.

And first of all the Sun, which has the chief rank among all the stars, is moved in such a manner that it fills the whole earth with its light, and illuminates alternately one part of the earth while it leaves the other in darkness. And it is the regular approaches and retreats of the Sun from which arise the regulated degrees of cold and heat.

— Cicero (circa 50 B.C.)

The border between day and night is called the **terminator** – a boundary that encircles the world, dividing the sunlit half of the globe from the dark half. We see sunrise when our location crosses the terminator into the light of day. We see sunset when our location crosses the terminator into the shadow of night. The Moon and the planets also have terminators, as we will later see.

Night retires into the regions opposed to the rays of the Sun, since it is by nature only the shadow of the Earth. Because, in the same way that, during the day, shadow is produced by a body which intercepts the light, night comes naturally when the air that surrounds the Earth is in shadow. And this is precisely what Scripture says, "God divided the light from the darkness."

– Basil of Caesarea (circa A.D. 360)

Far above the world, the Sun would be seen shining in a black sky. But from the ground, we see the Sun shine amidst the cheery bright blue of the daytime sky. This is because of the Earth's *atmosphere*. The atmosphere is the layer of air surrounding our world, giving us the air we breathe, the weather that brings the rains, and protection from radiation in space. The Sun "lights up the air" by scattering its blue rays throughout the daytime sky.

How does the Sun rule by day? Because carrying everywhere light with it, it is no sooner risen above the horizon than it drives away darkness and brings us day. Thus we might, without self-deception, define day as air lighted by the Sun. – Basil of Caesarea

The Sun and the blue sky are so bright that they hide the stars from sight during the day. But once in a while, the Moon passes in front of the Sun in an *eclipse*, blocking its bright rays. During an eclipse, the blue sky grows dim and we can see the Sun's place in a dark, starry sky.

Twilight is the time of transition between the blue daytime sky and the starry sky of night. Twilight is a band encircling the Earth on the shadow side of the terminator where the brightness of the daytime sky gradually fades into the darkness of nighttime. We pass through the twilight in the morning before sunrise and in the evening after sunset.

Morning twilight appears on the horizon before the sunrise, as the first rays of the Sun begin to light up the air. The twilight grows brighter as more of the Sun's rays filter into the morning sky. As the sky grows brighter, the clouds become tinted red and orange, Homer's "child of the morning, rosy-fingered dawn."

By twilight's end, a blue sky has rolled overhead. Another day begins as we cross the dawn terminator, and the Sun appears above the horizon once again.

Direction and the Sky

The Sun also ariseth, and the Sun goeth down, and hasteth
again to his place where he arose – Ecclesiastes 1:5

As the Sun crosses the horizon to begin another day, the "place" where the Sun rises is the **east**.

East is an Old English word that literally means "toward the sunrise." It is taken from the Old German word *ostar*, which is related to the ancient Greek word *eos*, which means "dawn." Many old maps use the Latin word *Oriens*, which means "to rise." The lands toward the sunrise, in the Far East, have long been called *the Orient*.

The east is one of the *directions* that we use to help find our way from one place to another. There are four principle directions that are used for navigation: *north, east, west* and *south*. These are known as the *cardinals*, or the *compass points*. The cardinal directions are found from the signs of the Sun and sky.

Just as it rises each day in the east, the Sun sets every evening in the **west**. This word comes from the Old German word *westar*, related to the Latin word *vesper*, which means "evening." The old maps use the Latin word *Occidens*, which means

"to set." For many years, Europe was known as *the Occident*. The western direction literally means "toward the sunset."

In addition to the Sun, *all* the celestial bodies in the sky rise in the east and set in the west. For this reason, the ancients called the east and the west "The Gates of the Heavens."

There are two gates of the heavens, the East and the West.
For by one the Sun appears, by the other he retires.
– Isidore of Seville (circa A.D. 600)

At midday, as it reaches the meridian, the Sun hangs high in the sky above the **south**. The word *south* is derived from the Old English word *suth*, which comes from the Old High German word *sunna* or Sun. The same old maps use the word *Meridies*, which, as we have seen, means "meridian" or "middle of the day." So "south" can be thought of as the direction toward the noon Sun!

At noon, shadows point **north**, away from the midday Sun. The English word *north* is related to the Greek word *nerteros*, which means "lower" or "under." Perhaps this is because the north is a "lower" direction where the Sun is never seen above the horizon (as seen from Greece). The old maps use the Latin name *Septemtriones*, which refers to the seven stars of the Big Dipper. We'll discuss that some more in the next chapter.

If you can follow the movements of the Sun, you can find your direction just as easily as people did in ancient times.

After observing the quarter in which the sun rises on any given day, at the middle of the day take your position in such a manner as to have the point of the sun's rising on your left; you will then have the south directly facing you, and the north at your back.

— Pliny the Elder (circa A.D. 70)

But you should locate direction by your own shadow and *not* by looking at the Sun! The shifting shadows always point in the directions *opposite* the Sun's direction.

You see what a shadow is during the day; that is precisely the nature of darkness during the night. If, at the appearance of a light, the shadow always falls on the opposite side; if in the morning it extends towards the setting Sun; if in the evening it inclines toward the rising Sun, and at midday turns toward the North. — Basil of Caesarea (circa A.D. 360)

If you watch your own shadow, you can easily find north at high noon. When the Sun is *highest* overhead, your shadow on the ground will be at its *shortest*.

The observer must then turn round, so as to look upon his shadow, for it will be behind him. Having thus changed his position, so as to bring the point of the Sun's rising on that day to the right, and that of his setting to the left, it will be midday, at the moment when the shadow straight before him is the shortest. — Pliny the Elder

These directions of the Sun determine the *exposures* of the sides of our houses. Windows that have an eastern exposure face the sunrise, and the morning light comes streaming in at breakfast. And windows that have a western exposure face the sunset, and the late afternoon sunshine streams in. Plants that like partial sunlight do well on walls with an eastern or western exposure. But the southern exposure receives full sunlight of the day, since it faces the noon Sun and

receives morning and afternoon sunshine. But the northern exposure can only receive indirect sunlight, since it is turned away from the Sun.

Attention must here be drawn to the fact that sunlight can enter any building from only three directions and never from the fourth. Windows facing the east and west will receive sunlight in the morning or afternoon, and windows to the south as well, since the whole path of the Sun is to the south of us, never will a north window admit sunlight because the Sun never invades the area and never approaching the border of the north-polar region, and consequently never pouring its light in from this direction. – Macrobius (circa A.D. 400)

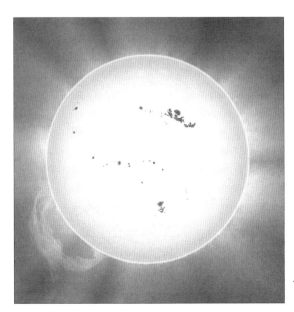

WARNING! Never look at the Sun!

In the course of this story, the Sun's position in the sky will be shown many times. But always remember, the Sun is *too bright* to look at and can *destroy* your vision! Don't use regular sunglasses either, since they won't give your eyes enough protection. Be sure to use only special filters designed for solar observing.

Bright objects, moreover, the eyes avoid and try not to see. The Sun actually blinds if you persist in staring against it, because its own power is great, and from on high through the pure air the images come heavily rushing, and strike the eyes so as to disturb their structure. –Lucretius (circa 50 B.C.)

The Horizon

When you are out in a wide-open place with no trees or buildings, and look off into the distance, you can see the **horizon**. The horizon is that distant place where the land ends and the sky begins. When we look toward the horizon, we are looking

in the "horizontal" direction – straight ahead, with our eyes level, not looking up or down. Out in a wide open space, with nothing to obstruct your vision, you can see the entire horizon. If you look around in every direction, through all the compass points, the horizon will always seem to be an equal distance away, as though you are standing at the center of a large *circle*. In Classical Astronomy, the horizon is regarded as a circle that divides the Earth and the sky.

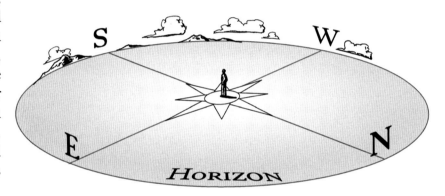

If you want to know the appearance of the other circle (the horizon), turn around and let your eyes easily gaze around you in a circle. It is where the higher sky comes exactly together with the lower earth, without any space or division, and restores and receives the shining stars from the sea. It encompasses the world with a thin line, a transverse limit of the world. – Manilius (circa A.D. 20)

The word *horizon* is taken from the Greek word *horizo* (ὁριζω), which means "limit." The horizon is simply the limit of our vision, the extent to which we can see over the curved edge of the Earth. The horizon shows us only that small section of the Earth's surface that can be seen in any particular direction.

Astronomical Alignments

Since ancient times, buildings such as the *pyramids* have been constructed to line up with the compass points. The great pyramids in Egypt are among the oldest buildings in the world. The sides of the pyramids are aligned very closely with the cardinal directions.

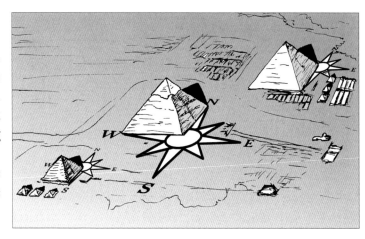

At a distance of 40 stadia from Memphis is a brow of a hill, on which are many pyramids, the tombs of the kings. Three of them are considerable. Two of these are reckoned among the Seven Wonders of the World.

—Strabo (circa 20 B.C.)

The Sphinx is also astronomically aligned to face the east. Every day for thousands of years, the Sphinx has watched the rising Sun.

In the year 1791, the city of Washington, D.C. was laid out to align with the compass points. A careful survey of the land was performed using measurements of the Sun, Moon, and stars to find direction. The numbered streets of Washington run from north to south, and streets designated by letters run east to west. Avenues, named for the thirteen original colonies, were laid out to follow diagonal lines.

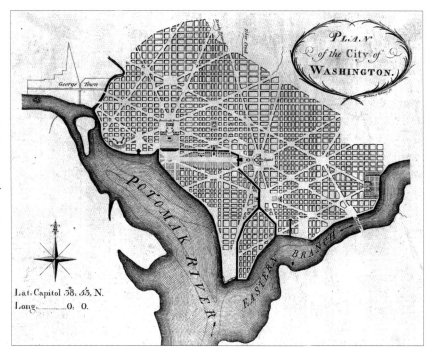

The National Mall in Washington, D.C., includes the U.S. Capitol, the Washington Monument and the Lincoln Memorial. These monuments are laid out along the Mall in a plan that extends from east to west. Like the pyramids, these monuments are astronomically aligned!

Throughout American history, as settlers moved west, new lands were also surveyed from the Sun, Moon, and stars. Many communities in the United States are also laid out to be aligned with the compass points.

Perhaps your neighborhood has also been planned out to follow the compass points. Maybe your house, sidewalk, and driveway are "astronomically aligned," just like the pyramids. The clues for finding direction are among the many signs that the LORD, in His abundant provision, has placed in the sky for our benefit.

Movements of the Sky

Everyone can see that the Sun rises in the east each morning and crosses the sky over the course of the day, setting in the west at evening. Throughout all history, this has been one of the plainest facts of life. In centuries past, when people lived closer to the land, it seemed pretty obvious that it was *the Sun* that moved, while the Earth remained still.

Under the ancient Greek astronomers, it became an established principle of astronomy that the entire sky, including the Sun, Moon, and stars, turned around the stationary Earth in a daily rotation. Around 350 B.C., the Greek philosopher Aristotle used a method of logic to devise a "geocentric" astronomy, which explained that the Earth was at the center of the universe, with the Sun moving around the Earth each day, in a westward motion.

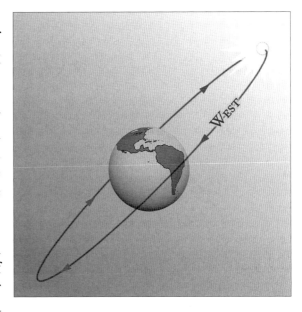

Aristotle's geocentric astronomy was an integral part of his overall description of nature. In about A.D. 150, an astronomer named Claudius Ptolemy created a mathematical arrangement based on the geocentric cosmology of Aristotle. For centuries, the earth-centered astronomy of Aristotle and Ptolemy was the standard way of understanding the sky.

If one should next take up the question of the Earth's position, the observed appearances with respect to it could only be understood if we put it in the middle of the heavens as the center of the (celestial) sphere. – Ptolemy (circa A.D. 150)

In A.D. 1543, an astronomer named Mikolaj Kopernik (better known as "Copernicus") proposed that it is *the Earth* that moves, which makes the Sun only *appear* to move across the sky. According to Kopernik's theory, our world is constantly rotating, and this rotation makes the Sun appear to rise and set. The Earth spins on its **axis** and completes one rotation every day, producing the 24-hour cycle from sunrise to sunrise.

For the daily revolution appears to embrace the whole cosmos... with the single exception of the Earth itself. But if one should admit that the heavens possess none of this motion, but that the Earth rotates from west to east; and if one should consider this seriously with respect to the seeming rising and setting of the Sun, Moon and stars, then one would find that it is actually true.

– Kopernik (A.D. 1543)

The Earth is constantly spinning toward the east, so it is actually the Earth's rotation that produces the variation between day and night. This rotation carries each place on the Earth from the bright daytime sunshine into the dark shadow of the night.

The eastward rotation of the Earth carries each place out of night's shadow and across the *sunrise terminator.*

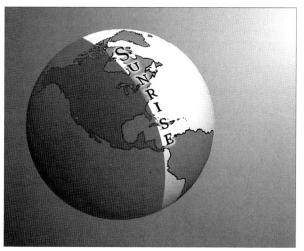

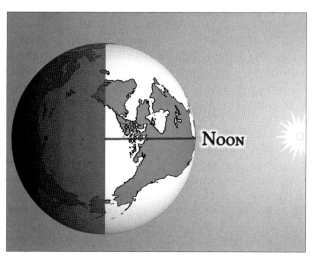

At high noon, we have reached the middle of the Sun's rays. As the day draws to a close, the eastward motion carries us across the *sunset terminator,* back into the Earth's shadow.

"And in the evening and the morning were the first day." Evening is then the boundary common to day and night; and in the same way morning constitutes the approach of night to day.

– Basil of Caesarea (circa A.D. 360)

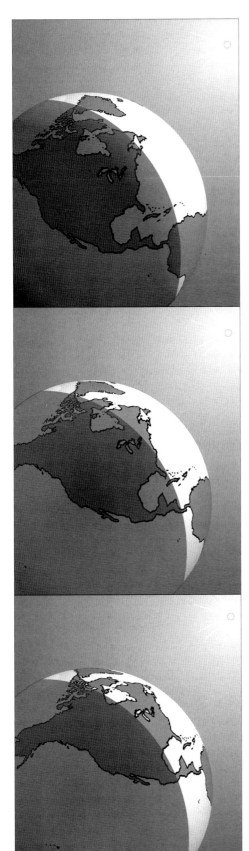

A Day Over Washington, D.C.

We can combine all the lessons of this chapter to understand the astronomy of an early spring day over the National Mall in Washington, D.C.

The eastward rotation of the Earth creates the *illusion* of the westward movement of the Sun. So when the Sun reaches the eastern horizon, behind the U.S. Capitol, it is simply the passage of Washington, D.C. across the sunrise terminator.

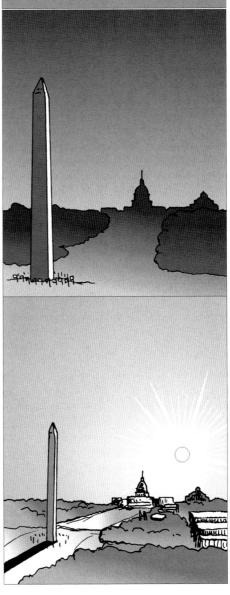

As the Sun rises higher in the sky, it is simply the effect of Washington being drawn farther into the Sun's rays with the rotation of the Earth.

In the early morning, as the Sun hangs low in the eastern sky, the shadows point toward the west. But as the Sun climbs higher, the Washington M o n u m e n t tracks the Sun's motion like the gnomon of a giant sundial.

At high noon, as the Sun hangs at the meridian, the Washington M o n u m e n t ' s shadow points north.

After noon, the Sun is now in the western part of the sky, and the shadows have turned toward the east.

As afternoon wears on, the westering Sun drops lower in the sky. As the day draws long, the shadows have circled to the other side of the compass, now pointing east.

As the day draws to a close, the setting Sun draws toward the Lincoln Memorial.

Washington, D.C. crosses the sunset terminator, and the Sun disappears below the western horizon.

Dusk twilight descends as the American capital passes deeper into the Earth's shadow.

Night falls, and the stars come out one by one.

Evening and morning and at noon, will I pray, and cry aloud: and He shall hear my voice.
– Psalm 55:17

Chapter 2
The Darkness He Called Night

The day's bright King now conquer'd does retire, Night takes possession on the vanquish'd fire;
The Moon her peerless light now doth display, Whilst Sol remains 'till next succeeding day;
The starry frames their equal power show, Around the sphere, with light that from them flow.
– "On Night" – Ames' Almanack for the Year of Our Lord 1786

As the glow of twilight fades, stars appear in the sky as the full shadow of night descends over the land. As the king of Israel wrote, the heavens do truly proclaim the glory of God. There is hardly a more majestic sight than a velvety black sky, studded at each point with stars that glitter like jewels, with the expanse of the **Milky Way** stretching overhead.

If, and whenever, your admiration has been excited when contemplating a grand circle ornamenting the sky, or if any one standing near you points out the Milky Way, bear in mind there is no other circle which exhibits a similar appearance. – Aratus (circa 275 B.C.)

In our generation, many people are not familiar with the true sight of a starry sky as its Creator intended it to be seen – a dark canopy, speckled with stars that shine more brightly than anything that can be seen on the ground. Such a sight can only be seen from the most remote locations, far from city lights.

Today, many people live huddled in the cities, where electric lights line every street and illuminate every corner. The city lights brighten the landscape and cast their glow back upon the skies. This results in a perpetual man-made orange twilight, through which even the brightest stars struggle feebly to be seen.

As a result of this **light pollution**, the glory of the heavens is largely hidden from our generation. The Milky Way is virtually unknown to urban-dwellers. Very few people today find the night sky to be a glorious sight. So the sky and its God-given signs go unnoticed and ignored.

Throughout most of history, the starry sky could be seen in its full glory. Though the secrets of the sky are mostly forgotten today, at one time they were well understood by the common people, especially shepherds, who slept each night under the stars.

Now whoso will know as the shepherds that keep sheep in the fields that hath no manner of learning, but even only by figures which is graved in small tables of wood. And thereby they have an understanding of heaven, and of the signs and stars, and also of the seven planets, and of their courses, their movings and properties and of many other things.

– The Shepherdes Kalender
(A.D. 1506)

The shepherds of old were well-acquainted with the many stars scattered across the night sky. Since the dawn of recorded history, patterns and shapes have been distinguished among the stars. These star patterns, called **constellations**, are "connect-the-dot" patterns meant to designate animals, persons, and other objects. Every culture in the world has included constellations in its fables and folklore.

There is a vast number of fixed stars, distinguished by the names of certain figures, to which we find they have some resemblance. – Cicero (circa 50 B.C.)

The word "constellation" comes from the Latin words *co* or "together" and *stella* or "star" – literally *co-stars*. As in ancient times, the constellations are still used today to divide the sky into convenient sections. In this way, the constellations provide a "road map to the stars." Like the shepherds of olden days, we can learn the courses, movings and properties of the heavens by observing these constellations.

The Bears

One of the most famous constellations in the sky is **Ursa Major**, the Big Bear. The constellation of Ursa Major includes many faint stars that form the head and legs of the Bear. Their faintness makes it difficult to see the outline of a starry bear, especially under the city lights.

However, nearly everyone can spot **The Big Dipper**, a star pattern made from

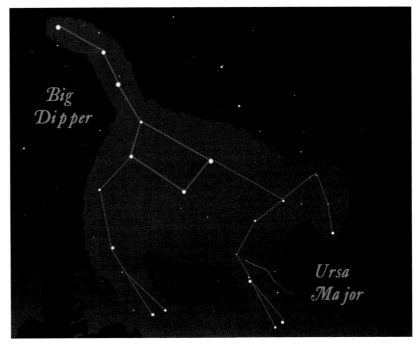

the seven brightest stars of Ursa Major. This familiar pattern of bright stars is easy to see from just about anywhere, even the city. In some European cultures, this pattern is seen as resembling a wagon or *wain* – an ox-drawn cart. But Americans have no trouble seeing the Dipper as a ladle for taking water from a container.

(It should be noted that the Big Dipper is not considered a true constellation, since it's only part of Ursa Major. It is considered an **asterism,** an informal grouping of stars made up of other constellations' stars.)

The Big Dipper faces **Polaris, the North Star**. This star remains in a fixed position above the northern horizon. Polaris is the brightest star in the **Little Dipper**, an asterism formed from the stars of **Ursa Minor,** the Small Bear. Except for Polaris, the stars of the Little Dipper are faint, and are best seen away from city lights.

The North Star has the unusual property of always being directly above the horizon at the point of *due north*. In this way Polaris has always been used for finding direction at night. For many centuries, the Big Dipper has been used to find the North Star. The outer stars in the "bowl" of the Big Dipper are *the Pointers*, and always point toward Polaris, thus pointing the way north.

The old maps indicate north by the Latin name *Septemtriones*. This strange name actually refers to the Big Dipper! The Latin word *septem* refers to the seven bright stars of the Dipper. *Triones* means a team of three oxen, which refers to the identification of these stars with a wain or a cart drawn by oxen. In many ways, the Bears have traditionally been associated with the north.

Sharing the northern sky, on the opposite side of Polaris from the Big Dipper, is the constellation **Cassiopeia**. The ancients saw Cassiopeia as a queen from an old myth. But it's much easier simply to spot the five stars of Cassiopeia that appear in the shape of a *W* or a *3*. The stars of Cassiopeia are about the same brightness as those of the Big Dipper and Polaris. So if you can spot these stars, you can also spot Cassiopeia.

Orion

Another famous constellation is **Orion**, the Hunter. Orion is probably the best known star pattern after the Big Dipper. Though not many constellations trace a clear picture in the stars, it's easy to see the shape of a man in the stars of Orion. Orion is formed of some of the brightest stars in the sky. Orion is easily spotted by the three bright stars of *Orion's Belt.* Also, Orion has a *sword* at his side, and a distinct upper and lower body, giving this star pattern a very human shape.

Seek him that maketh the seven stars and Orion, and turneth the shadow of death into the morning, and maketh the day dark with night: that calleth for the waters of the sea, and poureth them out upon the face of the earth: the LORD is his name. – Amos 5:8

In Winter evenings, Orion is seen high in the sky, facing **Taurus**, the Bull. This constellation includes a *V* shape of stars, forming the Bull's head. Taurus also includes the **Pleiades**, a beautiful cluster of seven little stars.

Canst thou bind the sweet influences of Pleiades, or loose the bands of Orion? – Job 38:37

At Orion's side is **Canis Major**, the Big Dog. The Big Dog is distinguished by the star **Sirius**, the brightest star in the sky. Sirius is the famous *Dog Star* of the Egyptian calendar (which we will learn about in later chapters). The Milky Way passes above Orion, and the stars in this part of the sky are among the brightest.

Orion lies obliquely to the region occupied by the Bull. Who will fail to observe him lying high upon a calm night? For he may be readily seen by any observant person looking towards the sky. – Aratus (circa 275 B.C.)

The Naming of the Stars

The Bible says that the LORD called the stars by name:

Lift up your eyes on high, and behold who hath created these things, that bringeth out their host by number: He calleth them all by names by the greatness of His might, for that He is strong in power; not one faileth –Isaiah 40:26

Except for a handful of constellations, the Bible does not provide us with the names the LORD gave to the stars. Only three star groupings are named in Scripture – *Kesil* (כסיל), which means "fool," is the name of *Orion* in Hebrew; *Kimah* (כימה), meaning "cluster of seven stars," is how the *Pleiades* are named in Scripture. *Ash* (עיש), meaning "group," is the biblical term for the *Great Bear*. In spite of some popular teachings, no other insights can be found from any Jewish or Christian historical writings. Any other information is lost to the sands of time.

Names notwithstanding, the constellations *as they are known* are very ancient. Prominent constellations like the Big Dipper and Orion were apparently known at the dawn of recorded history. Historical evidence such as inscriptions on clay tablets suggests that other traditional constellations were known in Mesopotamia by about 700 B.C., the time of the prophet Isaiah.

By the time the Greeks overthrew the nation of Troy (circa 1000 B.C.), the Bear and Orion passed with their fronts opposite - she content to twist in her circle around the Pole, he rising turned around from the Pole, as she circles around the world evermore. And in that time, one was already able to understand the signs of the dark night, and to tell the changes of the hours from the sky. –Manilius (circa A.D. 20)

Many cultures of the world have drawn the constellations differently than was done in classical western civilization. Though we can't have certain knowledge of the origins of the classical constellations, we can surely agree with this Christian writer:

But by whatever fashion of superstition these are named by men, they are nevertheless stars, which God made at the beginning of the universe and ordained to mark the seasons with regular motion. –Isidore of Seville (circa A.D. 600)

Our oldest reliable historical source for the classical constellations is the poem *Phaenomena*, written in about 275 B.C. by the Greek poet *Aratus*. Aratus was the poet whom the Apostle Paul quoted while evangelizing the Greek philosophers on Mars Hill in Athens:

For in Him we live, and move, and have our being; as certain also of your own poets have said, For we are also his offspring. – Acts 17:28

Aratus gives us a very colorful description of the constellations. Aratus's poem is famous for not teaching the superstition of *astrology*, for the pagan Greeks in that period did not practice the worship or divination of the stars. The constellations described in Aratus's poem are essentially the same constellations we still use today.

Some of Aratus's constellations, like the Bull, the Lion, and the Scorpion, actually do resemble the creatures for which they are named. Other constellations are obscure star patterns that bear no resemblance to their names. Mostly, the stars form arbitrary geometrical patterns – some triangles and a couple of square shapes. However they are drawn, the constellations can help observers find their way around the sky.

The constellations described by Aratus were used down through the centuries of the Christian era, though some Christian astronomers tried to rename them. In 1627, Julius Schiller of Germany created a star atlas called *The Christian Starry Sky* in which the pagan constellations were replaced by the Apostles and other heroes of the Bible. For example, Schiller renamed Orion after Jesus's father Joseph, and the Big Dipper became the Apostle Peter's Fishing Boat! However, Schiller's constellations never caught on. In his 1683 almanack, Cotton Mather wrote:

Though we don't go with Schiller to put Christian Names upon the Constellations, let it not be absurd to beseech the Readers of an Almanack to become Christian Men.

In addition to the forty-eight ancient constellations of Aratus, other constellations have been added in recent centuries. Today, eighty-eight constellations are recognized by the *International Astronomical Union*, a scientific astronomy organization.

The modern constellations all have Latin names, reflecting the Roman and medieval periods when astronomy was studied in Latin. Some stars have Greek names, reflecting the Greek roots of astronomy. Other star names and astronomical terminology have their roots in Arabic, following a five-hundred-year period when Arabic astronomy was preemininent. We may not be able to know the names that the LORD gave to the stars, but the names and astronomy terms we still use today reflect the long and rich heritage of Classical Astronomy in western civilization.

The Celestial Sphere

When you're under a clear, dark sky with stars all around in every direction, you can see that some stars are low to the horizon and some are high overhead. But no matter where the stars are in the sky, none seem to be any closer or farther away than any others.

It seems that all the stars are *equally* far away from the Earth, as though they are at the same constant distance. Though some stars are bright and some are faint, our eyes cannot tell if any of these stars are closer or farther away.

As a result, the starry sky has the appearance of being a great *dome* overhead, with all the stars studded on the dome's inside surface. Just as the horizon gives the illusion of being a great circle centered around an observer, the entire sky appears as a great concave bowl of stars, centered above the observer.

View yon majestic concave of the sky!
Contemplate well, those glorious orbs on high
There constellations shine, and Comets blaze;
Each glittering world the Godhead's pow'r displays!
– Benjamin Banneker's Almanack for the Year of Our LORD 1793

The spherical, dome-like appearance of the starry sky has been well known since ancient times. In fact, the ancients understood that the starry sky, if it could be seen in its entirety, would appear as a huge *sphere* – a **celestial sphere** with the Earth at its center. The celestial sphere is also called the vault of the heavens and the dome of the firmament.

The world and this, whatever name men have chosen to designate the sky whose vaulted roof encircles the universe, its shape has the round appearance of a perfect sphere... Our eyesight also confirms this belief, because the firmament presents the aspect of a concave hemisphere equidistant in every direction, which would be impossible in the case of any other figure. – Pliny the Elder (circa A.D. 50)

The word *celestial* comes from the Latin word *caelus*, which means "the heavens." The word *celestial* has historically been used to compare the things above with the *terrestrial*, the things down on the Earth.

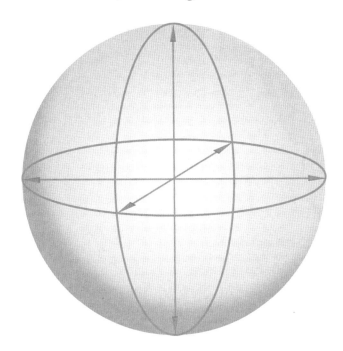

There are also celestial bodies, and bodies terrestrial: but the glory of the celestial is one, and the glory of the terrestrial is another. – 1 Corinthians 15:40

In geometry, a sphere is defined as a shape in which each point on its surface is an equal distance from its center.

For if an equal amount is added on every side, the extremity of the mass will be everywhere equidistant from its centre, i.e. the figure will be spherical.

– Aristotle (circa 350 B.C.)

In ancient and medieval times, the spherical appearance of the sky was so well understood that *the Doctrine of the Sphere* was an established foundational principle of Classical Astronomy. During this period, the **armillary sphere** was a common representation used to simulate the configuration and the motions of the celestial sphere.

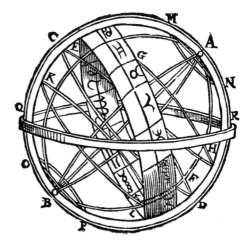

Armillary Sphere

In modern times, the *planetarium* is used to simulate the configuration and motions of the celestial sphere. A planetarium includes a domed ceiling for projecting images of the stars. According to the old philosophers, no other ceiling shape could be used to give a better simulation of the night sky.

Nowadays, it has been shown that some stars are closer to the Earth and others are farther away. So we now understand that the celestial "sphere" is simply another illusion in the sky based on appearances. After all, no stars are "close" as judged by the human eye. Even in ancient times, some philosophers understood that the celestial sphere was just an illusion.

Above all is the so-called sphere of the fixed stars, which includes the imagery of all the signs made up of fixed stars. But we must not suppose that all the stars lie on one surface, but rather that some of them are higher (i.e. more distant) and some lower (i.e. less distant). It is only because our sight can only reach to a certain equal distance that the difference is imperceptible to us.

– Geminus (circa 50 B.C.)

Even though the celestial sphere is known to be an optical illusion, it is still useful today to explain many appearances and apparent motions in the starry sky. Nevertheless, the celestial sphere remains a *powerful illusion*. Out in space, far above the Earth, the stars would still appear to be on the concave inside surface of a sphere.

The stars are *so* far away that the distances to the planets of the solar system are comparatively small. Every planet orbiting the Sun would see the same star-studded firmament with the same constellations seen from the skies of Earth.

In fact, the distance to the farthest planet is still like a *tiny speck* compared to the nearly infinite distance of even the closest stars. Even at billions of miles from Earth, the appearance of the starry globe would remain unchanged.

Is not God in the height of the heaven? And behold the height
of the stars, how high they are! – Job 22:12

From an understanding of the celestial sphere, we can learn the geometry of the sky. In fact, the great geometer Euclid wrote a book called *Phaenomena*, the first mathematical work on sky geometry. From this, we can discover many useful things from the sky. For example, the horizon can be considered a circle along the celestial sphere. Since the land blocks our view of half of the sky, the horizon is the celestial circle that divides the sky into visible and invisible halves.

Let the name "horizon" be given to the plane passing through our eye which is produced to the (extremities of the) universe, and separates off the segment which we see above the Earth. The horizon is a circle; for, if a sphere be cut by a plane, the section is a circle.

– Euclid (circa 300 B.C.)

A **great circle** is a circle that divides a sphere into two equal halves. Since the horizon divides the celestial sphere into equal visible and invisible halves, it is a great circle of the sky. Any other circle that cuts a sphere is **small circle**. We will see many other important great circles of the celestial sphere.

A Great Circle in the Sphere is one which, described on the surface of the sphere about its center, divides the sphere into two equal parts, while a small circle is one which, described on the surface of the sphere, divides it not into two equal but into two unequal portions.

– John Sacrobosco (circa A.D. 1230)

The Rolling of the Sphere

At a glance, the stars appear to hang motionless in the sky. But over a period of hours, it becomes clear that the stars are moving slowly across the sky.

The stars, each one, do seem to pause, affixed to the ethereal caverns, though they all forever are in motion, rising out and thence revisiting their far descents when they have measured with their bodies bright the span of heaven. – Lucretius (circa 50 B.C.)

But just like the Sun and Moon, the stars appear to cross the sky from east to west over the course of the night. The stars all move together, with none moving ahead of any of the others, with the steady motion of the entire celestial sphere.

That the sky revolves from east to west is signified by the fact that the stars, which rise in the east, mount gradually and successively until they reach the mid-sky and are always the same distance apart, and thus maintaining their relative positions, they move toward their setting continuously and uniformly.

– John Sacrobosco (circa A.D. 1230)

From ancient times, it was believed that the entire celestial sphere rotated each day toward the west, carrying with it the Sun, Moon, and stars.

The sphere of heaven, moving from the east toward the west, turns once in a day and a night, in the space of twenty-four hours, within which the Sun completes his swift revolving course over the lands and under the Earth. – Isidore of Seville (circa A.D. 600)

But in modern times, it is known that the sphere of stars does not move at all. This is another optical illusion resulting from the daily eastward rotation of the Earth.

And why are we not willing to acknowledge that the appearance of a daily revolution belongs to the heavens, (but) its actuality to the Earth? The relation is similar to that of which Virgil's Aeneas says: "We sail out of the harbor, and the countries and cities recede." For when a ship is sailing along quietly, everything which is outside of it will appear to those on board to have a motion corresponding to the movement of the ship, and the voyagers are of the erroneous opinion that they with all they have with them are at rest. –Kopernik (A.D. 1543)

The daily rotation of the sky can especially be seen from the constellations near the North Star. These stars are always elevated above the horizon and never rise and set. Over a span of hours, the northern stars change their positions around the North Star. It can be seen that the Big Dipper and Cassiopeia move *counter-clockwise* in a circle around the North Star.

The stars near the North Pole, which never sets for us, move continuously and uniformly, describing their circles about the pole, and are always equally near or far from one another. – John Sacrobosco (circa A.D. 1230)

As the Earth rotates, the Earth's axis is always pointed in the same general direction – toward the North Star. For this reason, the entire celestial sphere appears to turn around the North Star, like a big round wheel rolling around its axle.

The axis is a straight line north, which passes through the center of the globe of the sphere, and is called "axis" because the sphere revolves on it like a wheel. –Isidore of Seville (circa A.D. 600)

At the ends of the axis are the **poles**. Just as the globe of the Earth has a North Pole, the celestial sphere has a North Celestial Pole of its own. The North Star is very near the precise point of the North Celestial Pole. That is why the North Star is called *Polaris* or *the Pole Star*. The word *pole* comes from the Greek word *polos* (πολος) which means "pivot." As the pivot point of the sky, Polaris appears motionless as the entire sky turns around it.

But I am constant as the northern star, of whose true-fix'd and resting quality, there is no fellow in the firmament. The skies are painted with unnumber'd sparks, they are all fire and every one doth shine, but there's but one in all doth hold his place.

– William Shakespeare (circa A.D. 1600)

As the Earth rotates, the entire sky appears to pivot around Polaris. Suppose that at a certain time, Cassiopeia and the Big Dipper are on either side of the North Star.

After a few hours, as the Earth turns, the ground underfoot "tilts" as compared to the immovable stars. (Rotate the page to see the "movement" of the stars!)

As the Earth rolls on to the east, the stars appear to move counterclockwise around Polaris. With each complete rotation of the Earth, the Big Dipper and Cassiopeia complete a full circle in the northern sky.

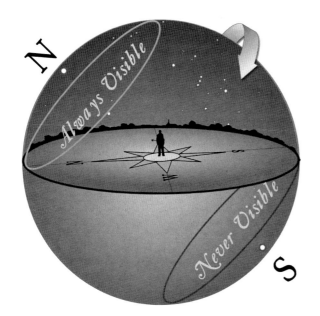

Always Visible, Never Visible

Just like the Earth, the celestial sphere also has both North and South Celestial Poles. From the Northern Hemisphere, the North Celestial Pole is **always visible** above the horizon. But the South Celestial Pole is always *below* the horizon, and is **never visible** from northern lands.

Also, the two poles terminate at either extremity; one indeed is not visible, but the other to the Northward rises high above the ocean. Surrounding it, two Bears lie circularly, which are usually called the Wains.

– Aratus (circa 275 B.C.)

The North Celestial Pole is said to be *elevated* while the South Celestial Pole is said to be *depressed*. In this way, the entire celestial sphere appears tilted. There is a circle of stars that lie between the elevated North Celestial Pole and the northern horizon. The Big Dipper and Cassiopeia are always seen within this circle from most of the Northern Hemisphere. These stars never actually set below the horizon but are *always visible* as they circle continuously around the North Star. This circle is called the **northern circumpolar circle**.

In antiquity, the *always visible* circle was originally referred to as the **Arctic Circle**, the Circle of the Bears (from the Greek word *arctos* (αρκτος) which means "bear.") Nowadays, this term refers to a latitude circle on the Earth that defines the boundary of the frigid north.

Now it is not the constellation of the Bear, but the Arctic Circle, which is the limit of the rising and setting stars...The Arctic Circle...extends to the signs which seem to our senses to touch in succession the most northern point of the horizon.

– Strabo (circa 20 B.C.)

Meanwhile, there is also a circle of stars that remains between the depressed South Celestial Pole and the southern horizon. These stars never rise above the horizon and therefore are *never visible* from the temperate latitudes of the Northen Hemisphere. Just as the Dippers and Cassiopeia are within the always visible northern circumpolar circle, unseen constellations such as **the Southern Cross** are below our horizon within a *never visible* southern circumpolar circle.

Although the celestial sphere is always revolving around the earth from east to west, the polar axis which holds the Great Bear, since it is above us, will always be visible to us, however much it turns in the swirl of the heavens. The south pole, on the other hand, once buried from our sight, as it were, by the location of our abodes, will never show itself to us, nor the stars with which it is undoubtedly adorned. – Macrobius (circa A.D. 400)

Since they are always above the horizon, the constellations of the Great Bear and the Small Bear have always been used to find north. And for centuries, Polaris, fixed above the northern horizon, has been a God-given sign that navigators on land and sea have always used to find their direction throughout the night.

The Circle of the Meridian

As they circle the North Star, the "always visible" stars rise to their highest points above the horizon, after which they descend again toward the tree tops. The other stars move like the Sun. They rise above the horizon and climb until they reach their highest point, after which they begin again to set.

Just like the Sun, the stars reach their highest points in the middle of the sky, at the **meridian**. Each celestial body has its own individual "noon" when it reaches the meridian. The meridian is actually another great circle of the celestial sphere that divides the spherical sky into two halves. Celestial objects are said to *culminate* or *transit* when they cross the meridian.

The meridian is defined as passing through the **zenith**, the point in the sky directly over the head of the observer, straight up above the ground. The circle of the meridian passes through the North Celestial Pole, so that the highest point reached by each celestial body is related to the pivot point of the sky.

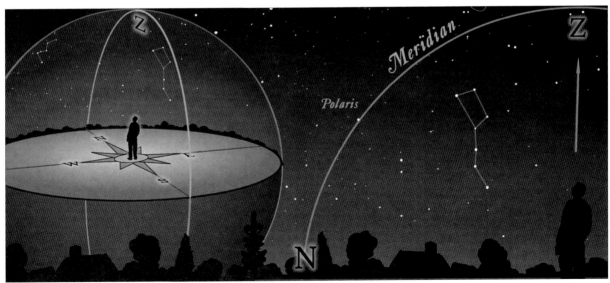

In this way, the meridian extends from the horizon, through the poles, and to the top of the sky. Thus, the meridian is the circle that defines the middle of the sky, dividing the "rising" half of the sky from the "setting" half of the sky. For this reason, the meridian is also known as the *midheaven*.

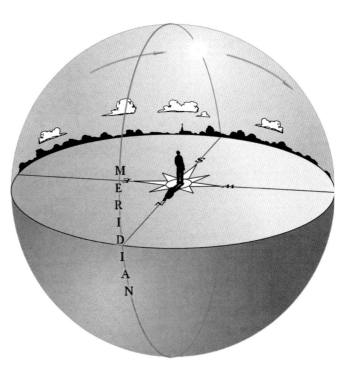

Meridian is a great circle imagined in the heaven which passes by the poles of the world and the point of the heaven and earth above our head the which is called zenith and always that the sun is coming from the east one to this circle, then it is midday.

– Shepherdes Kalender (A.D. 1506)

There is another point at the bottom of the celestial sphere, opposite the zenith. This is the **nadir**, the unseen extreme point below the horizon, in the invisible half of the celestial sphere.

The meridian encircles the entire sky, passing through the poles, along the zenith and the nadir. The **lower branch** of the meridian is the lowest point that a celestial body reaches each day. When the Sun sinks to the lower branch of the meridian, it is **midnight**, after which it ascends unseen toward the sunrise.

For it is called "meridian" and it is the middle of the circle of the earth, and the underneath which passes the point of midnight earthly opposed to the zenith. And when the Sun touches that part of the circle, it is called "midnight." – Shepherdes Kalender

And so we see that the meridian is an invisible celestial circle that arches overhead across the sky. Since it passes through the poles, the meridian crosses the horizon at due north and due south. For the experienced skywatcher, the meridian is yet another God-given sign for telling time and finding direction.

The heavens are thine, the earth is also thine: as for the world and the fullness thereof, thou hast founded them. The north and the south thou hast created them, Tabor and Hermon shall rejoice in thy name. – Psalm 89:11, 12

One can easily find the south by finding the highest point in the sky reached by any of the celestial bodies – Sun, Moon, or stars. In fact, in centuries past, a celestial body was said to be "southing" as it crossed the meridian.

I have added a column of the Southing of the Moon for every day and also the Southing of the Seven Stars, which may be useful to Planters, Watermen, etc. to know the time of the Night, etc. – Daniel Leeds Almanack for the Year of Christian Account 1694

As a great circle of the celestial sphere, the meridian divides the sky into east and west halves. The east half is the *A.M.* part of the sky, since everything on that side of the sky is rising. The sky to the west of the meridian is the *P.M.* half of the sky, since everything on that side is setting. So the meridian is also useful for indicating direction in the sky as well as on the land.

Thus, in the sky and on the Earth, *east* means east of the meridian, and *west* means west of the meridian. On the land and in the sky, the same directional arrows point to the same horizons. A compass hanging in the sky would be like a mirror image, showing east and west *reversed* compared to a compass on the Earth.

In Classical Astronomy, there are many ways that the sky is like a mirror of the world. As we've seen. the sky appears spherical and has North and South Poles. There are many more similarities between the Earth and the sky.

The Celestial Equator

Just as the Earth has an equator, there is also a **celestial equator** circling the sphere of the stars. The celestial equator, also called the *equinoctial*, is another great circle that divides the celestial sphere into two equal halves – a Northern Hemisphere and a Southern Hemisphere.

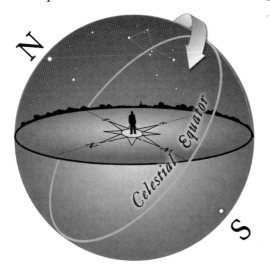 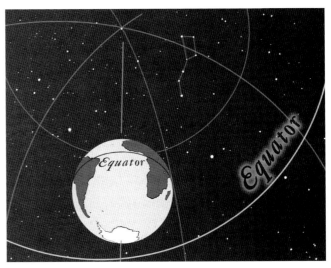

The celestial equator encircles the middle of the starry sky at an equal distance between the celestial poles, just as the terrestrial equator encircles the middle of the Earth at equal distances from the North and South Poles.

The equinoctial is a circle dividing the sphere into equal parts and equidistant at its every point from either pole. — John Sacrobosco (circa A.D. 1230)

A number of constellations lie on or near the celestial equator, but the brightest and closest are the stars of Orion's Belt, which lie just south of the celestial equator. In this way, Orion's "chest" is in the celestial northern hemisphere, and his "legs" are in the celestial southern hemisphere!

In the midst of both a girdle as large as the Milky Way revolves beneath the earth, bisecting, as it were, the sky, while therein both the days and nights are equal, that is, towards the end of Summer and the commencement of Spring. On it also appears the belt of magnificent Orion.

– Aratus (circa 275 B.C.)

Since the celestial equator is in the middle between the northern and southern extremities, it meets the horizon at the midpoints between the poles. Thus, the celestial equator crosses the horizon at due east and due west.

The celestial equator thus enables us to find more directional clues from the night sky. For example, if we spot Orion's Belt as it is rising, we know that we are looking directly to the east. And if we can find Orion's Belt as it sets, we know we are looking straight to the west. As we learn more about the stars and can find more constellations, we can develop a sense of direction from the stars.

In addition to simply learning the different constellations, it's also important to learn the arrangements between the constellations along the spherical sky. For example, when the Big Dipper is east of the North Star, Orion is southing high in the sky at the meridian. In this way, the Big Dipper can help you find Orion and vice versa. These relationships between the stars have been known since antiquity and have long been used to learn the sky and find direction at night.

Ulysses spread his sail before it, while he sat and guided the raft skillfully by means of the rudder. He never closed his eyes, but kept them fixed on the Pleiades, on late-setting Boötes, and on The Bear, which men also call the Wain, and which turns round and round where it is, facing Orion, and alone never dipping into the stream of the Ocean. –Homer's *Odyssey* (circa 700 B.C.)

In our modern world, it's easier than ever to find direction for learning the stars. If you live in an "astronomically aligned" neighborhood, you can use your sidewalks and driveways to find the directions to the stars.

Maybe you have a driveway or a sidewalk that runs north to south. Your meridian can be found by looking above and sighting down to the ends of your drive. Some people can find the North Star hanging over their garage!

A sidewalk or street that runs from east to west would be ideal for finding where the celestial equator crosses the horizon. Perhaps you can see Orion rising and setting at either end of your street.

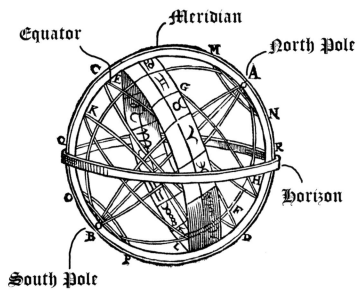

The celestial circles would be easier to imagine if we could actually see them in the sky. The traditional armillary sphere was used to represent these unseen circles and to find time and direction from the sky. But under a dark, starry sky, these circles can only be imagined in our minds or inferred from the useful signs that the LORD has placed in His firmament.

But even though these invisible circles can't be seen, the Sun, Moon, and stars nevertheless follow and cross the paths of these circles in their motions. These circular patterns are all part of *the Doctrine of the Sphere,* a very important part of Classical Astronomy, the key that opens the door to truly understanding the sky. There are many more invisible circles concealed in the sky, and this chapter is only the first step. But these things are truly worth searching out.

It is the glory of God to conceal a thing: but the honor of kings is to search out a matter.

— Proverbs 25:2

Chapter 3
The Cycle of the Month

When I consider thy heavens, the work of thy fingers, the moon and the stars,
which thou hast ordained, what is man that thou art mindful of him?
and the son of man, that thou visitest him? – Psalm 8:3, 4

The Moon's appearance is constantly changing. Sometimes we see the Moon as a thin crescent. Other times the Moon is full. At various times, the Moon can be seen in the evening, at midnight, and in the morning. Sometimes we can even see the Moon during the day. But there is an order and a progression to the Moon's changing appearance. This is *the Cycle of the Month.*

The Moon's changing appearance follows a cycle of **phases**. The word *phase* comes from the Greek word *phaiseis* (φαισεις) which means "appearance" or "shine." Each different phase of the Moon represents a different shining appearance. Every month, the Moon appears in its crescent phase, increases to a Full Moon, and diminishes back again. The Moon's phase changes slightly from night to night as it moves across the sky.

Furthermore seven stages, which are called phaiseis in Greek, mark the passage of a month: new moon, half-moon, gibbous, full moon, gibbous, half-moon, and conjunction, the latter being the stage at which the moon's light is completely invisible to us. – Macrobius (circa A.D. 400)

The Wandering Moon

The Moon is a companion world to the Earth. The Moon circles around our world in an **orbit**. When we follow the cycle of the Moon's phases from night to night, we are actually observing the Moon at different positions in its orbit.

The Orbit of the Moon

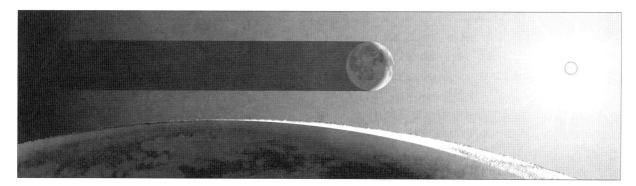

Just as the Sun shines on the Earth, the Sun is also shining at all times on the Moon. Therefore, half of the Moon always has a brightly lit "day" side, and half the Moon is in the shadow of its "night" side. Like the Earth, the Moon has a terminator that divides its bright side from its dark side. The earliest Greek philosophers understood that the Moon only shines with the reflected light of the Sun. So when we see the Moon shining in the night sky, we are simply seeing the Sun's rays reflected off the Moon's surface.

As sunlight striking the broad circle of the Moon, a borrowed light, circular in form,
it revolves around the Earth, as if following the track of a chariot.

—Empedocles (circa 450 B.C.)

Lunar Calendar

Just as the cycle of the day measures off short periods of time according to the rising and setting of the Sun, the cycle of the month measures longer periods of time. The Moon moves through its cycle of phases in a **lunar month** of about 29½ days.

The ancient Israelites were commanded by the LORD to celebrate their festivals according to the cycles of the Moon's phases. This is an example of a **lunar calendar**, measuring long periods of time by counting lunar months. Throughout history, many cultures have used a lunar calendar. But our western calendar is

a **solar calendar**, based on the Sun's annual cycle of **the year**. So the 30- or 31-day "month" we use in our solar calendar is not an actual lunar month, but simply a convention used to divide the year into twelve units.

Many wall calendars indicate principal phases of the Moon. This is a surviving relic of the days when everyone read the old colonial almanacks to tell time, track the seasons and follow interesting events in the sky.

The New Moon

During the time of the **New Moon**, we cannot see the Moon in the sky. The Moon at this time is at a place in its orbit between the Earth and the Sun. In the sky, the Moon is very close to the Sun and is lost in the Sun's bright glare. Also, when the Moon is new, its entire bright side is facing toward the Sun, and the dark side is facing toward the Earth. So even if the Moon was not hidden by the Sun's glare, it would not shine any light toward our world.

She is not seen in conjunction (i.e. at the New Moon), because, at that time, she sends back the whole stream of light to the source whence she has derived it.

—Pliny the Elder (circa A.D. 70)

Many wall calendars provide the date of the New Moon. This phase is symbolically depicted on the calendar as a black circle on a particular date because the New Moon cannot be seen from anywhere on the Earth. Since there is no bright edge, the Moon is an invisible black circle, just as shown on wall calendars.

New Moon

The Israelites were commanded to forever celebrate each New Moon as the beginning of another month. They celebrated by blowing trumpets and with burnt offerings at the temple.

Behold, I build an house to the name of the LORD my God, to dedicate it to Him, and to burn before Him sweet incense, and for the continual shewbread, and for the burnt offerings morning and evening, and on the Sabbaths, and on the New Moons, and on the solemn feasts of the LORD our God. This is an ordinance forever to Israel. – 2 Chronicles 2:4

The Waxing Crescent

As the Moon moves along its orbit, it circles around the Earth toward the east. After its New phase, the Moon moves east, away from the Sun's bright glare. It can now be seen hanging in the western sky after sunset. By this time, most of the bright side of the Moon is still turned toward the Sun. But since the Moon is not *completely* lined up with the Sun, a tiny edge of the bright side can now be seen.

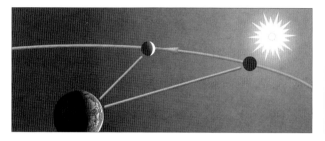 

In the days after the New Moon, the Moon is now in a **crescent** phase, appearing as a bright little fingernail in the evening sky. Traditionally, the lunar month begins on the evening of the first sighting of the crescent Moon. The ancient astronomers often said that the Moon has *horns* when in the crescent phase.

Do you not see when the Moon appears on the west side with thin horns that it marks the commencement of the month? — Aratus (circa 275 B.C.)

Whatever its phase, the brightly illuminated edge of the Moon always faces in the direction of the Sun, the source of its borrowed light. Therefore the "horns" of the waxing crescent Moon point *away* from the Sun, towards the east.

Clear it is, that the Moon always in her increasing, has the tips of her horns turned from the Sun toward the east. — Pliny the Elder (circa A.D. 70)

Each night, the Moon moves farther toward the east, and appears to move away from the Sun. We can then see a little more of the Moon's bright side, and so the crescent becomes thicker. During this period, the Moon is said to be **waxing**, an old-fashioned word that means "increasing." With each passing night, the waxing crescent Moon is a little *thicker* and a little *farther away* from the sunset.

The phase of the Moon simply depends on how much of the bright side is facing the Earth. As a waxing crescent, the Moon is at a section of its orbit "in front of" the Earth – more or less between the Earth and the Sun. As a result, most of the brightly lit part faces the Sun, and only a small portion is visible from the Earth. Since the Moon is in the general direction of the Sun, it can be found in the western half of the sky at sunset.

Earthshine

Sometimes, on a very clear night, you can look at a crescent Moon and actually see the outline of the dark side. The dark areas of the Moon seem to have a smoky glow, where the Moon's features can be made out. Though it may seem to be your imagination, this is real! This smoky light is called **earthshine**, and it is light that is reflected from the Earth onto the Moon, partially lighting the Moon's surface.

If we wish an evident proof that the Moon does not consume its body when at rest, we have only to open our eyes. If you look at it in a cloudless and clear sky, you observe, when it has taken the complete form of a crescent, that the part, which is dark and not lighted up, describes a circle equal to that which the full moon forms. Thus the eye can take in the whole circle, if it adds to the illuminated part this obscure and dark curve. – Basil of Caesarea (circa A.D. 360)

When the Moon is in its crescent phases, it is between the Earth and the Sun. The bright daylight reflecting off the Earth shines onto the Moon. This is enough light so that we actually see the lighted moonscape shining back on the Earth! The earthshine was first correctly explained by Leonardo da Vinci.

Some have believed that the moon has some light of its own, but this opinion is false, for they have based it upon the glimmer which is visible in the middle between the horns of the new moon, this brightness at such a time being derived from our ocean and the other inland seas, for they are at that time illumined by the Sun. The seas then perform the same office for the dark side of the moon as the moon when at the full does for us when the Sun is set.

– Leonardo da Vinci (circa A.D. 1500)

First Quarter

After about a week, the Moon is more or less "alongside" the Earth with respect to the Sun. The Moon is now evenly divided down the middle by its terminator. Half of the Moon is brightly lit, and half is in shadow. The Moon thus appears as a half-moon, hanging high in the evening sky at sunset. The First Quarter Moon can be found in the general vicinity of the meridian at sunset, depending on the time of year.

By now, the Moon has completed about one-quarter of its monthly cycle, so the waxing half-moon seen in the evening sky is called the **First Quarter**.

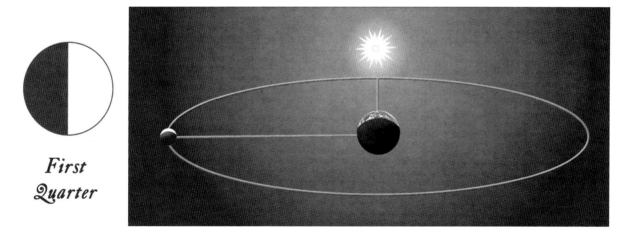

First Quarter

Wall calendars indicate this phase by a little circle, black on the left and white on the right. The First Quarter Moon is quite high in the evening sky, and about halfway from the sunset to the opposite horizon.

The Gibbous Moon

After the First Quarter, the Moon begins to swing *behind* the Earth. Now more than half of the Moon's visible surface is brightly lit. The Moon looks like a half-moon with an extra hump onto the dark side. For this reason, this phase of the

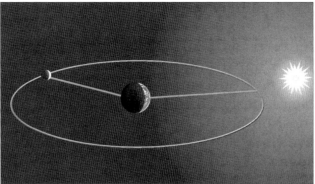

Moon is called **gibbous**, a term which comes almost directly from the Latin word *gibbus*, which means "hump."

The gibbous Moon can often be seen during the daytime, rising in the east in the evening before the Sun sets. During the gibbous phases, the Moon is always found in the eastern part of the sky at sunset. As it grows thicker each night in its gibbous phases, the Moon draws toward the eastern horizon.

With the progression of phases, the changing shape of the Moon's terminator proves that the Moon is actually spherical in shape, like the Earth. The Moon's terminator is curved inward when the Moon is crescent. When we see it "edge-on"

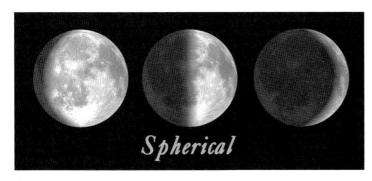

Spherical

at the half-moon, the terminator appears straight. But when the Moon is gibbous, the terminator is curved outward from the crescent phase. Even in ancient times, it was understood that no other shape besides a sphere could produce these appearances.

When the Moon is gibbous, the greater part of the Moon's surface is visible. By now, the dark areas on the Moon are clearly seen. These are called **maria** or "seas." These dark areas are not really water on the Moon. But with a little imagination, it's not difficult to see that the seas appear to form a "face" on the Moon's surface. Sometimes, people call this face *the Man in the Moon*. The face on the Moon seems to have a sad or worried expression, as though it is crying, woeful for having to constantly gaze upon a fallen world of sin.

Those whose sight is more acute and penetrating better descry the lineaments (on the Moon) and more perfectly observe the impressions of a face, and more evidently distinguish its different parts. – Plutarch (circa A.D. 100)

The Man in the Moon

The Moon's face is constantly turned toward the Earth as it orbits our world. This is because the Moon has more mass behind its face. The Earth's gravity tugs more strongly on this side, turning the face side toward the Earth as the Moon revolves in its orbit.

The Full Moon

The Full Moon occurs at mid-month, about two weeks after the first sighting of the crescent Moon in the evening sky. The Moon is now "behind" the Earth in its orbit, in the position opposite the Sun. The entire bright side is turned toward the Earth, and so the complete circle of the Moon's face can now be seen. Since it is on the opposite side of the Sun from the Earth, the Full Moon rises in the east just as the Sun sets in the west. Wall calendars show the phase of the Full Moon as a white circle.

Full Moon

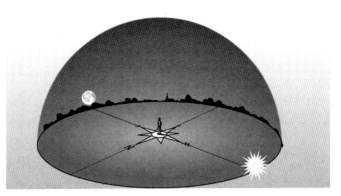

Now God commanded the Sun to measure the day, and the Moon, whenever she rounds her disc, to rule the night. For these two luminaries are almost diametrically opposed; when the Sun rises, the full moon disappears from the horizon, to reappear in the east the moment the Sun sets.

- Basil of Caesarea (circa A.D. 360)

Even though it is "the lesser light that rules the night," the Moon reflects quite a bit of light back onto the Earth. In the early part of the month, the Moon is quite dim and throws very little light. The half-moon is brighter and can cast shadows in the night. But the Full Moon is *very bright*, and lights up the whole landscape, casting strong shadows.

It is nonetheless true, that when at its perfection it makes the stars to turn pale and lightens up the Earth with the splendor of its light, it reigns over the night, and in concert with the Sun, divides the duration of it in equal parts. – Basil of Caesarea

It was during the first Full Moon of spring that the Israelites departed their slavery in Egypt on the night of the Passover. No doubt, the LORD, in His provision, wished Israel to depart when there would be much nighttime light to see by. And the LORD commanded that the Full Moon – *the fourteenth day of the month* – be the time forevermore for Israel to commence the weeklong Feast of the Unleavened Bread.

And ye shall observe the feast of unleavened bread; for in this selfsame day have I brought your armies out of the land of Egypt: therefore shall ye observe this day in your generations by an ordinance forever. In the first month, on the fourteenth day of the month at even, ye shall eat unleavened bread, until the one and twentieth day of the month at even. –Exodus 12: 17, 18

Since Jesus and His disciples celebrated the Passover the night He was betrayed, the Full Moon would have shone down on the LORD while He prayed in the Garden of Gethsemane.

After the night of the Full Moon, you can no longer see the Moon in the sky at sunset. You can look and look, but the Moon will be gone. In order to appreciate why the Moon disappears from the early evening sky, we need to understand that like the Sun, the Moon also rises and sets in a daily cycle.

The Rising and Setting of the Moon

In order to fully understand Classical Astronomy, it's very important to become an observer of the sky, as were the ancient philosophers and the founders of the American republic. To fully observe the Moon's cycle, we need to know that the Moon is sometimes visible in the evenings after sunset and that at other times it can be seen in the morning sky, around sunrise. Also, for most of the lunar month, the Moon can also be seen at some point during the day!

Because of the Earth's rotation, the Moon rises and sets in the sky, just like the Sun and stars. But as we rotate eastward along with the Earth, the Moon is also moving eastward in its orbit. So by the time we complete one daily rotation, the Moon has shifted to a place in the sky to the east of the previous day's position.

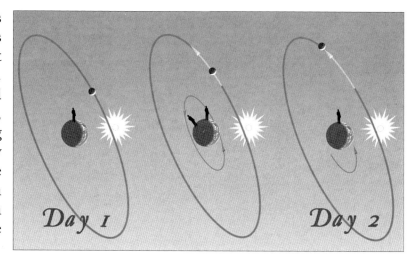

Like the Sun, the Moon has a "day" of its own. After rising, the Moon climbs higher until reaching its own "noon," where it crosses the meridian. Then the Moon moves into the western sky, where it finally sets. But these risings and settings happen at different times of the day, depending on the phase. For most of the month, the Moon rises or sets during the daylight.

When the Moon is new, it rises close to the same time as the Sun. The Sun and Moon cross the sky together, even though the Moon is lost in the Sun's bright glare. The Moon crosses the meridian with the Sun close to high noon, and sets invisibly sometime around the sunset.

As the New Moon moves in its orbit around the Earth, it is still moving progressively toward the east, away from the Sun. On the day after the New Moon, the moonrise occurs about 48 minutes after the sunrise. The Moon crosses the meridian about 48 minutes after high noon, and moonset is about 48 minutes after the sunset.

By the next day, the Moon has drawn a little more to the east in its orbit and rises about 48 minutes later than the previous day – about an hour and a half after the sunrise. The Moon also crosses the meridian and sets 1½ hours after the Sun. Each day thereafter, the Moon crossings will follow the Sun by another 48 minutes later than the day before.

About three days after the New Moon, the Moon is far enough away from the Sun to be easily seen in evening sky after sunset. Though usually unnoticed, the Moon rises in the blue skies of morning, nearly 2½ hours after the Sun. If you had a cloudless sky and a sharp eye and knew where to look, you could easily spot the slim crescent Moon in the daytime and follow its movement through the blue sky over the span of the day.

By the end of the day, the waxing crescent Moon arrives in the western sky and is easily seen in the evening twilight. The Moon sets 2½ hours after the Sun, sinking closer to the horizon as night falls. With each passing day, the waxing Moon is visible in the night sky for 48 minutes longer than the night before.

After a week, at First Quarter, the Moon rises about *six hours* after the Sun. So if the Sun rises at 6:00 A.M., the First Quarter Moon rises around high noon. On a clear afternoon, you can see the half-moon climbing higher in the eastern sky. The waxing half-moon reaches its own "noon" at the meridian sometime around 6:00 P.M. After sunset, the First Quarter Moon is then in the western half of the night sky, setting around Midnight.

(These rising and setting times as stated here only represent seasonal and global averages. Actual times can vary considerably with the date of the year and your location on the Earth's globe. The weather section of your local paper should have local rising and setting times for at least the Sun and Moon. This information is also available at many Web sites.)

After the First Quarter, in the gibbous phases, the Moon rises in the afternoon. It is very common to see the waxing gibbous Moon coming up in the east as the Sun sinks toward the sunset. The Moon is now visible for most of the night, crossing the meridian before midnight and setting before the sunrise. For most of us, the gibbous Moon sets unseen while we sleep, in the early morning hours before sunrise.

After the gibbous phases, the circle of the lunar face rounds off to a Full Moon. Having completed half a cycle of phases, the lunar month is now half spent. After two weeks, the Full Moon rises *twelve hours* after the Sun and comes up in the east just after the Sun disappears in the west. The Full Moon reaches its own "noon" at the meridian around midnight and goes down in the morning twilight as the Sun rises again.

The Waning Moon

The Moon rises later and later after the Full Moon. On the night after the Full, the Moon rises about 48 minutes *after* the sunset! The next night, the Moon rises 48 minutes after that, about an hour and a half after the Sun has set. On these nights, the Moon comes up in full nighttime darkness. Who hasn't seen the amazing sight of a big orange Moon rising large in the east during the late hours?

But as the Moon rises in darkness, it soon becomes clear that it is not full any longer. The Moon is now **waning**, an old-fashioned English word that means "decreasing." The Moon rises later and later each night as it passes through its waning phases. Only a few days after the Full Moon, the waning Moon is rising at bedtime!

After the Full, the waning Moon is once again gibbous. If you have learned to spot the face on the Moon, it is clear that the western edge of the Moon, which was bright during the waxing phases, is now dark. The Moon's eastern edge, which was hidden behind the darkness of the terminator in the early month, is now brightly lit. After the Full Moon, these bright edges are reversed.

Now she presents a perfectly rounded disc, now when diminished and lessened she shows a deficiency on one side. When waxing she is shadowed on one side, and when she is waning another side is hidden. – Basil of Caesarea (circa A.D. 360)

Waxing Gibbous   *Full Moon*   *Waning Gibbous*

The waning Moon now rises late after the sunset and crosses the meridian after midnight. The Moon crosses the sky over the span of the night but still has not set by morning! The waning Moon can be seen in the morning sky before sunrise, just as the waxing Moon can be seen after sunset.

In the waning phases, the Moon's relation to the Sun is exactly reversed from the waxing phases. The waning gibbous Moon can easily be seen in the morning at sunrise, far in the western sky, and the waning gibbous Moon sets in daylight as the Sun ascends in the morning sky. If you find yourself up early around the time of sunrise, look for the waning gibbous Moon.

During the waning phases, the Moon cannot be seen at all during the evening. The waning Moon can be seen rising during the nighttime, adding its feeble light to the bright sunshine during the day.

One while big and full, and another while all at once nothing to be seen.
Sometime shining all night long, and other times late it is when she
rises: she also helps the sun's light some part of the day.
– Pliny the Elder (circa A.D. 70)

Each night, the waning gibbous moon rises later and later after sunset and is higher and higher in the morning sky at the sunrise. You can notice that each morning, the Moon is a little *thinner* and a little *closer* to the Sun. Each night, the Moon rises 48 minutes *closer to the sunrise* than the night before.

Three weeks into the lunar month, a week after the Full Moon, the Moon reaches **Last Quarter**. The Moon has now waned to a half-moon, and rises in the late hours around midnight, about *eighteen hours* after the Sun. The Last Quarter ascends the eastern half of the sky through the wee hours and rides high in the middle of the sky in the early morning around sunrise. We can see that as the Moon wanes, it passes through a reverse order of its waxing phases.

Afterwards she shows her whole face, and the phases always declining
in an inverse order, she tells at each dawn what part of
the month is at hand. – Aratus (circa 275 B.C.)

The lunar month is now three-fourths over. The Last Quarter is shown on wall calendars as a circle, black on the right and white on the left – the reverse of the First Quarter. The Moon crosses the mid-sky and enters the western half of the sky in the morning, and goes down to its moonset around noon.

Last
Quarter

In the last week of the lunar month, the Moon has become a *waning crescent*. It is now an "old moon," rising in the wee hours before sunrise. The waning crescent Moon can be seen over the eastern horizon in the morning twilight, only a couple hours after rising. It's not very hard to spot a waning crescent in the daytime sky, especially in the midmorning when it crosses the meridian. You might even find it in the late afternoon, just a few hours before the sunset.

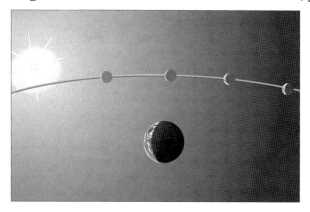 

The old waning Moon drops closer to the sunrise each morning. Now the Moon's *eastern* edge points toward the sunrise. The horns of the Old Moon point *west*, opposite from those of the waxing crescent.

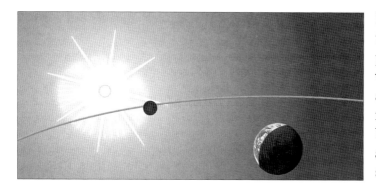

Finally, the Moon catches up to the Sun to complete its cycle of phases. One morning, the old waning Moon has disappeared again into the sunrise. The old month ends as the new month begins. The Moon is once again a New Moon, which rises and sets once again with the Sun.

And it shall come to pass, that from one New Moon to another, and from one Sabbath to another, shall all flesh come to worship before me, saith the LORD. – Isaiah 66:23

The next time you spot the Moon in the sky, make it a point to look again at the same time the next day. See how far the Moon travels across the sky in only a single day. If you see on the calendar that it is a New Moon, make it a point to observe the Moon in the coming evenings. Make a determined effort to observe the Moon on each clear night or morning for a month. You will begin to see the pattern of the Moon's cycle, and after a couple months, the cycle becomes clearer and clearer. Once you understand the Moon's cycle, you'll never forget it. Following the Moon will become a part of life, just as it was with farmers, sailors and common townfolk down through all history, when everyone understood Classical Astronomy.

Chapter 4
The Tabernacle for the Sun

The heavens declare the glory of God and the firmament sheweth his handiwork... In them hath he set a tabernacle for the Sun.... His going forth is from the end of the heaven, and his circuit unto the ends of it: and there is nothing hid from the heat thereof. – Psalm 19: 1, 4b, 6

With each rotation of the Earth, the Sun's *going forth* is from *the end of the heaven* at the eastern horizon, and it follows its *circuit* unto the other end, the western horizon. But the Sun's daily motion is *not* like the motion of the stars. The

stars of the celestial sphere are fixed in the sky, and they never change their positions among the constellations from day to day.

Like the Moon, however, the Sun can be found at a *different* position on the celestial sphere from the day before. Instead of jumping along through the constellations from night to night like the Moon, the Sun's apparent movement is very slow, hardly noticeable from day to day.

In addition to its daily rising and setting, the Sun also goes forth from one end of the celestial sphere to the other. Over a span of days, weeks, and months, the Sun can be seen to move north then south in the sky. Over the span of a *year*, the Sun makes a circuit of the starry sky which brings about many changes in our world – that annual cycle of light and dark and heat and cold that we call the **seasons**.

The Sun revolves in this determinate manner; and since the Sun revolves thus, the seasons in consequence come-to-be in a cycle, i.e. return upon themselves; and since they come-to-be cyclically, so in their turn do the things whose coming-to-be the seasons initiate. – Aristotle (circa 350 B.C.)

If we could see past the Sun's bright glare, we would observe that the Sun's path traces a circle around the celestial sphere. As the months and years go by, the Sun never departs from this circular path. This path is very much like a "tabernacle" – a dwelling in which the Sun can move, a "tent" that the Sun "pitches" amongst the stars from day to day. This tabernacle for the Sun is commonly known as the **ecliptic**.

The Ecliptic

The Sun follows a very regular path through the fixed stars along the ecliptic. The Moon also follows a very similar path, but slightly different from the Sun's, traveling above and below the ecliptic, but crossing at only two points.

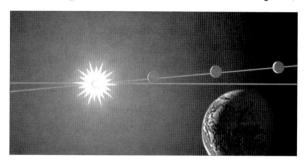 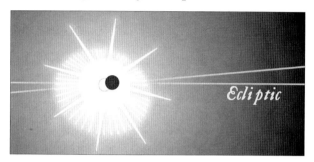

The Moon crosses the ecliptic over the course of the lunar month. Most of the time, nothing special happens. But once in a while, the Sun's cycle matches up with the Moon's, and the New Moon crosses the ecliptic when the Sun is nearby. At these times, the Moon covers over the face of the Sun, causing an **eclipse**. The ecliptic is so-named for being the circle in the sky where an eclipse occurs.

A third (circle), drawn through the middle is called the Ecliptic since, when both the Sun and Moon are pursuing their course along the same line at the same time, it is inevitable that one should suffer eclipse. – Macrobius (circa A.D. 400)

In addition to the Sun and Moon, a number of other bright celestial bodies can be seen moving among the fixed stars near the ecliptic. These are the **planets**, which comes from the Greek word for "wanderer." Many people are under the misconception that the planets are invisible without a telescope, but actually, they are among the brightest "stars" in the night sky. In fact, the classical planets are the brightest objects in the sky after the Sun and Moon.

We've seen that the Sun gives the illusion of moving toward the *west* as it rises and sets each day. But the Sun's motion along the ecliptic is toward the *east*, a slower second movement in the *opposite direction* to the daily rotation.

And since this is seen to be a great circle also because of the Sun's equal oscillation to the north and south of the equator... it was necessary to suppose a second movement different from the general one, a movement about the poles of this oblique circle or ecliptic in the direction opposite to the first movement. –Ptolemy (circa A.D. 150)

Like the Moon, the Sun also appears to move from west to east as it moves along the ecliptic. The Sun's changing position along the celestial sphere results in seasonal changes in the constellations. At each season of the year, certain constellations are seen in the evening after sunset. At other seasons, the same constellations are visible late at night or in the morning before sunrise.

The ancient philosophers such as Aristotle and Ptolemy taught that the Sun's movement was real – that the Sun actually did move from west to east along the ecliptic, with the Earth located at the center of this motion. But in his book *On the Revolutions of the Heavens*, Mikolaj Kopernik argued that if the Sun were motionless and the Earth rotated as it orbited the Sun, it would result in the illusion that the Sun and the stars moved in the sky over the course of the day and throughout the year.

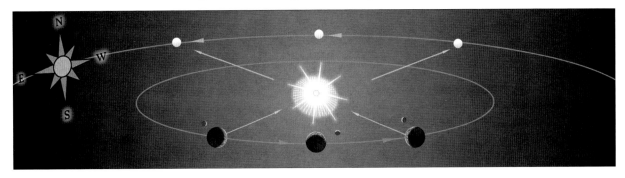

If one admits the motionlessness of the Sun, and transfers the annual revolution from the Sun to the Earth, there would result, in the same manner as actually observed, the rising and setting of the fixed stars, by means of which they become morning and evening stars. Finally, one will be convinced that the Sun itself occupies the center of the universe. And all this is taught us by the law of sequence in which things follow one upon another and the harmony of the universe; that is, if we only (so to speak) look at the matter with both eyes. – Kopernik (A.D. 1543)

The Sun's Motion along the Ecliptic

Just as the Moon orbits the Earth, our world is itself in orbit around the Sun. Our Earth is also a planet, a world in motion, continually "wandering" in a circle around the the Sun. If we could be far above our world, we would see the Earth joined by the other planets, other worlds that also orbit the Sun. The Sun and planets altogether form the **solar system**, the Earth's celestial neighborhood.

From far above the world, we could envision that the Earth's orbit lies within a plane, with the Sun also lying within that plane. The other planets in the solar system also circle the Sun near the same plane. The plane of the Earth's orbit is called the *plane of the ecliptic.*

Since the Sun and Earth lie within this plane, we can only perceive the plane of the ecliptic "edge on," so the ecliptic is perceived as a line across the starry sphere along which the Sun's path is found. Thus all the planets appear to line up with the Sun and are always found somewhere near the ecliptic. When we see the Sun, Moon, and planets along the ecliptic, we're actually looking out into the solar system from the Earth's surface.

The *classical planets* have been seen since the dawn of history and have been continuously observed since ancient times. The planet **Mercury** is the closest to the Sun, and it moves quickly through the sky as it wheels around the Sun.

Venus is the next closest, and alternates as the "morning star" and the "evening star" as it gleams brightly in our skies. Venus and Mercury, being closer to the Sun, never appear far from the Sun as seen from Earth.

The **Earth** is the third planet from the Sun. Beyond the Earth lies **Mars,** then **Jupiter** and **Saturn**. These outer planets are seen in any part of the sky, and they brightly dominate the lesser stars of the constellations they visit.

Beyond Saturn are the *modern planets*, **Uranus** and **Neptune**, along with *Pluto* and the other "dwarf planets." These bodies were discovered since the invention of the telescope and are very far away and dim, invisible to the unaided eye.

There is a band of constellations that lie along the plane of the ecliptic. The Sun, Moon and planets can always be seen moving among these constellations. These constellations are collectively known as the **zodiac**.

Often, when people hear the word *zodiac*, they think of **astrology** – an ancient pseudoscience that teaches that events in the world are influenced by the motions of the Sun, Moon, and planets. The practice of astrology is condemned by the Bible and discredited by modern science.

However, it should be understood that one of the many deceptions of the false science of astrology is that it is a *thief* that steals elements and terminology from the legitimate study of the sky. Many words that properly belong to *astronomy* are better known today as being associated with astrology.

Zodiac is such a word. The zodiac is simply the name of the ring of constellations that lie along the plane of our solar system, so that the Sun, Moon, and planets

appear to move through these constellations.

The word *zodiac* is derived from the Greek word *zoe* (ζωη), which means "life." Most of the zodiac constellations represent living creatures – human figures and animals – God's created things. The ancient Greeks envisioned a celestial "zoo" through which the Sun, Moon, and planets moved.

This foresaid heavenish Zodiak is called the Circle of the Signs, or the Circle of the Beasts, for zodia in the language of Greek soundeth like "beasts" in the Latin tongue. – Geoffrey Chaucer (circa A.D. 1400)

The word *zoe* turns up many times in the New Testament:

For God so loved the world, that he gave his only begotten Son, that whosoever believeth in him would not perish, but have everlasting life. – John 3:16

Though the actual word *zodiac* is not found in the Bible, it is generally understood that the Old Testament word *Mazzaroth* (מזרה) is the Hebrew equivalent. The use of this word in Job refers to the passing of the seasons, which results from the Sun's movement along the ecliptic:

Canst thou bring forth Mazzaroth in his season? or canst thou guide Arcturus with his sons? – Job 38:32

Also, a related word *Mazzaloth* (מזלה) is translated as "the planets" in 2 Kings 23:5 of the King James Version in connection with the idolatrous priests who worshipped the celestial bodies. The similarity of this word also points to the bodies that move through the constellations along the ecliptic.

Astronomy or Astrology?

As we've seen, the Sun, Moon, and stars were created for telling time and finding direction. Yet some Christians in our generation dismiss the legitimate study of God's sky because of confusion over astrology and the supposed pagan origins of the science of the stars.

While we certainly should be wary of corrupting influences, we should also make sure to distinguish *fact from fancy*. We should also take care not to hate God's creation in the sky simply because our generation confuses legitimate astronomy with ancient pagan superstition. According to the first-century Jewish historian *Flavius Josephus*, astronomy was first invented by the children of Seth:

> *Now this Seth, when he was brought up, and came to those years in which he could discern what was good, became a virtuous man; and as he was himself of an excellent character, so did he leave children behind him who imitated his virtues. All these proved to be of good dispositions. They also inhabited the same country without dissentions, and in a happy condition, without any misfortunes falling upon them till they died. They also were the inventors of that peculiar sort of wisdom which is concerned with the heavenly bodies, and their order.*

Therefore, Josephus indicates that astronomy was first developed by the servants of the LORD, the virtuous grandchildren of Adam. Josephus also says that the patriarch Abraham taught that the Sun and Moon were not gods, but powerless creations, subservient to God.

> *For which doctrines, when the Chaldeans, and the other people of Mesopotamia raised a tumult against him, he thought fit to leave that country; and at the command, and by the assistance of God, he came and lived in the land of Canaan.*

Josephus further states that it was Abraham who first taught astronomy to the Egyptians:

> *He communicated to them arithmetic, and delivered to them the science of astronomy; for, before Abram came into Egypt, they were unacquainted with those parts of learning; for that science came from the Chaldeans into Egypt, and from thence to the Greeks also.*

Though the writings of Josephus are not the revealed truth of Scripture, they nevertheless indicate that according to ancient Hebrew tradition, astronomy was an invention of God's servants, not idol-worshipping pagans.

In the time of Moses, about 1500 B.C., the heathen nations practiced the worship of the stars. Israel was commanded to worship the LORD alone, not created things like the celestial bodies:

And lest thou lift up thine eyes unto heaven, and when thou seest the Sun, and the Moon, and the stars, even all the host of heaven, shouldest be driven to worship them, and serve them, which the LORD thy God hath divided unto all nations under the whole heaven. –Deuteronomy 4:19

Centuries later, by about 700 B.C., the earlier pagan star worship had come to include finding *omens* in the sky – "bad signs" that were interpreted as predictions of trouble. Israel was commanded not to follow these pagan practices either:

Thus saith the LORD, Learn not the way of the heathen, and be not dismayed at the signs of heaven: for the heathen are dismayed at them. –Jeremiah 10:2

Modern devotees of astrology like to claim great antiquity for their superstition, that astrology in its current form goes back as far as 2000 B.C. or even earlier. Some Christian critics of astrology have suggested that it goes back to "Nimrod" and the Tower of Babel. However, there is no evidence for either belief, in the Bible or in any secular historical records. The fact is, the familiar *newspaper horoscope*-type astrology did not exist until about 50 B.C.! What we typically think of as "ancient" astrology is actually a relatively recent product of the Roman Empire, not Ancient Babylon!

In Rome, the Stoic philosophers were the first to develop a mathematical astrology. The Stoics taught *"cosmic sympathy"* – that everything in the world was interconnected and influenced everything else, beginning with the influence of the stars. The Stoics believed in *fate* – that emanations from the stars resulted in an inevitable human destiny, with no free will to alter the outcomes.

To support this view, the ancients noted the physical influence of the Sun and Moon in the natural world. They noted, as we do, that variations in sunlight and heat caused the changes in the seasons. They saw that the Moon raised the tide and that certain plants – *heliotropes* such as sunflowers – would turn to face the Sun as it crossed the sky. From that, they imagined that the celestial bodies exerted other influences over the world, including human affairs. The Stoics and their successors devised an elaborate scheme for assigning arbitrary meanings to the Sun, Moon, planets, and also the constellations of the zodiac, based upon flawed premises of Greek pseudoscience.

The idea of cosmic sympathy and the interconnectedness of all things led to all manner of bizarre divination and superstition. It was believed that *tea leaves* and *chicken entrails* could be "read" to tell the future. Even the paths of birds in flight were studied to discover new omens. The Romans were addicted to these superstitions. The Gospel of Christ first took root in this culture. No doubt the transforming power of Jesus released many Romans from the fatalistic tyranny of astrology.

The system of astrology is based on the assumption that there is some *meaning* to events in the sky. But the fact is, an *eclipse of the Sun* or a close passage of the Moon near a bright planet doesn't *mean* anything at all. These events are simply the result of the celestial bodies following their orbital paths as ordained by the LORD at their creation. The zodiac stars don't *mean* anything either. They are simply arrangements of stars in the sky observed to be part of God's creation.

The great Reformers understood the distinctions between CLASSICAL ASTRONOMY and astrology:

Astronomy is the most ancient of all sciences, and has been the introducer of vast knowledge; it was familiarly known to the Hebrews, for they diligently noted the course of the heavens, as God said to Abraham: "Behold the heavens; canst thou number the stars?" etc....I like astronomy and mathematics, which rely upon demonstrations and sure proofs. As to astrology, 'tis nothing....Astrology is no art; it has no principle, no demonstration, whereupon we may take sure footing; 'tis all haphazard work....Great wrong is done to God's creatures by the star-expounders. God has created and placed the stars in the firmament, to the end they might give light to the kingdoms of the earth, make people glad and joyful in the Lord, and be good signs of years and seasons. But the star-peepers feign that those creatures, of God created, darken and trouble the earth, and are hurtful; whereas all creatures of God are good, and by God created only for good, though mankind makes them evil, by abusing them. – Martin Luther, from *Table Talk*

In attestation of his wondrous wisdom, both the heavens and the earth present us with innumerable proofs not only those more recondite proofs which astronomy, medicine, and all the natural sciences are designed to illustrate, but proofs which force themselves on the notice of the most illiterate peasant, who cannot open his eyes without beholding them to investigate the motions of the heavenly bodies, to determine their positions, measure their distances, and ascertain their properties, demands skill, and a more careful examination; and where these are so employed, as the Providence of God is thereby more fully unfolded, so it is reasonable to suppose that the mind takes a loftier flight, and obtains brighter views of his glory. – John Calvin, from *The Institutes of the Christian Religion*

The ancient "science" of astrology has been utterly discredited by modern physics. Modern astronomy has shown that the only "influences" that emanate from the Sun, Moon, and stars are light, heat, and gravity. Although the Sun and Moon shine brightly and the Sun heats the Earth, the influence of gravity is small, at most merely raising the tide. People today have nothing to fear from astrology, since it lies on the ash heap of discarded ancient nonsense.

The Oblique Circle of the Zodiac

The Earth's axis of rotation is tilted to the plane of the ecliptic. This tilt is called the *inclination* of the Earth's axis. As the Earth revolves around the Sun, the axis remains inclined, pointing in the same direction, no matter what position it is at in its orbit.

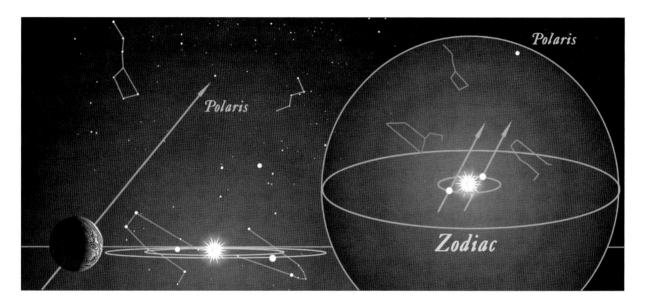

Wherever the Earth may be along its orbit, the North Pole of the axis *always* remains pointed at Polaris, the North Star. However, Polaris is not directly above the plane of the solar system, but is off to one side.

Imagine the solar system from the perspective of the Earth's axis, with the celestial poles and the celestial equator being upright. From this point of view, the zodiac would appear tilted as compared with the poles and equator.

The ecliptic is another great circle that bisects the celestial sphere. Being inclined to the celestial equator, one-half of the ecliptic is north of the equator and one-half is south. The ecliptic is therefore called the *oblique circle* of the celestial sphere. Historically, the terms *zodiac* and *ecliptic* have often been used interchangeably to refer to the oblique circle. The band of the zodiac is the most distinctive circle on the classical armillary sphere.

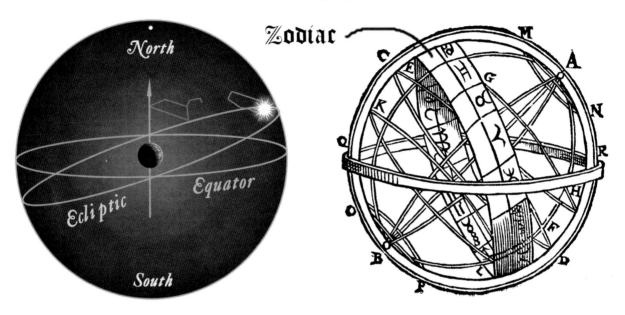

There is another circle in the sphere which intersects the equinoctial and is intersected by it into two equal parts. One half of it tips toward the North, the other toward the South. That circle is called "Zodiac" from zoe, meaning "life". – John Sacrobosco (circa A.D. 1230)

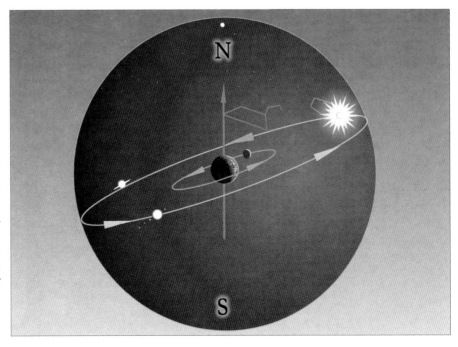

Compared to the celestial poles and equator, it seems that the Sun, Moon, and planets rise and fall from north to south along the ecliptic as they move along in their orbits. This results in the changes of the seasons and all the variations in the celestial cycles of the sky.

As seen from our place on the Earth's Northern Hemisphere, the northern extreme of the ecliptic rises to a point high in the sky overhead.

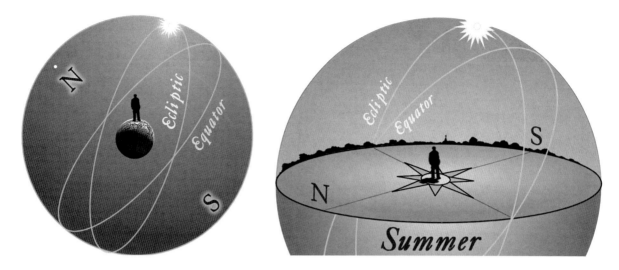

With the daily rotation of the sky, the southern extreme of the ecliptic reaches the meridian at a very low point, just above the treetops.

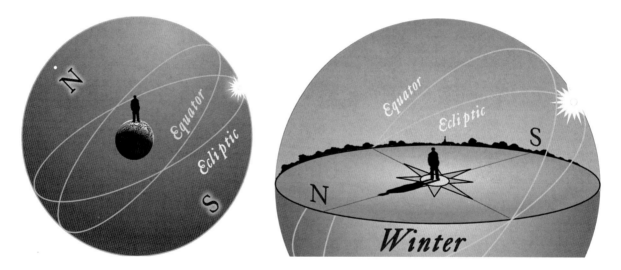

Twelve constellations have been traditionally associated with the zodiac. But stars can be grouped just about any way, so there is no special reason to find only twelve. The early, pre-astrological Greeks identified eleven zodiac constellations. The modern scientific scheme recognizes thirteen constellations that lie along the ecliptic.

Some zodiac constellations are composed of very bright stars that form distinct patterns. Other zodiac constellations are very faint and have patterns that are very obscure. But the zodiac constellations are useful in helping us find the place of the Sun in its tabernacle and find the Moon and planets in the night sky.

Following the Zodiac

Since the zodiac extends north to south, its traditional starting point is in between these extremes, at the point where the ecliptic intersects the celestial equator. This point of intersection is called the **vernal equinox**. In modern times, the vernal equinox is located in the constellation **Pisces**, the Fishes.

To the southward we find the constellation Pisces, one of them ever appearing brighter than the other, but it sooner feels the effects of the great northern blast. Both appear as though fastened by their tails, converging as one and at their junction shines a great and brilliant star, called a celestial tie. – Aratus (circa 275 B.C.)

Though the Fishes are the modern starting point for the zodiac, it is a hard pattern to find under the light polluted city skies. The stars of the Fishes are faint, and can best be seen under dark rural skies. The point of the vernal equinox is very near "the Circlet" in Pisces, a small circle of stars. Since Pisces lies along the celestial equator, it follows a similar path in the sky as Orion.

Heading east from the vernal equinox, the ecliptic ascends to the north, toward the brighter zodiac constellation **Aries**, the Ram. While the vernal equinox is found in the Fishes today, in the days of the ancient Greeks, the vernal equinox was in the Ram. In the 2000 years since then, the equinox has moved because of a phenomenon called *precession*.

Here also is the path of the fleet Ram, who, quickly moving, is not outrun by the more slowly moving Bear. – Aratus

As we move east, the constellations of the zodiac appear higher in the north. After the Ram, we encounter the constellations in the neighborhood of Orion, including **Taurus**, the Bull. Taurus is an easily recognizable constellation, formed of bright stars in a V–shape that resembles the horns of a bull. A V–shaped star cluster called the **Hyades** clearly forms a bull's head, and the bright red star **Aldebaran** (pronounced Al-DEB-a-ron) forms the Bull's eye.

Observe the huge horn of the Bull, where many other similar stars are located. Its head also is well defined, nor is any other conjecture required concerning it; besides there are the stars which shine on both sides of the head. Their name is often mentioned. Here, too, are the somewhat neglected Hyades which are spread over the forehead of the Bull. –Aratus

Between the Ram and the Bull's head, very near to the ecliptic, is the famous star cluster, the **Pleiades** (pronounced PLEE-a-deez). Besides nearby Orion and the Big Dipper, the Pleiades are among the few stars that the LORD names in His Word:

Canst thou bind the sweet influences of Pleiades, or loose the bands of Orion?

– Job 38:31

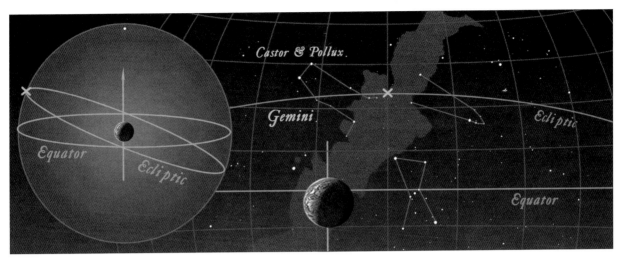

East of the Bull and above the head of Orion is **Gemini**, the Twins. The Twins are noted for two bright stars, underneath which are two parallel lines of faint stars, appearing double, like twins. These bright stars are called **Castor** and **Pollux**, after twin brothers in a Greek myth. Known together by their Greek name *Dioscuri* (Διοσκουρους), this was the name of the ship on which the Apostle Paul sailed from Malta on his way to Rome:

> *And after three months we departed in a ship of Alexandria, which had wintered in the isle, whose sign was Castor and Pollux.* – Acts 28:11

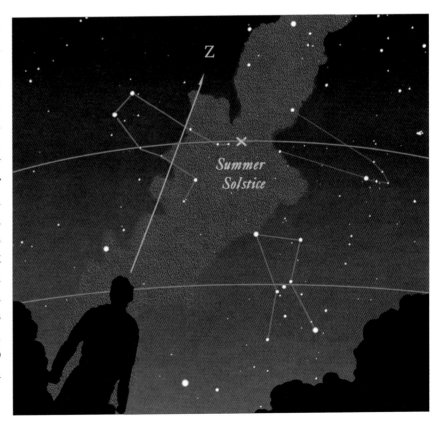

The Milky Way can be seen passing through the stars of the Twins. In modern times, the zodiac reaches its maximum northern extreme in the Twins, at a point in the sky called the **summer solstice**. As seen from the Northern Hemisphere, the Twins reach the meridian at a high point overhead in the sky, not far from the zenith. From this northern extreme, the ecliptic begins to descend again toward the south.

After Gemini comes **Cancer**, the Crab, an indistinct handful of very faint stars which are even harder to spot than Pisces. In ancient times, the point of the summer solstice was in the constellation of the Crab.

Near are the heads of the Twins, while below lies the middle portion of the Crab. – Aratus

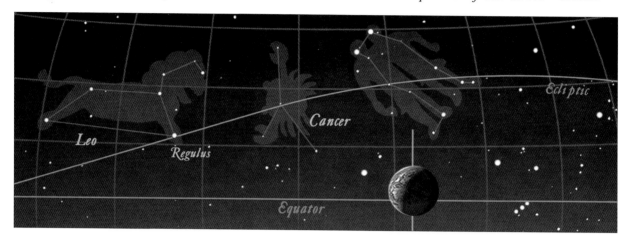

After the Crab follows the constellation **Leo**, the Lion. While the Crab is virtually invisible, the Lion is a very obvious constellation that looks very much like a lion jumping, like a great celestial *Aslan* of stars. The Lion appears to have a trapezoid-shaped body and a "sickle" asterism that forms its head. Leo is distinguished by **Regulus** (pronounced REG-you-lus) a bright reddish star that lies virtually right on the ecliptic.

Under both feet the Lion brightly shines; there also is the path of the scorching Sun. Then do the fields of corn appear empty at the first approach of the Sun to the Lion. – Aratus

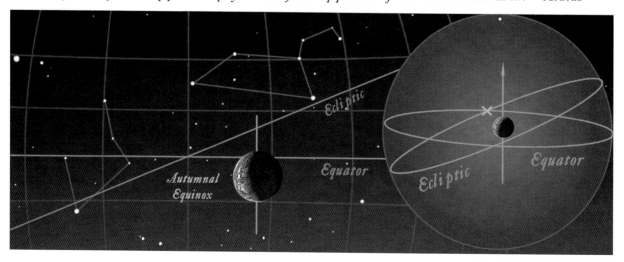

Continuing east from Leo, the ecliptic descends to the south until it again crosses the celestial equator. This point of intersection is called the **autumnal equinox**, which lies on the celestial sphere opposite the vernal equinox.

The autumnal equinox is in the zodiac constellation of **Virgo**, the Maiden. The Maiden is formed of bright stars, but they look more like a box-shape than a human figure. The Maiden is distinguished by the bright star **Spica** (pronounced "Spike-a"). Like Regulus, Spica also lies very near the ecliptic. And since Virgo also lies along the celestial equator, it also follows a similar path across the sky as Orion, from east to west, and climbs just as high above the horizon.

The Virgin appears, who holds in her hand the splendid star Spica.

— Aratus

The Southern Zodiac

Following to the east of Virgo, the zodiac extends down to the hemisphere to the south of the celestial equator. Here we find **Libra**, the Balance. Libra depicts a *balance* or a *scale* for weighing things. In ancient times, the autumnal equinox was in Libra. So Libra was taken to be the place where the daylight would be "balanced" with the darkness of night.

Then Libra, making the daytime equal with the nighttime, pulls along the Scorpion,
on fire with glittering stars. — Manilius (circa A.D. 20)

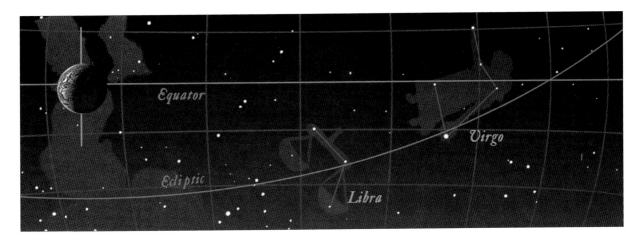

Libra is not a very distinct constellation and is defined by a fairly large triangle of modest stars. The Balance is the only constellation of the zodiac which does not depict a living creature. The ancient Greeks regarded the stars of Libra as belonging to the next zodiac constellation – **Scorpius**, the Scorpion. Thus, the Greeks only identified eleven zodiac constellations. The stars now associated with Libra were considered to be the *Chelae* or *Claws* of the Scorpion:

> *Observe the great Claws of the Scorpion; the stars therein are*
> *of moderate light and never very bright.* – Aratus

Libra is a late invention of the Romans, invented to honor Caesar Augustus. Libra was a constellation unknown to Aratus and the Greeks.

> *And you above all Caesar... whether you add yourself as a new star to the lingering months,*
> *where, between the Virgin and the grasping Claws, a space is opening (lo! For even*
> *now the blazing Scorpion draws in his arms, and has left more than*
> *a due portion of the heaven!)* – Virgil (circa 30 B.C.)

Like Orion and the Big Dipper, Scorpius strongly resembles the object for which it is named. The Scorpion is notable for its long, hook-shaped tail, formed of fairly bright stars. It has a head formed of a curved "Orion's Belt" of fairly bright stars. In this way, Scorpius is a large constellation that bears a strong resemblance to a real scorpion.

Scorpius is distinguished by the bright red star **Antares** (An-TAR-eez), which like Aldebaran, Regulus and Spica, lies near the Ecliptic. In fact, these stars can be used to locate the ecliptic in the sky.

Above Scorpius is a not-so-famous constellation called **Ophiuchus**, the Serpent Handler (pronounced Oh-fee-YOU-cus). While not a traditional zodiac constellation, it actually does cross the ecliptic, and the Sun, Moon, and planets pass among these stars. Traditionally, the ecliptic stars of Ophiuchus were associated with the Scorpion.

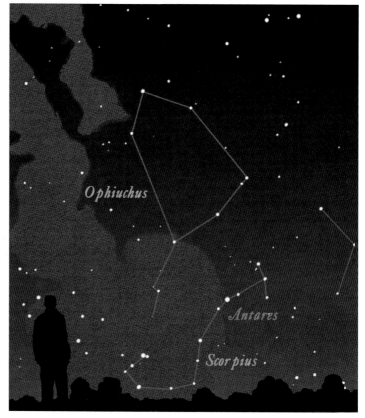

* Signs *

The ecliptic is not equally divided by the zodiac constellations. While the Scorpion is a very large constellation, only a tiny portion of it crosses the Ecliptic. Many other zodiac constellations are smaller but cover a larger section of the ecliptic. And as a *thirteenth* zodiac constellation, *Ophiuchus* messes up the traditional scheme of twelve constellations.

In ancient times, for timekeeping and other measurement purposes, it was convenient to divide the ecliptic into twelve equal sections corresponding to the twelve months in the year. These sections were called "signs." In another traditional usage of the word, a *sign* refers to the star pattern or a picture of the actual object supposedly depicted by the pattern of stars. Such sign-pictures were common on old star maps.

The word "Sign" is used in two senses: (1) for the twelfth part of the Zodiac circle, which is a certain distance in space marked off by stars or points; (2) for the picture formed by the stars, according to the resemblance and the position of the said stars. – Geminus (circa 50 B.C.)

In the first sense, each sign roughly corresponded to one-twelfth of the ecliptic, but did not correspond to the actual size of the constellations. Since some constellations were bigger than others, a zodiac "sign" might actually overlap adjoining constellations. But the term "sign" is very old-fashioned today and is no longer used in astronomy. Astronomers today use different mathematical schemes for finding position on the ecliptic.

But the signs made up of fixed stars are neither equal in size nor made up of an equal number of stars; nor do all exactly fill up their own allocated places in the "twelve parts." Some are deficient and occupy only a small part of the appropriate space, like the Crab; some overlap and encroach on certain portions of the preceding and following signs, for example, the Virgin. Again, some of the twelve signs do not even lie wholly on the Zodiac circle, but some are further north than it is, like the Lion, and some further south, like the Scorpion. – Geminus

The outdated astronomical use of *sign* is still used today in astrology to denote an equal, one-twelfth segment of the zodiac. But even in the early Church, it was understood that astrology was not intended in Genesis 1:14, where it states that the Sun and Moon were created for "signs and seasons, days and years." The "signs" referred to in Scripture have always been understood by Christian authors to refer to the visible indications of the passing seasons and other useful elements of the sky, not fatalism from the stars.

But those who overstep the borders, making the words of Scripture their apology for the art of casting nativities, pretend that our lives depend upon the motion of the heavenly bodies, and that thus the Chaldeans read in the planets that which will happen to us. By these simple words "let them be for signs," they understand neither the variations of the weather, nor the change of the seasons; they only see in them, at the will of their imagination, the distribution of human destinies. – Basil of Caesarea (circa A.D. 360)

Rounding Out the Circle

East of Ophiuchus is **Sagittarius**, the Archer.   The Archer is formed of stars about as bright as those of the Scorpion, and the stars of Scorpius extend toward Sagittarius from underneath. It may be hard to see an archer in these stars, but Sagittarius looks remarkably like a modern-day *teapot!* Since the "spout" lies in the Milky Way, it appears that "steam" is rising from the "teapot"!

Forasmuch as the Archer draws his great bow to the very point, but the Scorpion rising a little before him, abides near him and they ascend. – Aratus

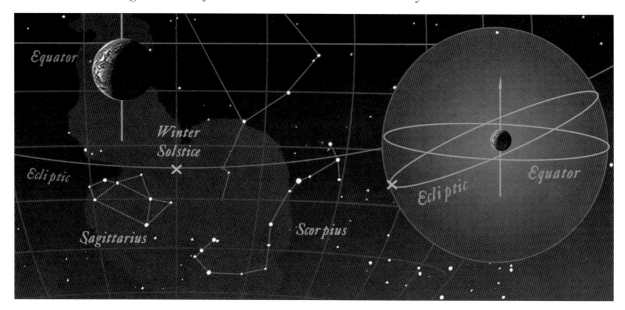

In modern times, the Archer is the home of the **winter solstice**, the extreme southern point of the ecliptic.   From the Northern Hemisphere, the stars of Sagittarius and Scorpius are low in the sky, grazing the treetops.   To the east of the Archer, the ecliptic begins to head north again.

Capricornus, the Goat is found east of the teapot. The Goat is a horn-shaped figure of dim stars, best seen under dark Milky Way skies.   In ancient times, the winter solstice point was in Capricornus.

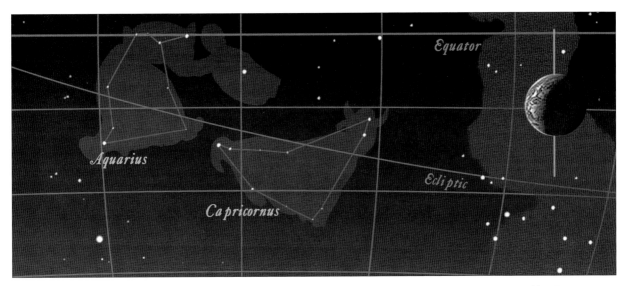

Aquarius, the Waterbearer is found east of the Goat. These constellations are in a part of the sky with few bright stars. Therefore, these patterns are not very distinct. The Waterbearer is best found by a little zig-zag of stars called the *Water Jar*, which lie above the ecliptic on the celestial equator.

In his neighborhood are the Pisces, while near his head is extended the right hand of the
Waterbearer and behind him is the Goat, standing farther off
where runs the Sun's path. – Aratus

As the ecliptic rises toward the equator, we again reach the vernal equinox in Pisces, completing our loop around the celestial circle of the ecliptic.

Next comes Capricorn, curled up with his cramped asterism, and after him from urn upturned
the Water Man pours forth the wanted stream. For the Fishes which swim eagerly into it; and
these as they bring up the rear of the signs are joined by the Ram. – Manilius (circa A.D. 20)

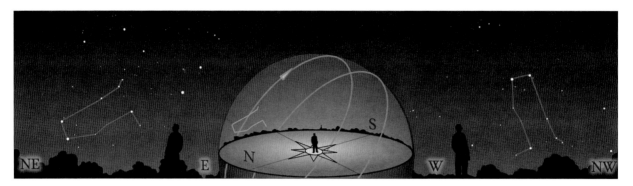

As we've seen, half of the zodiac constellations are to the north of the celestial equator, and half are to the south. Those that lie to the north rise and set toward the north and are high in the sky as they reach the meridian.

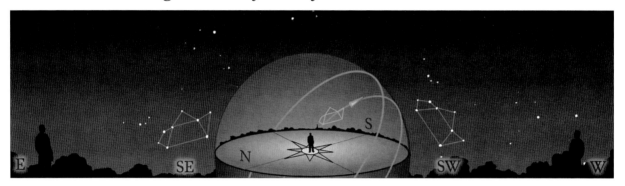

Similarly, those that lie to south rise and set toward the south and are low in the sky as they pass the meridian. Those that cross the equator rise and set due east and due west, and transit in the middle of the extremes.

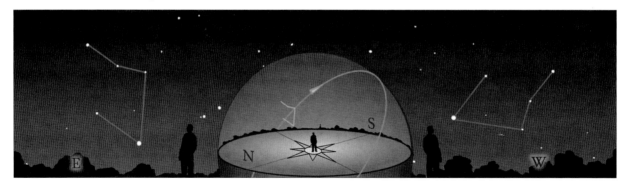

For this reason, the Sun, Moon, and planets can be seen rising and setting in different parts of the sky, passing high overhead or grazing the the treetops. As the Sun circles around in its tabernacle, its northern and southern variations result in the passage of the four seasons.

But have you ever known anything like the Sun or the Moon or the five planets? The Sun completes its annual course, defining its motion by the two extremities of a single orbit. The Moon, lit by the rays of the Sun, completes the same course in a month. – Cicero (circa 50 B.C.)

Chapter 5
The Cycle of the Year

Observe the circling Year, how unperceiv'd Her Seasons change! behold! by slow Degrees,
Stern Winter tam'd into a ruder Spring; The ripen'd Spring a milder Summer glows;
Departing Summer sheds Pomona's store; And aged Autumn brews the Winter storm.
– The North-American Almanack for the Year of our LORD CHRIST 1787

The annual cycle of the changing seasons is perhaps one of the most obvious facts of life, after the daily cycle of day and night. We all notice the signs that mark the passing seasons – the first appearance of the crocuses and daffodils, the warming and cooling of the air, the migrations of birds and butterflies, and the turning and falling of leaves from the trees.

But there are other signs in the sky that mark the seasons even more clearly than these signs on the ground – the lengthening and

From "The Shepherdes Kalender" – A.D. 1506

shortening of the daylight, the northern and southern risings and settings of the Sun, the drawing and withdrawing of the Sun overhead, and the constellations that accompany each season. In fact, these signs are all interrelated, and the seasonal changes on the land are all the result of the changing positions of the Sun over the span of the cycle of the year.

The Sun traverses the zodiac circle in a year. For a yearly period is that in which the Sun travels round the zodiac circle, and returns from the same point to the same point.... The yearly period is divided into four parts: Spring, Summer, Autumn and Winter. –Geminus (circa 50 B.C.)

- 93 -

The Sun Passage through the Zodiac

The orbital motion of the Earth around the Sun creates the optical illusion of the Sun moving eastward along the ecliptic. Like the Moon, the Sun moves from west to east through the constellations of zodiac. While the Moon rounds the zodiac circle in a single month, the Sun takes an entire year.

The Sun also moves from west to east, although its pace is much slower than the Moon's, crossing only one sign in the time that the Moon takes to traverse the whole Zodiac; nevertheless, it affords our eyes clear proof that it also has its own motion.   —Macrobius (circa A.D. 400)

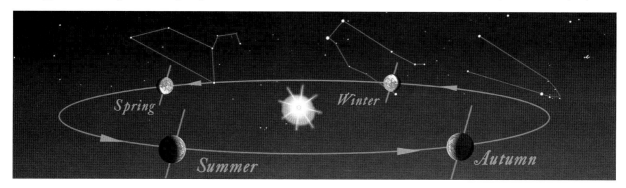

As the Earth orbits the Sun, the Earth's axis remains pointed at Polaris, and is inclined to the plane of the ecliptic. But from the perspective of the Earth's axis, it is the ecliptic that is obliquely tilted to the celestial equator and poles, so that the Sun rises and falls in our sky in the annual cycle of the seasons.

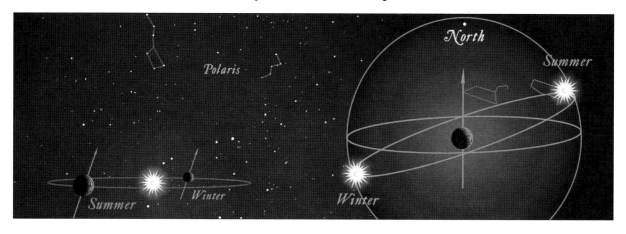

As the Sun follows its path through the zodiac, it rises to its highest altitude in the sky during the summertime, in the northern extremes on the ecliptic. The summer Sun is essentially "above" the northern half of the globe, and so the Northern Hemisphere spends more than half of each rotation in daylight. The Sun's ecliptic path carries it closer toward the elevated pole and the "always visible" circle of northern stars. Consequently, the Sun is above the horizon for a longer time than it is below, and the summer days are longer than the nights.

The Sun is at the southern extremes of the ecliptic in the wintertime, and so reaches its lowest altitudes of the year. The winter Sun is below the Earth's equator, and so the Northern Hemisphere spends more than half of each rotation in the Earth's shadow. In the sky, the Sun's path takes it closer to the depressed pole and the "never visible" circle. Thus, the Sun is above the horizon for a shorter time than it is below, and the winter nights are longer than the days. Spring and autumn are the seasons between these extremes.

The yearly cycle is made up of 365 daily revolutions of the Sun's orbit, with six hours added. But the Sun in its orbit swings now to the north and now to the south, bringing summer and winter in their turn, and spring and autumn. And from these four changing seasons derives the cause and origin of everything to which the Earth or sea gives birth. –Cicero (circa 50 B.C.)

We cannot directly observe the Sun's position against the stars of the zodiac. As we've seen, the Sun "lights up the air," giving up a portion of its sunlight to create the blue color of the sky. The scattering of the sunlight hides the stars, concealing the Sun's position on the ecliptic.

A sign that rises with the Sun and sets with it is of course never visible, and even nearby constellations are concealed by it. –Macrobius (circa A.D. 400)

The Sun's position on the ecliptic can only be seen directly during a total eclipse of the Sun. During total eclipse, the Sun is comparable in brightness to the Full Moon, and many bright stars can become visible. It is easy to find the Sun's position among the zodiac constellations during a solar eclipse.

The Sun's position on the ecliptic can also be confirmed during evening twilight. As the sky grows dim, we can see the zodiac constellation to the *east* of the Sun hanging above the sunset. In the morning twilight, we can see the zodiac constellation to the *west* of the Sun above the place of the sunrise. From this, we understand that the Sun is at a position on the ecliptic *between* the zodiac constellations seen before sunrise and after sunset.

March Hath XXXI Days

And now the Sun does on the middle shine,
And in the course mark the equinoctial line,
By which wise means we can the whole survey,
In the succession of a night and day.

– Entry for March, *The Connecticut Almanack for the YEAR of Our LORD 1780*

From "Poor Richard's Almanack" by Ben Franklin

As we all know, the New Year begins on January 1. But for astronomical purposes, the **tropical year** has traditionally been measured from the time when the Sun crosses the celestial equator. This event occurs every year on or around March 21. As we've seen, the **vernal equinox** is a point of intersection on the celestial sphere between the circles of the ecliptic and the celestial equator. However, in common usage, the day of the Sun's passage is also called the *vernal equinox*.

When the Sun is on the celestial equator, it is neither north nor south, but is perfectly balanced at an equal distance between the celestial poles. And so there is a perfect balance between daylight and darkness. On the equinox, there are twelve hours of day and twelve hours of night. From this derives the word **equinox**, which comes from the Latin words *aequus,* which means "equal," and *nox,* which means "night." For this reason also, the celestial equator is known as the *equinoctial circle.*

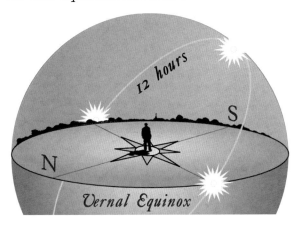

The word *vernal* comes from the Latin word *vernalis*, which means "pertaining to the spring." The day of the vernal equinox is the *first day of spring* for those who live in the Northern Hemisphere. The seasonal signposts have traditionally been reckoned according to such astronomical events. Astronomically speaking, the equinox occurs at the precise moment when the Sun is centered on the celestial equator.

When, returning from the southern regions, the Sun is in the middle of the heavens and divides day and night into equal parts, the more it sojourns above the Earth, the more it brings back a mild temperature to us. Then comes spring, which makes all the plants germinate, and gives to the greater part of the trees their new life, and by successive generation, perpetuates all the land and water animals. – Basil of Caesarea (circa A.D. 360)

As we've seen, the vernal equinox today lies in the constellation of the Fishes, though in centuries past it was in Aries. On the first day of spring, as the Sun lies on the equator, its bright rays hide the stars of the Fishes. The Sun therefore rises *due east*, at around 6:00 A.M., and sets *due west* twelve hours later, around 6:00 P.M. (as we saw in Chapter 1).

The middle circle is called the Circle Equinoxial, upon which turneth the heads of Aries and Libra. And understand well that evermore this circle equinoxial turneth justly from very east to very west....This same circle is called the equator of the day, for when the Sun is in the heads of Aries and Libra, then the days and the nights are alike of length in all the world. – Geoffrey Chaucer (circa A.D. 1400)

If one lives on or near a street that runs from east to west with a clear horizon, the Sun can be seen rising and setting at the ends of the street! If we approach God's creation with our eyes open, we can appreciate that the Sun's rising due east and setting due west are actually "signs" of the coming season. This is a sure sign of the coming of spring, just as clear and apparent as melting snow, crocuses and daffodils, and the return of the red-breasted robins.

April Hath XXX Days

And dripping, more or less, it does remain,
Eer since (to cause Noah's Flood) it first did rain,
Before which time the Earth (so Moses says),
Was watered by a Mist, no other way:
The Rain-bow also proves it unto me,
For without Clouds no Rain-bow could there be.
– Entry for April, *Leeds' Almanack for 1694*

As spring progresses, March gives way to April. As the Earth's motion steers the North Pole toward the Sun, the Sun appears to move into the stars of the Ram, higher and higher into the northern sky.

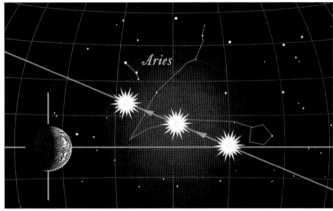

The Sun rises and sets increasingly toward the north, so that morning and evening shadows point somewhat toward the south. The Northern Hemisphere spends more time in the Sun's rays, resulting in a longer period of daylight.

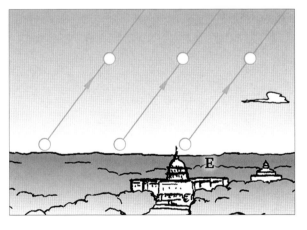

In March, we reset our clocks as we go on *daylight savings time*. During the longest days, the Sun would rise about 4:30 A.M. and set at 7:30 P.M. Most people are not yet awake at 4:30 A.M., and would rather have extra daylight in the evening to extend the time for outdoor activities.

So as the days grow longer, the civil authorities decree each year that we set our clocks ahead one hour in the springtime. We set our clocks to *spring forward* in the spring so that the Sun rises and sets an hour later. However, with daylight savings, the Sun reaches the meridian at about 1:00 P.M. instead of 12:00 P.M. This is one of the ways that "clock time" is separated from "sundial time."

May Hath XXXI Days

Now May the sweetest month in all the year,
With all her pomp and duty doth appear,
Rise up betimes, view nature's lovely bloom,
Which late was buried in cold winter's womb.
– Entry for May, *The Connecticut Almanack* for 1780

During May, the Sun has moved from the Ram into the Bull. Each day, the Sun draws higher and higher overhead in the noon skies of the Northern Hemisphere as it passes the meridian. As the Sun moves north, the days grow longer and the land is warmed by the additional hours of exposure to the Sun's rays.

As the Sun rises higher throughout the spring, the Sun's increasing altitude in the noon sky can be measured by the shortening of the noon shadows. On the vernal equinox in the midnorthern latitudes, the noon shadows can be nearly as long as the height of the person or object casting the shadow. But over the course of the spring, the noon shadows grow shorter as the Sun draws higher overhead. The noon shadows are thus the yardstick for measuring the invisible rise and fall of the Sun through the zodiac constellations.

Since the Sun is in the northern half of the celestial sphere from the first day of spring until the first day of fall, the Sun rises and sets toward the north during the spring and summer.

And understand well that all signs of the Zodiac, from the head of Aries to the end of Virgo, are called signs of the north from the equinoctial; and these signs arise betwixt the very east and the very north in our horizon generally forever. –Geoffrey Chaucer (circa A.D. 1400)

On spring mornings, as the Sun rises northerly, the sunrise shadows point toward the south! After rising, the Sun passes *above* due east. As the Sun rises farther to the north, it passes higher above the due east horizon, so that the morning shadows point due west. On an "astronomically aligned" street, the shadows of trees, utility poles, and people fall parallel with the street and sidewalk. Likewise, in the evening, the westering Sun hangs over due west so that the shadows point due east.

June Hath XXX Days

Now is Majestic Sol in's highest clime,
And greatest altitude in tropic sign,
Affording hottest beams and melting rays,
To make the season teem with summer Days.
– Entry for June, *The Connecticut Almanack* for 1780

The spring days grow longer throughout the beginning of June as the Sun passes in front of the stars of the Bull. Towards month's end, the Sun enters the constellation of the Twins. Finally, on or about June 21, the Earth reaches the place in its orbit where the North Pole is most inclined toward the Sun. In the sky, the Sun reaches the northern extreme of the ecliptic – the point of the **summer solstice**. As is also similar to the vernal equinox, the day of the Sun's crossing is itself called the *summer solstice*.

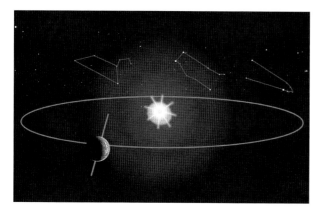

The day of the summer solstice is *the first day of summer* and *the longest day of the year*. In accordance with ancient tradition, summer begins on the day with the most daylight of the entire year.

Many large cities such as New York, Washington, Cleveland, Chicago, and San Francisco are near the latitude of 40 degrees north. On the longest day, these places bask in the Sun's rays for *fifteen hours*, and pass through the Earth's shadow for a brief *nine hours*. With daylight savings, the Sun rises at about 5:30 A.M., crosses the meridian at around 1:00 P.M., and sets about 8:30 P.M. (depending on one's location).

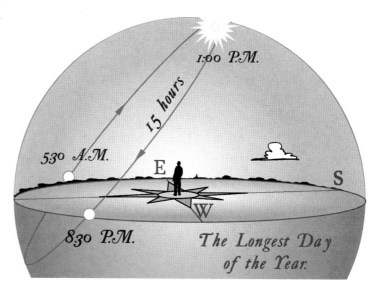

The Longest Day of the Year.

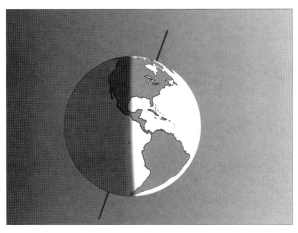

As seen from above the globe, sunlight covers most of the Northern Hemisphere, pushing back the sunrise and sunset sides of the terminator. Far to the north, there is a circle of continuous daylight around the North Pole. This is the terrestrial **Arctic Circle**. On the summer solstice, locations to the north of the Arctic Circle experience twenty-four hour daylight. As the Earth rotates, these places are never carried into the Earth's shadow, and the summer Sun never sets in the Arctic. This region is called "The Land of the Midnight Sun."

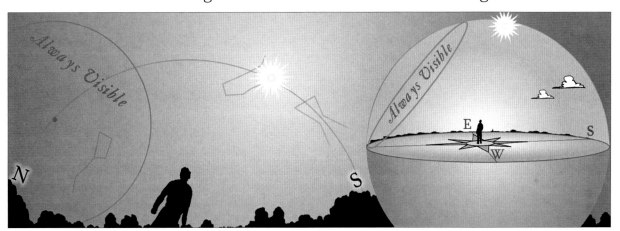

On the first day of summer, the Sun is at the point on the ecliptic which is closest to the North Star and the "always visible" circle. Thus, the bright luminary is at its highest in the noon skies of the Northern Hemisphere and is above the horizon for the longest period of time, as compared with every other day of the year. On the summer solstice, the shadows at noon are the shortest of the year. In the midtemperate northern latitudes, the shadows are about one-quarter the length of the objects casting them.

The Summer Solstice occurs when the Sun comes nearest to the region where we live, describing its most northerly circle and producing the longest day of all days in the year, and the shortest night. – Geminus (circa 50 B.C.)

On the solstice, the Sun rises at its farthest extreme to the northeast and sets at its farthest point to the northwest. During the longest days, the period of twilight is also the longest of the year. The sky still retains the Sun's glow for a long time after the sunset. In the morning before sunrise, the sky starts to glow quite a while before the Sun actually rises. During these weeks, the Sun appears to ride close below the horizon. If you watch the twilight very closely, you can see the twilight glow move far to the north of the place of the sunset, indicating the Sun's position.

In places to the north of the continental United States, like Canada, Europe, and Alaska, the *white nights* can be seen in late spring and early summer. After sunset, the Sun scoots underneath the northern horizon, and a patch of twilight is always seen over the short summer night. The sky never gets completely dark because evening twilight merges with morning twilight!

The word *solstice* comes from the Latin words *sol*, which means "Sun," and *stit*, which means "stand" – literally "the Sun stands." The ancient Romans used this name because on the solstice, the Sun goes no further north but "stands still" in the sky.

The Greek word for the solstice is the **tropic**, from the word *tropos* (τροπως), which means "turning." After the solstice, the Sun turns from its northern extreme and begins to head south again, through the descending part of the zodiac. As with the term *solstice*, the *tropic* also refers to the extreme points of the ecliptic. The word also refers to the celestial circles corresponding to the tropic point above the celestial equator.

Wherefore it is called the "Circle of the Summer Solstice" or the "Summer Tropic" from tropos, which is "turning" because then the Sun begins to turn toward the lower hemisphere and to recede from us. – John Sacrobosco (circa A.D. 1230)

Just as there are poles and an equator on the Earth and in the sky, there is also a "summer tropic" circle on the Earth and sky. The terrestrial tropic is called the *Tropic of Cancer* and passes under the celestial solstice point.

The terrestrial Tropic of Cancer defines the northern extreme of "the tropics", the zone of warm climate. Along the Tropic of Cancer, the noon Sun passes directly overhead at the zenith, and the noon shadows more or less disappear. Contrary to popular belief, the Sun is never directly overhead in the regions north of the tropics.

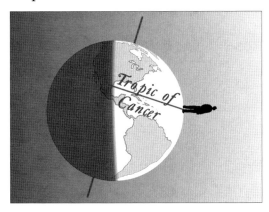 

You might wonder why the northern tropic is named after *Cancer* since the Sun is really in *Gemini*. As mentioned previously, in classical times, the solstice point really was located in Cancer. Over the centuries, the solstice has moved into Gemini due to the phenomenon of *precession*, which has also moved the vernal equinox from Aries to Pisces. While we don't say "The Tropic of Gemini," the term "Tropic of Cancer" is still used today more because of tradition than any astronomical reality. Old astronomy habits die hard!

July Hath XXXI Days

Observe the Bee for she instructs us all,
And preaches labor to both great and small,
In time she gathers to increase her store,
And when that's gone she toils abroad for more.
– Entry for July, *The Connecticut Almanack* for 1780

During July, the Sun passes through the stars of the Twins and by month's end enters the Crab. During the long days of late spring and early summer, the length of daylight doesn't change very much from week to week. In most places, the length of daylight is only a few minutes different in the weeks before and after the longest day.

In the spring, the Sun moves north through the zodiac as though climbing a hill. As the Sun reaches the top of its northern "climb," it begins to "level out," and doesn't move much further to the north between May and June. As the Sun again heads south

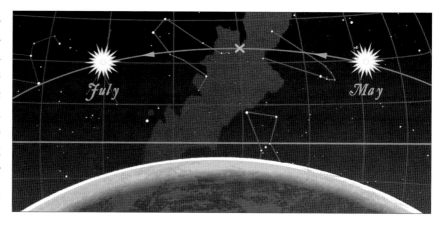

across the sky after the longest day, it takes until late July for it to again reach the position of mid-May. For this reason, the length of daylight is just about the same for about a month on either side of the longest day.

August Hath XXXI Days

Preferments are but children's toys,
As years increase decrease our joys,
For as a shadow pleasures pass,
A tale of that which never was.

– Entry for August, *The Connecticut Almanack* for 1780

As summer wears on through August, the Sun moves through the Crab and into the Lion, drawing again toward the south. The seasonal signs of spring now become reversed. The Sun's risings and settings move away from the north. The noon Sun is increasingly lower in the sky, and the noon shadows grow longer once again.

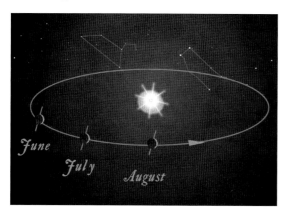

As the Earth moves along its orbit, the North Pole draws away from the Sun, and the distribution of the Sun's light between the hemispheres becomes more even. The circle of continuous twenty-four hour daylight recedes from around the North Pole, and the Northern Hemisphere days grow shorter again.

Summer Heat

The Sun shines with a considerable amount of light, but it produces even more heat. About two-thirds of the Sun's radiation is in the form of heat radiation. The intense heat of the Sun is responsible for the warming that occurs during summer. Since the land receives more light in summer, it also receives more heat, and so summer is the warmest season. But the late days of summer, during August, are much warmer than the early days in June. However, in June, the amount of sunlight (and heat) is greatest.

Why isn't it hotter in June and cooler in August, when the solar radiation is less? This phenomenon is called **the lag of the seasons**. Like everything else, the Earth gains heat slowly. A teapot on a stove needs time to absorb heat from the burner so that the water will reach the proper temperature to boil. The Earth responds to heat in the same way.

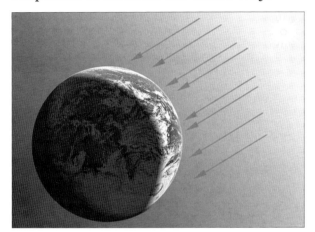 

The Earth gains heat by **insolation**, from the Latin word *insolatio*, which means "to expose to the Sun." The land and seas of the Earth need the span of the summer to absorb the Sun's heat. Consequently, the seasons lag behind the Sun by about two months, and August is usually much hotter than June. The Earth loses heat in the same way. February is usually a much colder month than December, when the days are shortest.

We can observe the same warming effect during the daytime. It's always much cooler in the morning than in evening. Noon is never the hottest time of day. The ground and air don't reach their hottest temperatures until about 3:00 or 4:00 P.M. during summer afternoons. Just ask anyone who works outside during the warm months!

The Sun generates the difference of heat and cold over the seasons, because in the Summer it comes nearer, not to us, but to the point of our zenith, and in the Winter it departs from it again. – Simplicius (circa A.D. 500)

September Hath XXX Days

Now glittering Sol doth more and more decline,
And now doth cross the Equinoctial Line,
The nights do then exceed the days in length,
The heat abates and the cold doth gather strength.
– Entry for September, *The Connecticut Almanack* for 1780

Throughout September, the Sun passes from the Lion to the Maiden. The Sun reaches the **autumnal equinox** on or around September 23. As with the other seasonal benchmarks, the day of the Sun's second equator crossing is also called the *autumnal equinox, the first day of fall.*

The Autumnal Equinox occurs when the Sun in its passage from north to south is once more on the equinoctial circle, and makes the day equal to night. – Geminus (circa 50 B.C.)

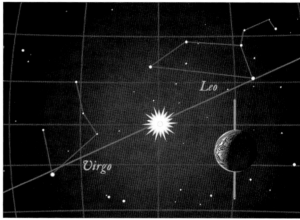

As summer yields to fall, the Northern Hemisphere is again equally divided between illumination and shadow, and the world once again collectively experiences a global twelve-hour day. The whole world again sees the Sun rise due east and set due west as the Sun again ascends equally between the celestial poles.

By the end of September, the days are an *hour and a half shorter* than at the beginning of the month! From week to week, the Sun sets much earlier than it did the week before. Though the days may still be warm, the mornings are now very chilly, since the Sun's light and heat are greatly diminished from the warmest days. These are celestial signs of the changing seasons, presaging the falling of the leaves from the trees and the southern migration of the geese, signs of even cooler months yet to come.

October Hath XXXI Days

At length forsaken by the solar rays,
The drooping nature sickens and decays,
In hoary triumph unmolested reigns,
O'er barren hills and bleak untrodden plains,
Hardens the globe, the shady globe deforms,
Brings on the cold and shakes the air with storms.
– Entry for October, *The Connecticut Almanack* for 1780

The Sun now dips into the southern stars of the Balance and darkness prevails over the Northern Hemisphere. The Sun now rises and sets to the south. As the days grow shorter, the shadows grow longer, and the Sun never reaches very high along the meridian at noon.

The Sun now rises later and sets earlier. The early sunrises of summer are long past, and the morning light arrives later and later. In order to provide an earlier time of sunrise, daylight savings comes to an end. We "fall back" by setting our clocks backward one hour, so that we get back that hour of sleep we lost in the spring. But since the Sun already sets so much earlier than in summer, evening twilight arrives before dinnertime.

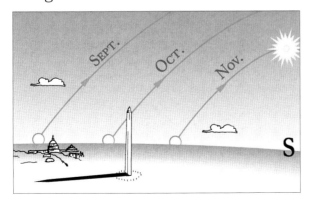

Autumn

Over span of the year, the shadows on the sundials also grow long and short with the seasons, which can make the sundial hard to read. To compensate, the sundial gnomon is inclined so that it points toward the elevated North Celestial Pole. In this way, the sky rotates around the gnomon and the gnomon is centered on the circle of the Sun's daily motion throughout all the seasons.

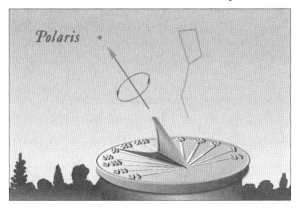

While a flat dial with an inclined gnomon works well, the shadows still are a bit distorted. The best sundial design is an **armillary sundial** with a circular dial. An armillary sundial, like the armillary sphere, imitates the shape of the firmament and best corresponds to the Sun's circular path across the sky.

Standard Time

Throughout history, time was measured according to *local time*. Twelve-noon was simply the time when the Sun reached its highest point in the sky at the meridian. Each person saw noon at a unique time for that location. One sundial would point to noon while a sundial 50 miles away would read a time different by a few minutes.

This system worked fine for centuries. But in the modern world, the inventions of the telegraph and the railroad enabled high-speed transportation and communication. It became difficult to manage the many small differences in local time across short distances.

In 1884, the nations of the world agreed to adopt a system of *standard time* in which the whole world is divided into twenty-four *time zones*. With standard time, cities separated by hundreds of miles share a common clock time, though their sundials may read differently by as much as an hour.

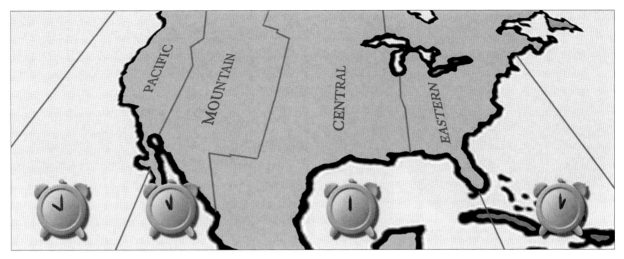

As a result, on any day of the year at any latitude, the times of actual sunrise and sunset vary depending on your location within a time zone. The Sun rises and sets earlier in the eastern end of a time zone and later in the western end of a time zone. Almost everywhere within each time zone, the Sun no longer reaches its highest point in the sky at precisely twelve-noon.

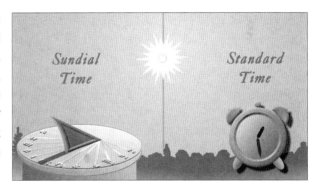

Standard time and daylight savings provide a common standard reference for telling time across a high-speed world. But between standard time and the extra hour of daylight savings, the Sun can reach "high noon" in the sky as late as 1:30 PM. While convenient for modern life, standard time conflicts with the reading of sundials.

In our high-tech world, timekeeping is now decoupled from the *Two Great Lights* that God has placed in the sky for "signs and seasons, days and years." As a result, few people today appreciate our classical astronomical heritage. Sundials can be corrected for standard time and daylight savings, but not many correctable sundials are commonly available. Nowadays most sundials are simply lawn ornaments and not very useful for telling time.

November Hath XXX Days

The bird quite mute, the trees quite leafless are,
Good housewives now their rousing fires prepare,
Much cut throat work abounds, where swine are killed,
Those who have none, with pout and carp are filled.
– Entry for November, *The Connecticut Almanack* for 1780

Throughout autumn, the Sun is lower in the noon sky. The Sun now passes from the Claws to the Scorpion. As the Sun rises and sets to the south, it never passes above the east or west horizons. The Sun's daily circle extends only a bit above the horizon, making the days very short.

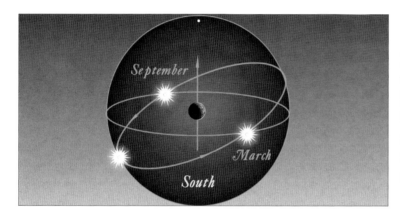

During the autumn and winter months, the Sun is in the southern zodiac. From the first day of fall until the first day of spring, the Sun is south of the celestial equator and lies low to the horizon.

And all the signs from the head of Libra unto the end of Pisces are called signs of the south from the equinoctial; and these signs arise evermore betwixt the very east and the very south in our horizon. – Geoffrey Chaucer (circa A.D. 1400)

By early November, the days are nearly at their shortest. Now in the "valley" of its southern course, the Sun's southerly descent "levels out" as it approaches

its extreme. Though the actual shortest day is still to come, in most places the length of daylight will only differ by a few minutes from early November until about late January. But if skies are clear, the earlier nightfall offers a prime season for evening stargazing, especially for small kids with early bedtimes!

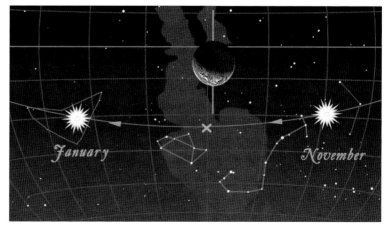

December hath XXXI Days

Leaf-less it brings the ancient Year to Grave,
And layes him in another out to have,
Let us, poor Men, consult as Time requires,
Temperance in Meat & Drink, warm Cloathes, good fires.
– Entry for December, *Leeds' Almanack for 1694*

In early December, the Sun passes quickly from the Scorpion through the Serpent Bearer, and into the Archer. On or around December 21, the Sun reaches the southern extreme of the zodiac at the **winter solstice**. It is now *the first day of winter, the shortest day of the year.*

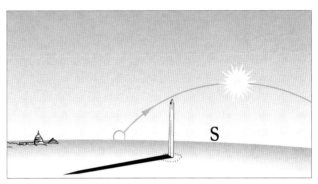

By the shortest day, many folks in the northern United States will see the Sun grazing the treetops at noon, and the noon shadows will be at their longest of the year, double the length of the objects casting them.

As winter begins, the Earth is on the opposite side of the Sun from the summer solstice. The North Pole is pointed *away* from the Sun. The Sun is on the far side of the ecliptic from Polaris, and so the Sun is closest to the depressed southern pole. Darkness covers its maximum extent over the Northern Hemisphere.

The Winter Solstice occurs when the Sun is furthest away from the place where we live, and is lowest relatively to the horizon, describing its most southerly circle, and producing the longest night of all nights and the shortest day. – Geminus (circa 50 B.C.)

The lengths of the days and nights are exactly reversed from the summer solstice. The winter nights are as long as the summer days, and vice versa. In the mid-northern latitudes, the Sun's rays shine for a mere nine hours, rising at about 7:30 A.M. and setting around 4:30 P.M. Nighttime lasts for fifteen hours.

The longest day is equal to the longest night, and the shortest day to the shortest night.
– Geminus (circa 50 B.C.)

On the winter solstice, the Sun rises and sets far to the south and never approaches the east or west horizons. The Sun's daily circle across the sky is at the end of the ecliptic closest to the "never visible" circle of southern stars.

On the shortest day, the Sun again "stands" in the sky. But since it is now at the winter tropic, the Sun hereafter turns north and begins again to climb the ecliptic. On the winter solstice, the Sun reaches the zenith above the *Tropic of Capricorn*, the other end of the tropics from Tropic of Cancer.

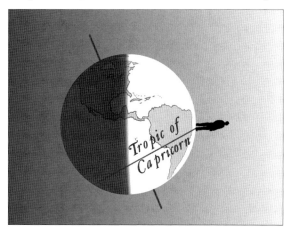

Two thousand years ago, the winter solstice was in the Goat, but as with all the other seasonal signposts, it has moved into the Archer due to precession. The name "Tropic of Capricorn" persists from ancient tradition.

Arctic Noon -- Winter Solstice

Since the lands around the North Pole are in total darkness, the extreme short day can be found at the Arctic Circle. On the December solstice, people in Alaska, Iceland, and Scandinavia may see the Sun momentarily rise due south right around noon, only to set quickly. Except for a long twilight on either side of this noon sunrise/sunset, the Arctic nights of early winter are long and dark.

January Hath XXXI Days

Begin the year with serious thought,
How many the last to the grave were brought,
Thy turn may come thou knowest not when,
Be sure thou art prepared then.
– Entry for January, *The Connecticut Almanack* for 1780

As the dwellers of the north endure the winter, the Earth revolves back to the place of the spring equinox. As the Sun hides the faint stars of Capricornus, it again heads north toward a March rendezvous with the equator. The Sun now creeps toward the north, only to set just as far north at the western horizon. The cold winter days are slightly longer than the shortest day, though they are not longer by very much.

Even as our air snows down flakes of frozen vapors, when the horn of the Goat of heaven
touches the sun, so, upward, I saw the aether become adorned. – Dante (circa A.D. 1300)

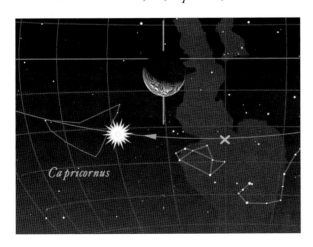

Capricornus

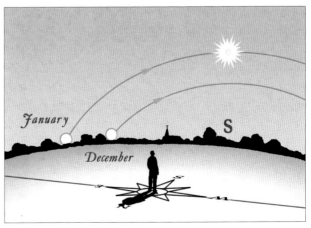

January

December

S

February Hath XXVIII Days

The weather being cold and raw,
Let not thy beasts want hay or straw,
For if thou dost, thou mayest not fail,
To lift them up then by the tail,
And if in that state long they bide,
Your greatest gain will be their hide.

— Entry for February, *The Connecticut Almanack* for 1780

By February, the days are growing noticeably longer. As the Sun passes before the stars of the Waterbearer, it now again draws north and tends toward the east and west at its risings and settings. The Sun passes higher at noon, and the noon shadows grow short again.

In that part of the young year when the sun tempers his locks beneath Aquarius,
and now the nights decrease toward half the day. — Dante (circa A.D. 1300)

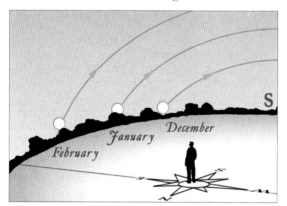

Darkness recedes from the Northern Hemisphere, and the Sun's daily circle above the horizon has increased from its solstitial minimum.

Wintertime

Just as the Earth warms up slowly during the summer, it also cools down slowly during the dark days of winter. The Earth loses heat throughout the dark months, and the temperatures continue to lag behind the seasons. The coldest temperatures of winter are usually reached during February, not December.

March Again

In March, the Sun approaches the equator again, and the daylight again equals out across the globe. As the days grow longer, the plants again begin to bud, and the robins and geese are again sighted. On and on the ancient cycle of the year continues. The Signs & Seasons accompany the Sun's annual rise and fall in the blue sky above, in its invisible course along the ecliptic.

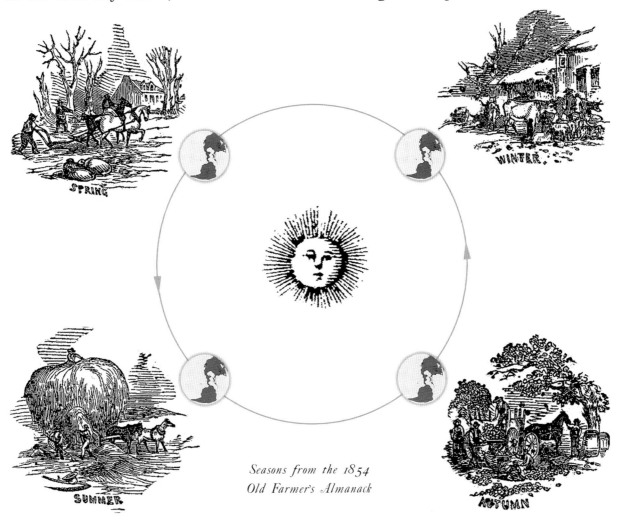

Seasons from the 1854
Old Farmer's Almanack

The seasons will roll along through our lives, just as they always have since the dawn of history. If we only stop to notice, we will always observe the Sun's annual back-and-forth motion, across the horizons and in the noon sky, drawing our shadows long and short, until history is no more.

While the Earth remaineth, seed time and harvest, and cold and heat, and Summer and Winter, and day and night shall not cease. – Genesis 8:22

Chapter 6
The Seasonal Skies

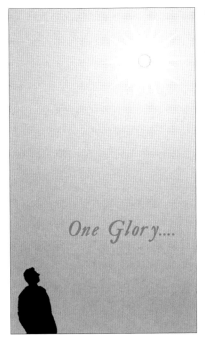

One Glory....

The celestial bodies are very different from the things we see on the Earth, since they can only be perceived as lights in the sky. And what differences there are between these lights! The brilliant Sun blazes down from on high, lighting our days, while the shining Moon casts a silvery glow onto the land. The stars spangle the firmament, some twinkling as bright, glittering jewels in the night sky, others as faint sparks, barely visible.

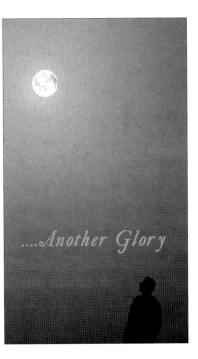

....Another Glory

Traditionally, the various brightnesses of the celestial bodies have been measured according to a scale of **magnitudes**. In antiquity, the great astronomer Claudius Ptolemy compiled a catalog of the visible stars and sorted the stars into categories according to their brightness. The brightest stars are those of *first magnitude*. Many of the bright first magnitude stars are in the neighborhood of Orion. The next brightest stars are of *second magnitude*, and are also quite bright. The Big Dipper, Cassiopeia and Polaris are all second magnitude stars, easily seen from under the city lights.

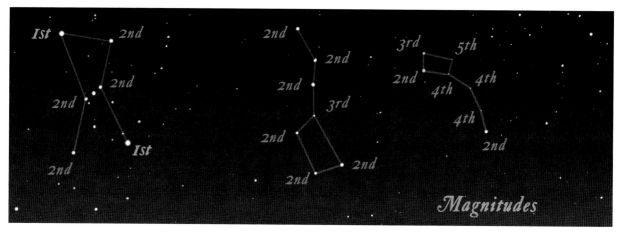

Some of the less obvious constellations are formed of *third* and *fourth magnitude* stars. These are harder to see from the city, but easy to find under dark rural skies. The faint stars are *fifth magnitude,* and background stars are *sixth magnitude,* the dimmest that can be seen with the human eye.

Altogether there are 1022 stars, of which 15 are first magnitude.
– Ptolemy (circa A.D. 150)

Ptolemy counted fifteen of the brightest stars as being of first magnitude. Ptolemy's magnitude categories were used throughout late antiquity and the medieval period.

Let him imagine, who desires to understand well that which I now saw... fifteen stars which in different regions vivify the heaven with brightness so great that it overcomes all thickness of the air. – Dante (circa A.D. 1300)

However, with the modern telescope, thousands more stars have been counted than Ptolemy ever knew. Also, not all of Ptolemy's first magnitude stars are visible today from the midnorthern latitudes. And for whatever reason, some of the brightest stars we see today were not reckoned as first magnitude by Ptolemy.

Today we can still count fifteen of the brightest stars visible in the northern skies, each of which are about first magnitude in the modern scheme. These stars can be used to find the brightest constellations and as a road map for navigating the night sky. Can you learn only fifteen stars over the course of a year? If so, then you'll be able to find many of the seasonal constellations.

First Magnitude Stars

Sirius	*Betelgeuse*
Rigel	*Pollux*
Procyon	*Capella*
Regulus	*Spica*
Arcturus	*Vega*
Deneb	*Altair*
Antares	*Fomalhaut*
Aldebaran	

Rolling through the Seasons

As the Sun rolls along its seasonal circuit of the ecliptic, the bright luminary continually overtakes the stars that lie to its east. In turn, each zodiac constellation appears above the western horizon and disappears into the sunset as the Sun advances. In the mornings, the zodiac constellations emerge from the sunrise as the Sun continues its easterly path through the stars.

The twelve signs of the Zodiac suffice to show the termination of the nights, and during all the year the proper season for tillage, seed-time and planting. All these announce that we are everywhere watched over by Providence. – Aratus (circa 275 B.C.)

Because of the Sun's apparent motion along the ecliptic, the morning and evening stars are constantly shifting over a period of months, another sign of the passing seasons. Consequently, we associate certain "skies" with each season.

Why are the Summer nights always adorned with the same stars, and winter the same way, and certain figures in the sky repeat on the same days, and depart unchanged? – Manilius (circa A.D. 20)

The Winter Sky

Orion and **Taurus** rule the evening skies of February and March. The Twin stars of **Gemini**, **Castor** and the first magnitude **Pollux**, are high up overhead. The Milky Way passes through the neighborhood of Orion, and this area includes some of the brightest stars in the sky. Orion himself includes the first

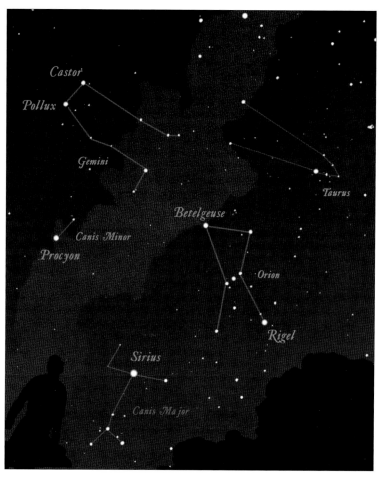

magnitude stars **Betelgeuse** (pronounced BEETLE-juice) and **Rigel** (RYE-jell). The other stars of the Hunter's body, and also Orion's Belt, are of second magnitude, and form a very conspicuous human pattern of stars.

Near Orion and low to the south is **Canis Major**, the Big Dog. This constellation is notable for including the famous and historic star **Sirius**, (pronounced "serious"), the Dog Star, the brightest of all the stars in the sky. Sirius was the calendar star of the Egyptians, observed to create the world's first solar calendar. Besides Sirius, the other stars of the Big Dog are less conspicuous, of second magnitude or dimmer.

Such a keeper is he (Orion) that under his proud back the Dog shines, standing upright upon both feet, nevertheless he is not conspicuous, especially about his belly, although, near the upper part of his jaw, is a very remarkable and brilliant star of a scorching nature which is called Sirius. – Aratus

Above of the Big Dog, under the Twin stars, and to the east of Orion is the first magnitude star **Procyon** (PRO-see-yon) the bright star defining **Canis Minor**, the Little Dog. This star lies somewhat to the north of the celestial equator. Procyon, Sirius, and Betelgeuse form a great triangle of stars in the winter sky.

Here beneath the Twins, brightly shines Procyon. These you may see in after years returning in order and in due time. – Aratus

Above Orion and the Bull is the constellation **Auriga**, the Charioteer. Auriga features the first magnitude star **Capella**, the fourth brightest star visible from the Northern Hemisphere. Auriga passes almost directly overhead in the mid-northern latitudes. While it may be hard to picture a man driving a chariot,

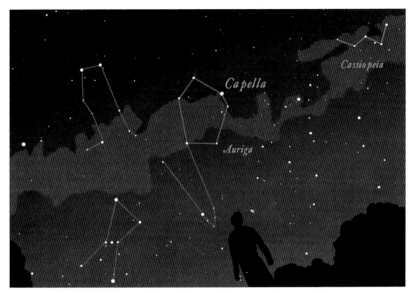

Auriga does appear as a lopsided hexagon of mostly second and third magnitude stars.

When Orion is near the meridian, the Big Dipper is to the east of the North Star and Cassiopeia is to the west. If we follow the Milky Way overhead across the sky from Orion through Auriga, we can see it passing through the stars of Cassiopeia.

These bright stars near Orion are easy to learn. If you can learn these constellations, they will help you to learn the stars of the coming season. If you learn the new constellations as they arrive with the coming seasons, you will learn all of the primary constellations over the span of a year. Learning the constellations is the key to mastering the ancient techniques of celestial timekeeping and navigation.

The Spring Sky

In April and May, **Leo**, the Lion is high near the meridian in the hours after sunset. In the trapezoid of Leo, the bright star at the lower right is the first magnitude star **Regulus** (REG-you-lus). Besides Regulus, the basic outline of the trapezoid is formed of second magnitude stars and should be easily visible from under city lights. More faint is the "sickle" of Leo, an arc of third and fourth magnitude stars that form the Lion's head.

East of Leo is **Virgo**, the Maiden. While not looking much like a young girl, Virgo is formed of mostly third magnitude stars in a somewhat rectangular shape. The brightest star in Virgo is the first magnitude star **Spica** (SPIKE-a), seen to the lower left of the Lion. Spica is only the fifteenth brightest star seen from Earth, but it is one of the brightest stars in the evening this season.

To the south of the Lion and the Maiden is **Corvus**, the Crow, a fairly distinct third magnitude constellation. Nearby **Crater**, the Cup, is more of a challenge, being formed of fourth and fifth magnitude stars.

Between the Lion and the Twins is the faint, indistinct constellation **Cancer**, the Crab. This star pattern is formed of dim fourth magnitude stars and cannot be easily picked out except under dark rural skies. Cancer is only famous for being a zodiac constellation and former home of the summer solstice. If it had been in another part of the sky, the Crab would not have been very famous.

While looking at the Lion high in the midheaven, if you lean way back, you can see the Big Dipper "above" the stars of Leo. While the Big Dipper is not very close to the Lion, there are no prominent constellations between them. And if you turn around to face north, you can see that the Big Dipper is at its highest above Polaris. So just as we can use the Big Dipper to help us find the North Star, we can also use it to find Leo, on the opposite side from the North Star.

As Virgo turns to the west, **Libra**, the Balance trundles to the meridian. High above Libra is the first magnitude star **Arcturus** (ark-TUR-us). This orange-colored star is the *second brightest star* visible from the mid-northern latitudes. Arcturus is in the constellation **Boötes**, (BO-oo-teez), the Herdsman. This constellation is shaped like an elongated "kite" of mostly third magnitude stars. Arcturus helps locate its less-bright neighbors to the south.

Nor shall the Claws, although faintly shining, pass long unnoticed, since the bright constellation of Boötes rises suddenly, illumined by Arcturus.
– Aratus

The name "Arcturus" turns up twice in the book of Job in the King James Version of the Bible:

Canst thou bring forth Mazzaroth in his season? or canst thou guide Arcturus and his sons?
– Job 38:32

However, this passage does not refer to the star known as Arcturus. The Hebrew word *Ash* (עיש) translated as *Arcturus* means "group" or "crowd" and is identified with the Great Bear, i.e. the Big Dipper.

Other translations render *Mazzaroth* as "constellations" and call "Arcturus and his sons" the "Bear with its cubs." However the scholars wish to render this verse, it seems that all readings of Job 38:32 make reference to the portion of the sky visible overhead in the evenings of late spring and early summer.

In Greek, *Arktouros* (Αρκτουρος) means "bear watcher." Aratus mentions this star by name in *Phaenomena:*

After Helice, Arctophylax, very like a waggoner, is borne along commonly known by the name Boötes, because he appears to drive the Wain of the Bear, and appears conspicuously bright. Beneath his girdle rolls Arcturus, the most brilliant of stars. – Aratus

When Arcturus is near the meridian, the Big Dipper is west of Polaris. If we look straight up to the zenith, we can see the "handle" of the Big Dipper pointing in that general direction. The Big Dipper's handle can help us find the bright first magnitude stars of early summer.

If you follow the curve of the arc of the Big Dipper's handle, it will lead to Arcturus. From there, if you "spike" straight down in the same general direction, it will point toward Spica. If you can find the Big Dipper in the sky in any season, you only need to remember this rule:

Follow the "arc" to Arcturus, and follow the "spike" to Spica.

The Summer Sky

During the evenings of June and July, **Scorpius** is now found low to the south. This figure is best seen from the first magnitude star **Antares** (an-TAR-eez). This star is a ruddy orange color that closely resembles the planet Mars. In fact, its name in Greek means "anti-Ares" or "the Rival of Mars." The Scorpion is also notable for its *head*, a slightly curved arc of third magnitude stars that form a sort of faint, sideways Orion's Belt in the summer sky.

The Scorpion has a very distinct tail formed of second and third magnitude stars. But Scorpius lies low in the south, and its tail drags the treetops, just missing the "never visible" circle. In the northern temperate latitudes, a clear, flat horizon, such as over water, is required to see the whole Scorpion.

High above Scorpius is **Vega**, in the constellation **Lyra**, the Lyre (LEE-ra). Vega is a blue first magnitude star, the next brightest star to the east of Arcturus. The orange-colored Arcturus and the blue-colored Vega offer a chance to compare and contrast a color difference in the stars.

Between Arcturus and Vega is **Corona Borealis**, the Northern Crown, a tight arc of third and fourth magnitude stars just to the upper left of bright Arcturus. To the east of the Crown is **Hercules**, best seen by finding the *Keystone*, a small trapezoid of third magnitude stars near Vega.

Near this revolves a form like to a man toiling with which no one is thoroughly conversant; neither is it known for whom he labors, but it is usually called Hercules, and like to a man kneeling, for he struggles on his knees; his hands are lifted up higher than both his shoulders and extend as far as he can reach. In the midst, the sole of his right foot is placed upon the head of the winding serpent. – Aratus

Between Hercules and the Scorpion is **Ophiuchus**, the Snake Handler, formed of third magnitude stars. The **Serpent's Head** is near the foot of Herculus. As we've seen, Ophiuchus is actually the thirteenth constellation of the zodiac, since part of it crosses the ecliptic.

As the summer progresses into August and September, **Sagittarius**, the Archer is at the meridian in early evening. Above the Archer, an asterism called *the Summer Triangle* is high overhead, a giant celestial triangle formed of three first magnitude stars. **Vega** (VAY-ga) is the high star to the west corner of the

Triangle. To the east is **Deneb** (DEN-eb), the brightest star in the constellation **Cygnus** (SIG-nus), the Swan.

Cygnus is sometimes called *the Northern Cross* since the fainter stars form a cross-like shape, with Deneb at the head of the Cross. However, *Deneb* means "tail" in Arabic, and this star is supposed to be the tail of the swan. If you can see a line of stars extending from Deneb, they might look like the neck of a swan. The lower star of the Triangle is called **Altair**, and it is the bright star in **Aquila**, the Eagle.

As seen from a dark site, the Milky Way passes through the middle of the Summer Triangle and down to the Archer, disappearing below the horizon. The thickest part of the Milky Way is in Sagittarius, but near the Triangle, the Milky Way is divided, and *the Great Rift* is visible between the two branches.

It is easily seen that the Milky Way is not simply a circle but a zone having quite the color of milk, whence its name; and that it is not regular and ordered, but different in width, color and density, and position; and that in one part it is double. – Ptolemy (circa A.D. 150)

To the east of the Milky Way is **Delphinus**, the Dolphin, a small diamond-shaped pattern of fourth magnitude stars with a "tail." Within the Milky Way, the Summer Triangle includes the fourth magnitude **Sagitta**, (SAJ-itta), the Arrow.

The Autumn Sky

In October and November, the Summer Triangle has moved into the western sky, and the **Great Square of Pegasus** is high in the evening sky. **Pegasus** is easily found by this geometrical pattern of four stars of second magnitude. The Great Square is surrounded by **Pisces**, the Fishes, and Pegasus can help you find the fainter zodiac constellations in that part of the sky.

To the south, below the Great Square and the Summer Triangle, lie the Goat and the Waterbearer. The fourth magnitude stars of **Capricornus** and **Aquarius** are best seen on clear nights from a dark site. Under these zodiac constellations is **Fomalhaut** (FOE-mall-hoot), a bright first magnitude star in the constellation **Piscis Austrinus**, the Southern Fish. Fomalhaut lies far to the south and skims the tree tops.

Beneath the Goat, and to the southward, swims another fish called the southern fish Another star, beautiful and brilliant, may be seen below the feet of the Waterbearer. – Aratus

As the days grow shorter into December, the stars to the east of the Great Square roll into the evening sky. The constellations in this part of the sky have traditionally been associated with the ancient Greek myth of *Perseus*. In this ancient fairy tale, Perseus is a great hero who slays evil monsters, rides the winged horse *Pegasus*, and rescues the beautiful princess Andromeda, the daughter of King Cepheus and Queen Cassiopeia. This storyline is not very different from many Hollywood action movies!

The constellations **Perseus** and **Andromeda** are each defined by trails of third and fourth magnitude stars and Andromeda is between Cassiopeia and Pegasus. Shining very faintly near the "knee" of Andromeda is the **Andromeda Galaxy**, a great pinwheel of stars, visible as a fuzzy blob in a pair of binoculars.

For there a sad object is observed – Andromeda – adorned with stars, beneath her mother...
Moreover, just above her head the great Horse rolls, lightly touching her where a star shines,
common to both at a certain point, viz. at his at navel and at the crown of her head. – Aratus

Perseus is found next to Andromeda, between Cassiopeia and the bright star **Capella**. The shape of Perseus is like a diagonal line of stars, extending from upper right to lower left, with two branches extending downward.

At the left shoulder of Andromeda, and very near, you find the more northern fish (of Pisces),
while both her feet point towards her spouse Perseus, on whose shoulders they rest.
To the north he stands conspicuous above all with his right hand extended
towards the seat of his mother-in-law's chair. – Aratus

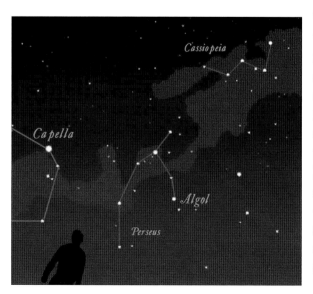

There is a star in Perseus named **Algol**, which represents the head of the slain monster Medusa. Algol is a variable star, and it varies in brightness from a dim fourth magnitude to a bright second magnitude! Algol varies in a cycle of only *three days*, and changes over this period, from the dimmest star in Perseus to the brightest. Algol is a type of star known as an "eclipsing binary" – actually *two stars* – where a dimmer star passes in front of a brighter star, eclipsing it and making Algol appear to change in brightness over the nights.

Perseus, Father of the Persians

While Perseus is best known as a myth, there may in fact have been a real man upon whom the legend is based. In 400 B.C., the Greek historian Herodotus wrote that Perseus was the father of the Persian people. Without a doubt, the descendants of mythical Perseus have played a prominent role in history.

The Old Testament has much to say about the Persian empire, especially in the books of Daniel and Ezra. After the conquest of Babylon, it was *King Cyrus* of Persia who ended the Babylonian Captivity of the tribe of Judah. Cyrus showed great kindness to God's people in this time, allowing the walls of Jerusalem and the Temple to be restored. His successors continued this kindness. One hundred years after Cyrus, the Persian *King Ahasuerus* was the husband of Esther and allowed the Jews to defeat their enemies.

In later centuries, the Persians conquered Greece. At the frontier of their empire, the kings of Persia were at war with kings of Macedonia, in the northern part of Greece. In about 330 B.C., a Macedonian king named *Alexander the Great* rose up and eventually conquered the entire Persian empire, from the *Mediterranean Sea* to the *Ganges River* in India. After Alexander, a new Persian empire arose, ruled by the Greek descendants of Alexander's generals.

In 146 B.C., Rome conquered Greece, becoming the imperial power in the Mediterranean for the next 750 years. Though Rome eventually conquered all the western lands of Alexander's Greek empire, Persia remained as the one enemy that Rome could never defeat. For centuries, many Roman emperors fought to a standstill against the Persians. After the Roman capital moved to Constantinople, the Byzantine emperors remained at war with Persia for centuries more.

About A.D. 600, the Byzantine and Persian empires had fought each other to exhaustion. With no strong armies to protect them, both weakened empires were at the mercy of a new power in the region – *Islam*. In A.D. 632, the armies of Mohammed spilled out of the Arabian peninsula, fighting both Byzantium and Persia. The weakened Byzantine army was defeated, and the Christian lands of Israel, Syria, and Egypt were lost to the Muslim Caliphs. Though the Byzantine empire lasted another 800 years, the Persian empire was conquered completely.

The lands of the former Persian empire are today the nations of *Iraq, Iran* and *Afghanistan*, and they remain Muslim to this day. However, many Persians who escaped the Arab conquest of Persia settled in Bombay, India, and preserved the traditional Persian culture and religion. These people are today known as the *Parsees*, another name for "Persians."

So when you look up at the constellations of Cassiopeia, Pegasus, and Perseus, don't think of the far-fetched pagan myth. Instead, think of the Persian kings Cyrus and Ahasuerus, who were used mightily by God to protect the nation of Israel. Think of the great Persian empire that played a prominent role in the history of the world for 1200 years. And pray for the Persian people alive today who might still claim the mythical hero Perseus as their ancestor.

The Winter Sky Again

In the cold evenings of January and February, the stars of **Aries**, the Ram, and **Taurus**, the Bull, are near the meridian as darkness falls. The red first magnitude star **Aldebaran** (al-DEB-aran) marks the bright eye of the Bull, and the V-shaped star cluster, the *Hyades* (HI-a-deez) forms the Bull's head. Near the "knee" of Perseus and near the Ram is that famous cluster of stars, the *Pleiades*. Keen eyesight can reveal six or seven stars in this tight little knot of stars.

Near his left knee all the Pleiades are gathered together. A small space contains them all.
Their light is by no means brilliant, but they are of fair renown. – Aratus

The Pleiades are very famous, and are among the few celestial objects named in the Bible.

He is wise in heart, and mighty in strength: who hath hardened himself against him,
and hath prospered?....Which maketh Arcturus, Orion, and Pleiades,
and the chambers of the south. – Job 9:4, 9

As winter wears on, mighty Orion turns again to the middle of the sky. The constellations have come full circle through the evening sky and have brought their signs of each passing season. Not only has the evening sky changed with the seasons, but also the midnight sky and the morning sky.

Over the seasons, each of the constellations is visible at different hours of the night. In one season, a constellation is seen in the early evening, in another season, after the sunset. Sometimes a constellation can be found in the early morning, before the sunrise. At still other times, it can be high in the sky, near the meridian.

The Annual Courses of The Stars

The seasonal changes of the constellations can best be understood by observing the annual course of a single constellation, such as Orion. During late spring and early summer, Orion rises and sets invisibly with the Sun as the bright luminary passes through nearby Taurus and Gemini.

By the end of July, the Sun has rolled into Cancer, moving to the east of Orion. One morning, Orion emerges from the morning twilight. This is the **heliacal rising** of the stars of Orion. The heliacal rising of a star is its first appearance before the sunrise, when it rises just before the Sun. As we will later see, the heliacal rising of Sirius was very important in ancient Egypt.

Heliacal or solar rising occurs when a sign or star can be seen by departure of the Sun from it, which previously could not be seen because of the nearness of the Sun. –John Sacrobosco

As the Sun rises, the stars of Orion quickly disappear in the brightening blue twilight. Orion invisibly crosses the blue sky and sets unseen before the Sun, to be seen again the next morning. But Orion rises earlier over the coming weeks and months and is higher in the sky at sunrise.

By the autumnal equinox in September, Orion rises around midnight and is in the midheaven at the morning twilight. Orion goes down invisibly throughout the morning and sets unseen by noon.

Throughout the autumn, Orion rises before midnight, each night earlier than the night before. Orion reaches the meridian during the nighttime, and moves farther into the western sky by morning as each new day dawns in the east.

Into November, Orion rises in the early evening, after sunset. When a star rises visibly in the night sky, it is called the **temporal rising** of the star.

Chronic or temporal rising occurs when a sign or star, after sunset, emerges above the horizon from the east at night. It is called "temporal rising" because astronomical time begins with sunset. – John Sacrobosco (circa A.D. 1230)

Finally, by the winter solstice, Orion rises so early that the Hunter comes up in the east just as the Sun sets. At this time, Orion is opposite from the Sun in the sky. Orion climbs the sky as the evening twilight fades and is southing at midnight. Orion is westering throughout the wee hours and sets in the west just before the sunrise, still opposite the Sun.

Throughout the winter, Orion rises invisibly before the sunset and is visible in the eastern sky as evening twilight fades. This is traditionally called the **cosmic rising** of stars, when stars rise unseen behind the blue daylight sky.

Cosmic or mundane rising takes place when a sign or star ascends above the horizon from the east by day. – John Sacrobosco

Even though we can't observe a star's cosmic rising, we infer that it did in fact rise when it appeared as the night falls. Thus, when we see Orion and his neighbors high in the sky after dark, we understand that these stars rose invisibly during the daytime.

In the wintertime, Orion reaches the meridian before midnight and is prominent in the evening skies of winter. Orion moves into the western sky in the early hours and sets before the next sunrise.

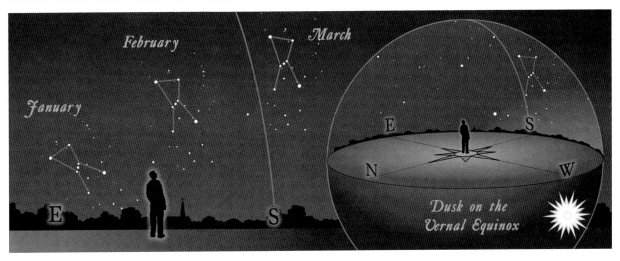

By the vernal equinox in March, Orion rises invisibly at about noon and is near the meridian in the evening twilight after the Sun sets. Orion is in the western sky in the early evening and sets by midnight.

As the spring days grow longer and warmer, Orion rises early and reaches the meridian in daylight, appearing farther to the west in the evening twilight. As the Sun again approaches Aries and Taurus, the stars of Orion draw closer and closer to the sunset with each passing night. By May, Orion reaches its *heliacal setting* and disappears into the Sun's evening glow. Orion will not be seen again for a couple of months, until its next heliacal rising.

Progression of the Seasonal Skies

Each constellation moves in a cycle similar to Orion, heliacally emerging from the sunrise in one season, rising at midnight in the next, rising and setting opposite the Sun in the season following, and rising invisibly at noon in the season after that. On any given night, we can see each of the constellations at different hours of the night, in different places in each of their own cycles.

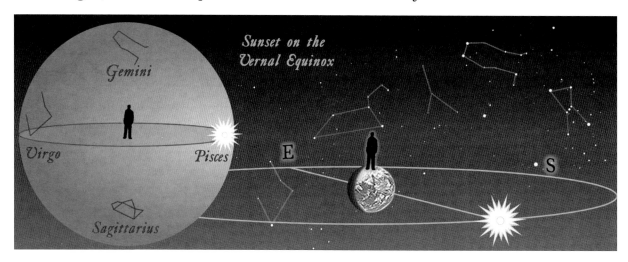

As the Sun rises in early spring, its bright rays hide the stars of the Fishes. The zodiac constellations that follow – the Ram and the Bull – occupy the western sky at sunset. The summer solstice in Gemini is in the midheaven. The zodiac constellation opposite the Sun rises as the Sun sets. So on the first day of spring, Virgo is rising at sunset and Leo is above the eastern horizon as night falls. The winter solstice in Sagittarius is invisible at the lower meridian.

Orion hangs high in the sky while Gemini passes the meridian. As we gaze up at these Twin stars, we can imagine that this is the place in the sky where the Sun will soon be in the early days of summer. In this way, we can see that *the evening sky shows the Sun's place in the season that is coming.*

The stars of Virgo and Leo reach the meridian by midnight on the first day of Spring. This is another clue that helps us know the Sun's position on the ecliptic, since the autumnal equinox passes the meridian at midnight when the Sun is in the opposite end of the sky at the vernal equinox.

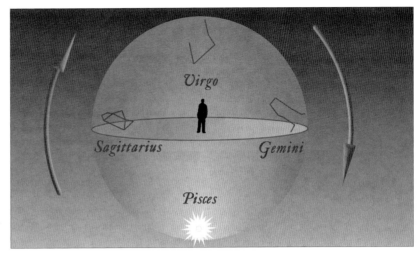

If it be enquired, How we can know the Place of the Sun among the Stars, since all the Stars near it are lost in the Sun-Beams? 'Tis answered, that we can see plainly what Constellation or what stars are upon the Meridian at Midnight, and we know the Stars which are exactly opposite to them and there must be upon the Meridian (very nearly) the same Day at Noon; and thereby we know that the Sun at Noon is in the midst of them. –Isaac Watts (A.D. 1726)

At midnight on the equinox, when Virgo and Leo are near the meridian, the Big Dipper is high above the North Star. Cassiopeia, if it can be seen at all, is lost in the treetops. Whenever the sky is turned in this manner, *Capella* and *Vega* can be seen together in the sky at the same distance above the horizon. These first magnitude stars are of similar brightness, though Capella is yellowish in color, and Vega has a distinctly bluish color. Capella is above the northwest, while Vega is at the same distance above the northeast, on the opposite side of the sky from the North Star. It's always interesting to see these bright northern stars "balanced" along the northern horizon, Capella indicating the departure of the winter sky, and Vega heralding the coming of the summer sky.

By the morning, the aspect of the sky has changed again. The Archer is southing and indicates where the Sun was three months before at the winter solstice. In this way, *the morning sky shows the place where the Sun has been in the season that is departing.* The Goat and the Waterbearer are above the place of the sunrise, further confirming the Sun's place in Pisces.

As spring rolls along, the Sun continues moving eastward into the stars of the Ram. During April, the stars of the Bull and Orion are drawn toward the sunset. Into May, as the Sun enters the Bull, the Twin stars Castor and Pollux draw toward the western horizon.

Let us suppose that the Sun is in Aries. Taurus is seen near the western horizon, for the Pleiades and the Hyades, the brighter constellations of Taurus, set shortly after the Sun. In the following month, the Sun has gone back into the sign behind Aries, that is Taurus, and so we do not see the Pleiades or any other constellation of Taurus during that month. – Macrobius (circa A.D. 400)

Through the spring, as the Sun departs from Pisces, Aries, and Taurus, these constellations can be successively seen heliacally emerging from the glow of the sunrise. In this way, the early morning sky shows us the zodiac constellations that the Sun passed throughout the spring.

By the summer solstice, the Sun has moved into the constellation Gemini. Castor and Pollux have now been swallowed by the sunset, and Orion and his neighbors rise *cosmically* with the Sun. In evening twilight, the Lion faces toward the western horizon and will leap into the sunset in the coming season.

> *A month later Gemini is no longer seen, which means that the Sun has gone into it. And so it becomes evident that the Sun had crossed three signs, Aries, Taurus and Gemini, and has receded through half a hemisphere.* –Macrobius (circa A.D. 400)

The Balance is southing as twilight fades. Boötes and Hercules shine overhead. The teapot asterism of the Archer temporally rises in the southeast as the Summer Triangle hangs over the eastern horizon.

With standard time and daylight savings, astronomical midnight occurs around 1:00 A.M. By this time, the Milky Way stretches overhead through the Summer Triangle, and the Archer is near the midheaven. At midnight on the summer solstice, Sagittarius marks the opposite solstice from the Sun.

In the north at astronomical midnight, the Big Dipper is west of Polaris. Cassiopeia is to the east, and the Great Square rises nearby in the northeast.

Pisces rises after midnight, and in the wee hours of the summer mornings, the Ram rises temporally above the horizon, followed by the Bull. The Pleiades rise heliacally on a morning in early summer.

By the day of the autumnal equinox, the Sun has moved into Virgo, and bright Arcturus lies to the west above the evening twilight. As the twilight deepens, the stars of the Big Dipper come out. If we follow the Big Dipper's handle, we can *follow the arc to Arcturus and follow the spike to the sunset!*

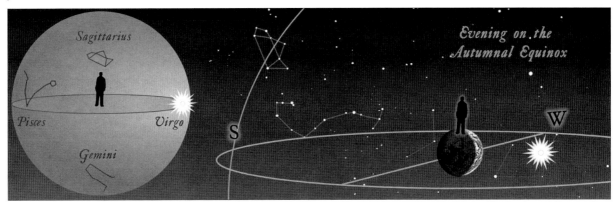

As the days become cooler, the teapot of Sagittarius at the meridian is a sure sign of the coming season, when the Sun will soon reach its southern extreme at the winter solstice. The Summer Triangle shines brightly overhead. Pisces rises opposite from the sunset and reaches the meridian at astronomical midnight with the Great Square.

At midnight on the equinox in the north, Cassiopeia hangs high overhead, near Pegasus. Capella rises in the northeast, while in the northwest, Vega hangs just about as low above the horizon, again "balanced" on opposite sides of Polaris.

In late September mornings, Orion and his neighbors rise about midnight and nearly reach the meridian by sunrise. Leo hangs low above the sunrise, revealing where the Sun has been in recent months. The early morning appearance of Orion is as sure a sign as the geese flying south that the summer heat is over and that the cooler days of autumn have arrived.

As the days shorten and nighttime prevails over the land, the sunset has reached its southernmost extent of the year. The Goat and the Waterbearer lie low in the southwestern sky, and perhaps Fomalhaut can be seen through trees that have lost their leaves. During the evening of the long nights of early winter, the faint stars of the Fishes, near the vernal equinox, are visible near the meridian with the brighter Square of Pegasus.

Orion and Gemini rise opposite the Sun in the east as night falls, with Orion climbing to face the Bull. The Big Dipper is low in the trees while Cassiopeia wheels around overhead. Orion reaches the meridian by midnight on the first day of winter. The Big Dipper has again swung around to the east as Leo climbs the eastern sky.

As another winter morning dawns, Orion sinks into the west, and Leo and Virgo share the midheaven. The Big Dipper is high overhead, near the zenith, and the handle's arc swings east toward Arcturus. In the following months, the sky swings back around again to the signs of spring, and the seasonal cycle of the stars begins again.

Each day brings a change of its own, and the sky can look as many different ways as there are days of the year and hours of the night. Stars emerge from the Sun's morning glow and disappear back into the evening glow months later, as the solar body traces its seasonal course. Over the months, each constellation of the zodiac enjoys its turn at the middle of the sky at early evening.

The Sun, indeed, travels over all of them during the year, and making a long circuit, approaches sometimes one and sometimes another, sometimes when he rises, sometimes when he sets, according as one star or another greets the dawn. – Aratus

Learning the stars and following their cycles is the surest way to understand the comings of the seasons and to get the true sensation of astronomical timekeeping. By observing the changes in the Sun, Moon, and stars, and by following the benchmarks of seasonal change, we can follow the heavenly bodies as they trace out their ancient paths. In this way, we can practice the methods that our ancestors used for centuries to measure the passage of the seasons and the years.

Thou canst always add the signs of the passing season, comparing whether at rising or at setting of a star the day dawn such as the calendar would herald. – Aratus

Chapter 7
The Wandering Stars

Once we become familiar with the constellations of the starry sky and as we learn to know the first magnitude stars by name, we can then learn to identify the planets. The five classical planets are among the brightest "stars" in the sky, and some can be much brighter than even Sirius! Most people have probably seen the planets but didn't realize that they were not just ordinary stars.

Unlike the **fixed stars** that form the constellations, the planets are **wandering stars** that change their positions in the sky against the background constellations. Sometimes the planets move forward to the east, sometimes they stand still in the sky, and other times they move backward through the zodiac toward the west.

The other wandering stars have their courses round the Earth in the zodiac, and rise and set in the same manner; their motions are sometimes quick, sometimes slow, and often they stand still. There is nothing more wonderful, nothing more beautiful. – Cicero (circa 50 B.C.)

However, these celestial bodies are not really wanderers. Like the Sun and Moon, the planets are near the ecliptic, and they move in a very regular and predictable manner through the zodiac. The planets appear as bright stars amidst the zodiac constellations, brilliant visitors that temporarily alter the well known patterns of the stars.

But most worthy of our admiration is the motion of those five stars which are falsely called wandering stars; for they cannot be said to wander which keep from all eternity their approaches and retreats, and have all the rest of their motions, in one regular constant and established order. –Cicero (circa 50 B.C.)

The Classical Planets

Like the Sun and Moon, the five wandering stars were seen to move north and south as they traced their paths through the zodiac. Originally, the ancients counted seven planets – the five wandering stars and also the Sun and Moon – so that the word *planet* included all the celestial bodies that moved along the zodiac.

In their earliest period, the Greeks gave descriptive names to the wandering stars. The planet now known as Saturn was originally called *Phainon*, "The Shining Star." The planet

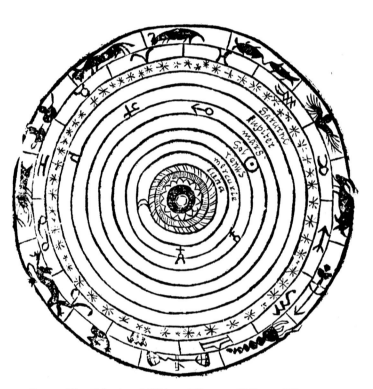

From "The Schoole of Skil" – Thomas Hill – A.D. 1599

Jupiter was called *Phaethon*, "The Bright Star." The planet Mars was originally *Pyrois*, "The Fiery Star." The planet Venus was known by two names – when it was seen in the morning before the sunrise, it was called *Phosphoros*, "The Light Bearer," and when seen in the evening after the sunset, it was called *Hesperos*, "The Evening Star." The planet Mercury was *Stilbon*, "The Gleaming Star."

The planets are stars which are not fixed in the heavens like the rest, but move along in the air. Sometimes they move towards the north, generally in the direction opposite to that of the universe, sometimes with it, and their Greek names are Phaeton, Phaenon, Pyrois, Hesperus, and Stilbon. –Isidore of Seville (circa A.D. 600)

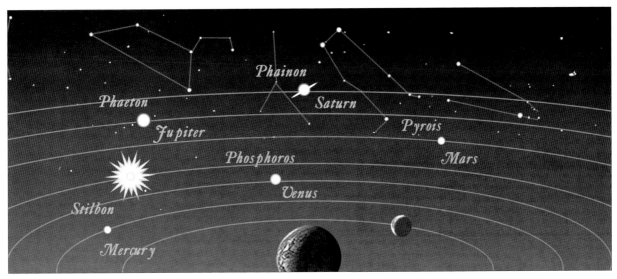

After the Greek general Alexander the Great conquered Babylon (circa 330 B.C.), Greek astronomy absorbed Babylonian astronomy and astrology. After that, the wandering stars came to be associated with the pantheon of pagan gods. The Romans, who were addicted to astrology, continued this practice and named the wandering stars after their corresponding pagan deities.

Saturn a.k.a "Father Time"
from "A Pocket Almanack" - A.D. 1779

The Shining Star *Phainon* became associated with *Kronos,* whom the Romans called *Saturn.* The Bright Star *Phaethon* was renamed for *Zeus* or *Jupiter.* *Pyrois,* the Fiery Star, became *Ares,* known to the Romans as *Mars.* *Phosporos/Hesperos* was named for *Aphrodite* or *Venus,* and the Gleaming Star *Stilbon* was associated with *Hermes* or *Mercury.*

To these the Romans have given the names of their gods, that is, of Jupiter, Saturn, Mars, Venus and Mercury. Deceiving themselves and wishing to deceive others into worship of these gods, who had bestowed upon them somewhat in accordance with the desire of the world, they pointed to the stars in heaven, saying that that was Jupiter's star, that was Mercury's and the empty idea arose. This erroneous belief the devil cherished, but Christ destroyed. –Isidore of Seville (circa A.D. 600)

In spite of 2000 years of Christian civilization, these celestial bodies are still known by their pagan names to this day. These ancient astrological planet names have been officially adopted by the International Astronomical Union, the scientific authority that assigns names to celestial bodies.

The Modern Planets

In the modern scientific world, it is understood that the planets move in their own orbits around the Sun, and that Earth itself is a wandering star in orbit around the Sun. The combination of the other planets' orbits and the Earth's orbit give rise to the various planetary motions.

All of the planets, including the Earth, move in an eastward direction in their orbits around the Sun, with respect to the celestial sphere. The planets therefore all appear to move eastward against the background stars of the zodiac, since our line of sight between the planets and the zodiac constellations is constantly changing. Some planets move quickly, some slowly, but they each move at their own rate. Compared to the immense distances to the stars, the planets are *very close* to our world and are illuminated by the dazzling light of the Sun. The planets therefore shine very brightly in our night sky several magnitudes brighter than most of the brighter stars.

There are two types of planets that we can observe from the Earth – **superior planets** and **inferior planets**. Superior planets are the worlds that lie beyond the orbit of the Earth, while the inferior planets are inside the Earth's orbit, between the Earth and the Sun. The superior planets orbit the Sun more slowly than the Earth, while the inferior planets move faster than the Earth.

The Superior Planets

Saturn is the most distant planet of the solar system that can be seen with the unaided eye. The Shining Star *Phainon* shines at first magnitude and is about as bright as many of the brightest stars in the sky. Saturn moves very slowly through the zodiac, passing through a single constellation in two and a half years, taking nearly *thirty years* for a complete circuit of the zodiac. A child that sees Saturn in a certain constellation will see

it there again in middle age and once more in old age. Most of us can only hope to see two complete cycles of Saturn in a lifetime! Even a small, inexpensive telescope reveals the rings of Saturn, a very remarkable feature.

Next below the sphere of the fixed stars lies the Shining Star "Phainon" which goes by the name of Kronos (Saturn). This star traverses the Zodiac circle in 30 years, very nearly, and a single sign in two years and six months. –Geminus (circa 50 B.C.)

Jupiter is the king of the planets, the largest world in the solar system. Jupiter is indeed "The Bright Star," since it shines much more brightly than first magnitude, more than twice as brightly as Sirius! *Phaethon* is the fourth brightest visible object in the sky, after the Sun, Moon, and Venus, and the brightest of all the superior planets. Jupiter circles the zodiac in twelve years, visiting one

zodiac constellation each year. A child seeing Jupiter in a certain constellation will see it there again in young adulthood and again in middle age. Even a small telescope shows bands of color on Jupiter, and also the four Jovian moons first seen by Galileo.

Under the Shining Star, and lower than it, revolves the Bright Star "Phaeton", called the star of Zeus; this traverses the Zodiac circle in twelve years, and one sign in one year. –Geminus

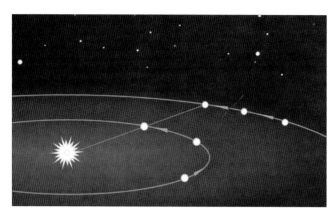 

Mars is the most unusual superior planet. Mars moves quickly through the zodiac, completing the circle of the ecliptic in only about two and a half years. Over the course of its cycle, Mars changes dramatically in brightness. When it is far from Earth on the opposite side of the Sun, Mars shines dimly at about second magnitude, displaying a fiery orange color. As the Earth and Mars draw toward the closest points in their orbits, the Fiery Star *Pyrois* brightens almost *fifty times*, rivaling Jupiter and shining with a bright copper color. Through a telescope, Mars appears as a small orange dot, not a very impressive sight compared to Jupiter and Saturn.

Under this is ranged the Fiery Star "Pyrois," that of Ares. This traverses the Zodiac circle in two years and six months, and a sign in two and a half months. – Geminus

The Inferior Planets

Venus is an extremely bright celestial body, the brightest object in the sky after the Sun and Moon, over *fifteen times brighter* than Sirius! Venus can be spotted at times in the morning or evening sky. As the Morning Star, the Light Bearer *Phosphoros* appears in the night sky before the sunrise. At other times, it is *Hesperos,* the Evening Star, the first star to be seen after the sunset. Venus is so bright, it is often confused with an airplane or even a UFO! Through a telescope, Venus displays phases similar to the Moon.

Next lower than this lies "Phosphorus," the star of Aphrodite, and this moves at approximately the same speed as the Sun. – Geminus

While Venus is nearly impossible to miss in the sky, Mercury is another story. The Gleaming Star *Stilbon* can vary in brightness from first magnitude to the brightness of Sirius! However, Mercury is always seen low in the sky, in the bright glow of the sunrise or sunset. Also, Mercury orbits very quickly and is found in a different place from night to night. Mercury is often hard to identify even for experienced stargazers! Through a small telescope, Mercury never looks like much more than a bright dot.

> *Below this lies the Gleaming Star "Stilbon," the star of Hermes, and it also*
> *moves at equal speed with the Sun.* – Geminus

Motions of the Inferior Planets

Since the inferior planets lie between the Earth and the Sun, these planets are never far away from the Sun. At various times in their cycles, Venus and Mercury lie in the same general direction as the Sun and are invisibly lost in the Sun's glare. This is called a **conjunction**, from the Latin word *conjunctus,*

which means "joined together." This is similar to a New Moon, where the Moon is in conjunction with the Sun. At times, the inferior planets are on the far side of the Sun with respect to the Earth. This is a **superior conjunction**.

Since they move more swiftly than the Earth, the inferior planets appear to move out from behind the Sun. A planet's apparent separation from the Sun is its **elongation**, from the Latin word *elongare,* which means "to be far from." After superior conjunction, a planet is seen to the east of the Sun and therefore has an *eastern elongation*. When Venus or Mercury have an eastern elongation, they are seen in the evening sky, to the east of the sunset.

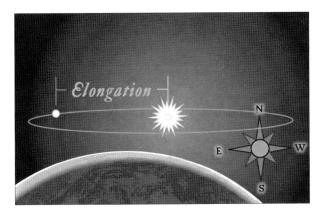
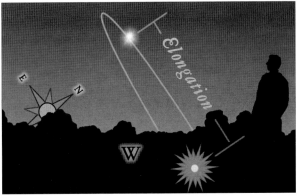

As an inferior planet "rounds the bend" in its orbit, it reaches a point of greatest separation from the Sun. This is the **maximum elongation** of the planet. At *maximum eastern elongation*, the inferior planets reach their maximum distance above the sunset in the evening sky. Though Mercury always remains near the bright glow of the Sun, Venus can extend very far from the Sun, over one-half the distance to the meridian!

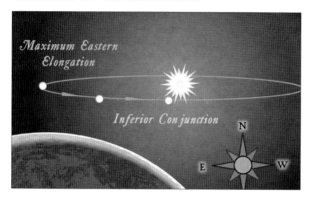

After maximum eastern elongation, Venus and Mercury begin to overtake the Earth, and they reach a **station** where their movement through the zodiac appears to stop, after which they reverse direction through the zodiac and draw again toward the sunset. The inferior planets eventually disappear into the sunset as they pass between the Earth and the Sun. Mercury and Venus are at **inferior conjunction** when they line up with the Sun.

After inferior conjunction, Venus and Mercury overtake the Earth in its orbit. When they again emerge from the Sun's glare, they are now seen to the west of the Sun, and have a *western elongation*. At western elongation, the inferior planets rise before the Sun, appearing in the morning sky before the sunrise.

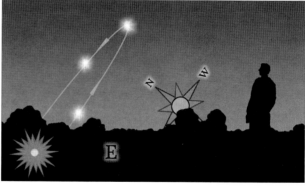

The inferior planets reach their *maximum western elongation*, where they rise earliest before the Sun and are farthest from the place of the sunrise. After their western maximum, Venus and Mercury are again stationary and again drop toward the Sun. Eventually, the inferior planets move again into the Sun's glare, and disappear behind the Sun in another *superior conjunction*. Swift Mercury completes this cycle in about three and a half months. However, this cycle of Venus takes about a year and seven months.

Motions of the Superior Planets

The superior planets lie *outside* the orbit of the Earth; these planets can appear in any part of the sky. Like the inner planets, the superior planets are also seen at **superior conjunction**, on the far side of the Sun from the Earth. The outer planets move more slowly in their orbits than the Earth, and they generally appear to remain in their host constellation as it emerges from the Sun's glare over the months of the passing season.

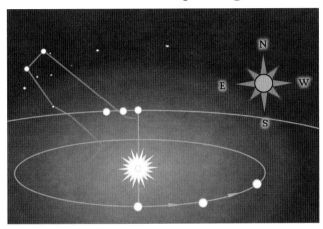

After superior conjunction, the superior planets also have a heliacal rising where they appear one morning above the sunrise. When a superior planet reappears in the morning, a new **apparition** of the planet has begun. After heliacal rising, the superior planets have a western elongation and are seen among the morning stars. Since the motion of the outer planets through the zodiac is much slower than the Sun's apparent motion, these planets rise earlier and earlier as the months pass, moving along with their host stars.

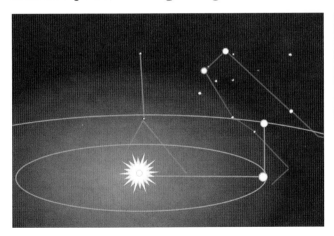

After several months, the planet and its constellation rises around midnight and is at the meridian around sunrise. At this point, the planet is one-quarter of the zodiac circle away from the Sun. This point is therefore called **quadrature**, since the planet is now in a different quadrant of the sky from the Sun. Quadratures are the same idea as the quarters of the Moon's phases.

In the season after quadrature, the planet rises before midnight with the seasonal advance of the stars and arrives in the western half of the sky by sunrise. With each passing day, week, and month, the planet rises earlier and earlier. Soon it is rising in the early evening, an hour or two after sunset. The planet culminates in the hours after midnight and is in the western sky by the time the Sun rises.

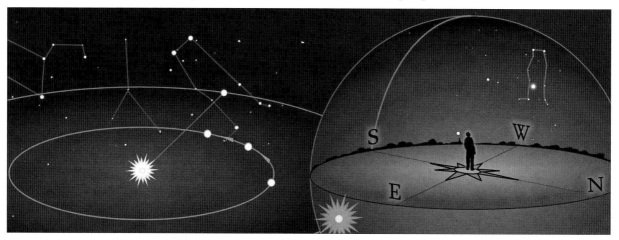

The Earth's orbital motion has now carried our world around to the other side from the place where we observed the superior conjunction. Instead of being on the *far side* of the Sun, the Earth is now on the *same side* of the Sun as the superior planet. The Earth approaches a place where it will *pass between* the Sun and the superior planet. This is the **opposition** of the planet, where it appears *opposite* from the Sun in the skies of Earth. At opposition, the planet rises as the Sun sets. The planet ascends in the eastern sky, culminating at midnight and setting the next morning as the Sun rises. The planet is in the same relation to the Sun as the Full Moon, which is the opposition of the Moon.

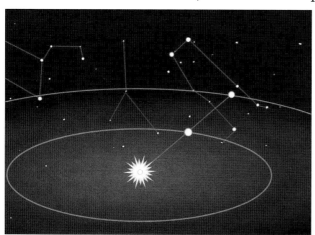

During opposition, the Earth is between the Sun and the superior planet, so the Earth is closer to the planet than at any time of the year. A planet appears at its brightest at opposition, and is at its largest as seen through a telescope. This is especially noticeable in the case of Mars, which is *six times* closer to the Earth at opposition than at superior conjunction.

At all times in their cycles, the superior planets can be seen moving eastward through the stars of the zodiac. But as a superior planet approaches opposition, an unusual thing happens. The planet begins to slow down, become stationary, and then reverse its motion through the sky, moving again toward the west! This is **retrogradation**, the retrograde motion of the planets.

Remotio or retrogradio of stars is when a star, while moving on its regular orbit, seems at the same time to be moving backward. – Isidore of Seville (circa A.D. 600)

As the Earth begins to approach and then pass the planet, the line of sight of the planet changes as compared to the background stars. By the time of opposition, the retrogradation has already begun and continues for many weeks afterwards. Eventually, the Earth "rounds the bend" in its orbit, and the superior planet appears to again move eastward through the zodiac.

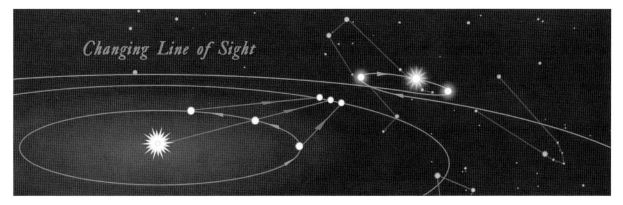

The retrogradations are especially noticeable if the planet is near one of the first magnitude stars along the ecliptic, Aldebaran, Regulus, Spica, or Antares. If a planet is to the east of a bright star when retrogradation begins, it will draw near the star as it moves to the west and draw away when it moves eastward again. The retrogradations are best explained today by the heliocentric Kopernikan model of the solar system. But in ancient times, the retrogradations and other movements of the planets were a source of great wonder and mystery.

What is yet more wonderful in these stars which we are speaking of is that sometimes they appear, and sometimes they disappear; sometimes they advance towards the Sun, and sometimes they retreat; sometimes they precede him, and sometimes follow him; sometimes they move faster, sometimes slower; and sometimes they do not stir in the least, but for a while stand still. –Cicero (circa 50 B.C.)

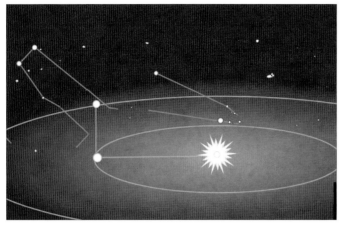

After opposition, the planet has an eastern elongation from the Sun. The planet rises "cosmically" in the daytime and is found in the night sky after sunset. In the following months after, the planet is found higher in the night sky at sunset. After some months, the superior planet is at evening quadrature and is high in the midheaven as the Sun sets.

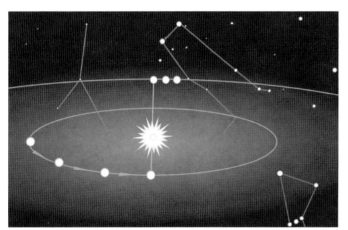

Following quadrature, the superior planet is in the west and draws toward the sunset with the passing weeks and months. The Earth has swung again onto the far side of its orbit, and the planet is now dropping toward the opposite side of the Sun. The planet's apparation draws to a close at heliacal setting, and vanishes again into the sunset, invisibly approaching the next superior conjunction.

The Dance of the Planets

As the planets circle the Sun, they appear at every spot along the zodiac at one time or another. Since the planets circle the Sun at different rates, sometimes they appear to move toward other planets. Like the other "wanderers," the Moon also moves through the constellations of the zodiac as it circles the Earth each month.

From time to time, the celestial bodies appear to pass near each other in the night sky, when they generally line up along the same line of sight. These events are also *conjunctions*, since the Moon and the planets appear "conjoined" in the sky. But these aren't like the inferior and superior conjunctions with the Sun, where the Moon or planets disappear into the Sun's glare. The Moon and planets are very bright celestial objects, so *lunar* and *planetary conjunctions* are always easily visible and interesting sights to see.

There are several types of conjunctions. In some instances, the Moon can be seen passing the bright planets and the bright first magnitude stars of the zodiac. The Moon makes the fastest circuit of the night sky, zooming through the entire zodiac in only a month. Since the planets move much more slowly, the Moon passes by the planets each lunar month. The Moon draws near to a planet over a period of nights as it changes in phase. The Lesser Light is in conjunction with the planet on the night when it makes its closest approach. In the nights after, the Moon pulls away from the planet.

The planets can also approach each other and also the first magnitude stars. It is a beautiful sight to see brilliant "twin stars" close to each other, and it is interesting to watch these planets draw close to each other over a period of nights and then pull away again in a celestial ballet.

It's always a dazzling sight to see a thin crescent Moon pass near bright Venus in a twilight sky. It is also exciting to see Jupiter or Mars near opposition, rising with a thick gibbous Moon. Sometimes these conjunctions can be quite far apart, but other times they can be very close.

But the planets are seen now in one region of the sky and now in another, and often, although
two or more have come together in close proximity, they later leave the place in which
they were seen together and in time separate from each other. Therefore, we may be
sure, as our eyes attest, that the planets are not fixed in the celestial sphere.
Consequently, they have motions of their own; and no one will be able
to deny what his eyes verify. –Macrobius (circa A.D. 400)

At other times the Moon may even pass *in front* of a star or planet and cover it for a few hours. This is called an **occultation**, from the Latin word *occultare*, which means "to hide." It's not uncommon to observe occultations of Aldebaran, Regulus, Spica and Antares, since these bright stars lie close to the ecliptic.

As an occultation approaches, the slight motion of the Moon through the zodiac can be easily observed as the distance shrinks between the Moon and the star or planet. Later, the star appears like a little flea riding on the edge of the Moon. Finally, the star winks out and disappears! At a later time, the star or planet can be seen again, this time on the opposite side of the Moon's limb.

Lunar occultations of the planets can be very interesting sights as seen through a telescope. As the Moon draws closer, the planet appears to hover over the Moon's edge. The planet disappears behind the Moon as the occulation begins.

In the perpetual motion of planets, some meet in a more rapid course, others make slower revolutions, and often in an hour we see them look at each other and then hide themselves.
– Basil, Bishop of Caesarea (circa A.D. 360)

Though conjunctions between the planets are not monthly occurrences as are lunar conjunctions, planetary conjunctions are nevertheless very common. During each annual apparition of Jupiter, there is usually at least one conjunction with Venus, in the morning or evening – sometimes both. It can be a remarkable sight to see these two brightest "stars" glittering together in the twilight before the sunrise or after the sunset. However, conjunctions of Venus and Mars are unimpressive, since Mars is far away and faint, nearly on the opposite side of the Sun, when it lines up with Venus. Since Mercury is faint and low into the Sun's glow, conjunctions with Mercury are not very noticeable.

With the superior planets, conjunctions of Jupiter and Mars are impressive when the Fiery Star is near opposition, and the two bodies are of nearly equal brightness. However, this is infrequent, since Mars moves around so much in the night sky. Conjunctions of Jupiter and Saturn are rare, only happening about every twenty years, since the zodiacal motions of these planets are so slow. But Jupiter approaches and moves away from Saturn slowly, taking years to pass the ringed planet.

All of the planets come close to the bright ecliptic stars during their cycles. Occasionally three planets will come together in a *triple conjunction* or *trio*. These events are rare, and any particular combination can occur only once in a century. On the other hand, it is fairly common to see *planetary alignments*, where the planets gather in a general area of the sky.

When we see conjunctions of the planets, especially gatherings of multiple planets, we can get a sense of looking out into space, out over the edge of the solar system. Also, such conjunctions can be a useful tool for helping us learn the constellations of the zodiac and find the planets. Learning the zodiac is an important step towards understanding and appreciating "the clockwork of the heavens," the remarkable celestial order that the LORD has ordained.

The Moon as a Classical Planet

As we've seen, the Sun and Moon were regarded as classical planets in antiquity, since they also "wandered" through the stars. The Moon also follows the path of the zodiac, mimicking the annual motion of the Sun, sometimes appearing high in the sky and at other times appearing low above the trees.

The Moon completes the same course every month which the Sun does in a year. The nearer she approaches to the Sun, the dimmer light does she yield, and when most remote from it she shines with the fullest brilliancy; nor are her figure and form only changed in her wane, but her situation likewise, which is sometimes in the north and sometimes in the south. But this course she has a sort of summer and winter solstices. —Cicero (circa 50 B.C.)

The Sun and the Moon appear to be about the same size in the sky, though the Sun is *one million times brighter* than the Full Moon! So when the Moon traces the Sun's path, you can gaze up at the sky and imagine the place of the Sun among the stars hidden by the bright daytime sky.

When the Moon is in Gemini at the meridian, you can imagine how high in the sky the Sun is on the summer solstice. The shadows cast by the Moon are very short, just as those cast by the Sun would be on the longest day of the year. Conversely, when the Moon is in Sagittarius at the meridian, you can picture the noon Sun low above the horizon on the winter solstice. The Moon shadows are very long, as are the Sun's shadows at the beginning of winter.

When the Moon is on the celestial equator at the equinox points, the shadow lengths are between their two extremes. From night to night, the Moon can be seen climbing north through the zodiac as it passes through Pisces, simulating the Sun's motion from winter to spring. The Moon descends south through the zodiac as it passes Virgo, just as the Sun rolls from summer into autumn.

The Seasons of the Moon's Phases

Over the course of the seasons, each phase of the Moon appears in each of the zodiac constellations. Near the *vernal equinox*, when the Sun is in Pisces, the First Quarter Moon is high overhead in Gemini. In this way, *the First Quarter shows the season that is coming*, where the Sun will be in three months.

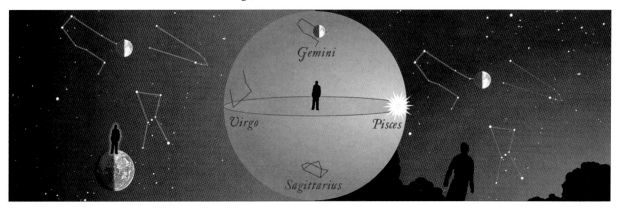

The Full Moon, being at opposition from the Sun, is at the autumnal equinox in Virgo. In this way, the Full Moon is always opposite the Sun and offers another clue to the Sun's unseen position along the zodiac.

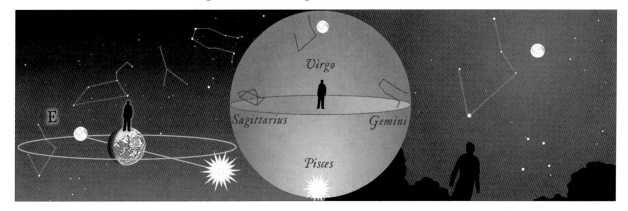

On the morning of the Last Quarter of early spring, the waning Moon is low to the trees in Sagittarius. In this way, the *Last Quarter shows the season that has departed*, where the Sun was three months ago.

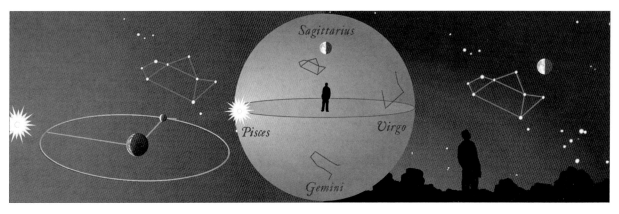

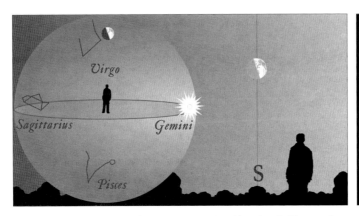 

The quarters of the Moon similarly follow the advance of the seasons. At the time of the *summer solstice*, the First Quarter Moon is in Virgo. Since the summer days are several hours longer, the Moon reaches the meridian while the Sun still shines and is in the western sky when the Sun finally sets.

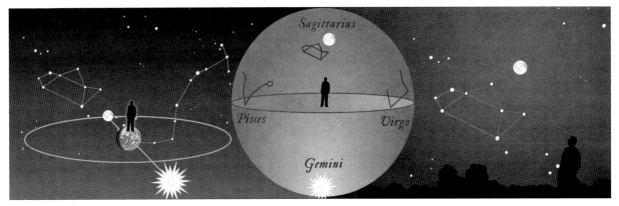

The first Full Moon of summer is in Sagittarius, at the *opposite solstice* from the Sun. Thus, as the Sun reaches its highest point of the year in Gemini, the Full Moon is at its lowest place in the sky.

 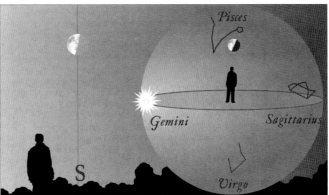

At the Last Quarter of early Summer, the Moon is near the point of the vernal equinox in Pisces. The Moon is seen in the eastern sky as the Sun rises at its earliest times of the year. The Last Quarter Moon crosses the meridian in daylight, sometime in the early morning hours after the sunrise.

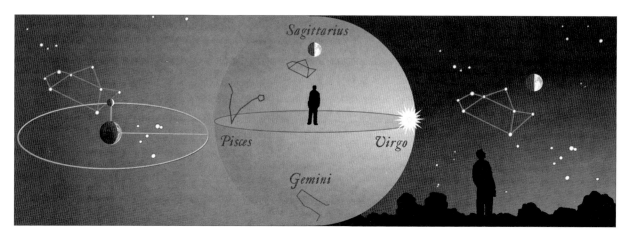

Near the time of the *autumnal equinox*, when the daylight and the nighttime are equal, the First Quarter Moon is at the meridian as the Sun sets. Here at its evening quadrature, the autumn Moon is low along the meridian in Sagittarius.

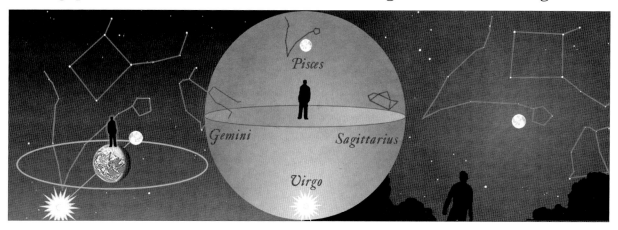

Every Full Moon occurs when the Moon is at *opposition* from the Sun. So when the Sun is near the autumnal equinox, the Full Moon of autumn is at the opposite point on the celestial equator, near the vernal equinox in Pisces.

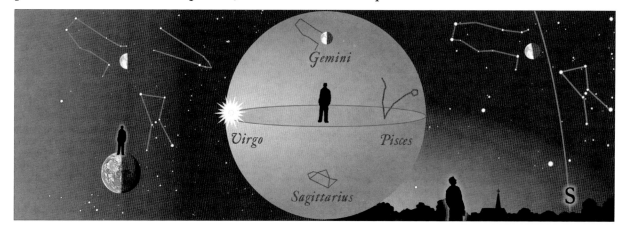

At Last Quarter, the Moon is at its morning quadrature to the equinoctial Sun. The waning half moon of fall shares the meridian with Orion as the Sun rises, high overhead in Gemini.

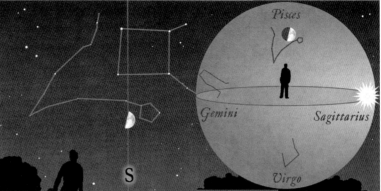

During the dark days near the *winter solstice*, the First Quarter Moon is near Pisces. Since the Sun goes down so early in these shortest days, the waxing half-moon is in the eastern sky at sunset and crosses the meridian after dark. In winter and all seasons, whether in daylight or in darkness, the First Quarter is at the meridian at about 6:00 P.M. (or 7:00 P.M. during daylight savings).

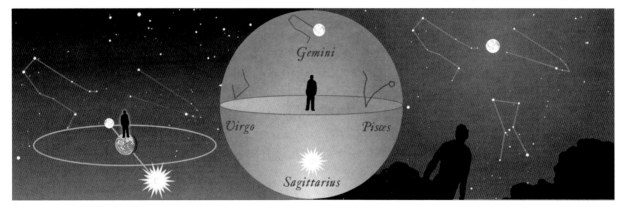

When the Sun is low in the short days nearest the winter solstice, the Full Moon is near the point of the summer solstice in Gemini. The early winter Moon is high overhead at midnight, casting short shadows over the winter landscape.

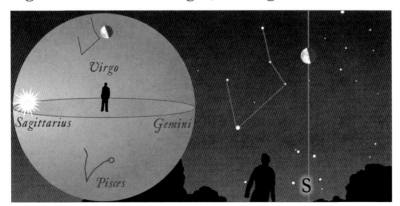

The Last Quarter nearest the winter Solstice is in Virgo. The waning half-moon crosses the meridian in darkness and is west of the meridian at the rising of the winter Sun. As in all the seasons, the Last Quarter Moon reaches the meridian around 6:00 A.M. (or 7:00 A.M. during daylight savings).

Throughout *Signs & Seasons*, we've observed the simple yet elegant order of the Sun, Moon, stars, and planets. We've learned to observe the passage of time in the sky, in the daytime and the night. In these ways, we can observe the celestial signs and follow their changes as they circle across the seasons. We are now prepared to approach the sky with *understanding*, as our ancestors did for centuries, and see the *Glory of God* as declared by the Heavens.

He appointed the Moon for seasons: the Sun knoweth his going down. Thou makest darkness, and it is night: wherein all the beasts of the forest do creep forth. –Psalm 104:19, 20

Epilogue
The Calendar

Lift up your eyes on high, and behold who hath created these things, that bringeth out their host by number: he calleth them all by names by the greatness of his might, for that he is strong in power; not one faileth. –Isaiah 40:26

We've seen the signs and seasons and days and years that are drawn from the *Two Great Lights* in the sky above. We've seen the order that the LORD has established in the sky and the recurring cycles that divide and limit our lives. Over the course of human history, these cycles have been studied for many different reasons. In ancient times, pagan cultures centered their religion on the stars. In modern times, astronomers study the stars for their own sake. Today, as well as in times past, some people just seek to marvel at the natural beauty of the stars. But down through history, there has been one very important practical reason for studying the stars: in order to develop and maintain the **calendar**.

A "calendar" is not simply a chart of days in a month that hangs on the wall. A calendar is a mathematical system for measuring time – to calculate the cycles of the seasons and to find the dates of important events, such as planting and harvesting or celebrating religious feasts. Our wall calendars are simply a printed record of that mathematical system which allows us to easily find the days of the month and track the seasons between equinoxes and solstices.

Calendar Page from The Shepherdes Kalender (A.D. 1506)

Our modern calendar is the product of centuries of astronomical observation. In our calendar, the **year** is measured by the **tropical year**, the time between successive crossings of the vernal equinox. Over the centuries, this has been found to be *365.2422 solar days*, or rather *365 days, 5 hours, 48 minutes and 45 ¼ seconds.* For most common purposes, the year can be rounded to *365 ¼* days.

The period of the Moon's phases, the **synodic month**, is *29.5306 solar days on average*, or rather *29 days, 12 hours, 44 minutes, 4 seconds* (roughly *29½ days*). The synodic or **lunar month** only roughly corresponds to the calendar month of 30 or 31 days. Our modern calendar year is based on the Sun's period, not the Moon's, since there is not a precise number of lunar months in the solar year. Because of this imprecision, the cycles of the Sun and Moon have been closely studied over the centuries to learn their order and to understand their motions.

But Sun and Moon, those watchmen of the world, with their own lanterns traversing around the mighty, revolving vault, have taught unto mankind that seasons of the years return again, and that the thing takes place after a fixed plan and order fixed. –Lucretius (circa 50 B.C.)

The Lunar Calendar

As we've seen, the ancient Israelites were instructed by the LORD through Moses to observe a calendar based on the Moon's phases. Even at the grey dawn of secular history, a **lunar calendar** was already in use in Mesopotamia. In the most elementary manner, the annual seasons of *birth, growth and death*, recur after twelve cycles of the Moon's phases. Since the lunar month is 29½ days, it is common to count a "hollow" month of 29 days followed by a "full" month of 30 days.

For this reason the civic months are alternately reckoned as "full" (30 days) and "hollow" (29 days) because two months contain 59 days.
       – Geminus (circa 50 B.C.)

The Moon's Phases
Hans Holbein the Younger (A.D. 1534)

But twelve lunar months add up to only 354 days, 11¼ days shorter than the actual solar year of 365¼ days.

The Moon-year and the solar year are different things, as the solar year is the time of the Sun's revolution through 12 signs, that is, 365 1/4 days, while the Moon-year contains 12 lunar months, that is, 354 days. – Geminus

To correct for the shortfall and keep it from falling behind the actual seasons, a lunar calendar requires the occasional addition of an extra thirteenth month, an **intercalary** month (from the Latin word *intercalo,* which means "to call among").

After only three years, the lunar calendar has a 33¾ day shortfall. The addition of one intercalary month still leaves a remainder of about four days. Over a period of decades, this difference would also add up to produce quite a shortfall. Thus, the ancients discovered rules for adding intercalary months in order to permit long-range timekeeping so that the months would not fall in the wrong seasons.

Lunar Cycles - from
"Byrhtferth's Manual" (A.D. 1011)

Since then, neither the month nor the solar year consisted of a whole number of days, the astronomers sought for a period which should contain a whole number of days, a whole number of months, and a whole number of years. – Geminus

The Greek philosopher Meton, who lived in 440 B.C., is traditionally credited with discovering a method for harmonizing the lunar and solar periods. Meton discovered that 235 lunar months was nearly equal to 19 solar years.

For they found by observation that in 19 years there were contained 6940 days and 235 months, including the intercalary months, of which in the 19 years, there are 7. – Geminus

By properly selecting "full" and "hollow" months, the Metonic cycle worked out to 12 years of 12 lunar months and 7 years of 13 lunar months. Some scholars believe the 19-year cycle was first known to the Babylonians and only borrowed by Meton and the Greeks. Other scholars believe Meton may have discovered it first. At any rate, a lunar calendar based on the Metonic cycle was in widespread use throughout the ancient world by the fifth century B.C.

You know, also, how the nineteen annual revolutions of the bright Sun agree, and as many stars also, as night allows, from the belt to the end of the feet of Orion and to his impudent dog. – Aratus

The modern Hebrew calendar is a luni-solar calendar also based on the 19-year cycle. *Rosh Hashana*, the Jewish New Year, occurs at a New Moon, and *Passover* occurs at the Full Moon, 6½ lunar months later. The 19-year cycle is not set forth in the books of Moses, and Scripture doesn't otherwise indicate a calendar method for keeping track of the Passover and other Hebrew holidays over a span of years. However, the 19-year cycle was universally understood and used in antiquity by everyone, including the tribe of Judah.

The Solar Calendar

Our modern civil calendar is based on a solar calendar, taken from the annual cycle of the Sun. In our solar calendar, the solstices and equinoxes arrive on the same dates every year. The first solar calendar was developed by the Egyptians. Our modern calendar is ultimately descended from this early Egyptian solar calendar.

Egypt is a very dry, desert place that gets very little rain. Throughout history, only the lands near the banks of the River Nile have had enough water to allow farmers to grow crops. Egyptian farmers have always dug irrigation ditches from the Nile to water their fields. During the hottest days of summer, the water level in the Nile would begin to run low. But at the end of each summer, with great predictability, the Nile would flood, overflowing its banks, bringing water and nutrient-rich soil that would save the crops for the harvest.

Sirius

The ancient Egyptians observed a connection to the summer heat and the brightest star Sirius. Each year, Sirius vanished into the sunset with the Sun's advance through the zodiac. The hottest days of summer would always arrive during the forty days when the Dog Star Sirius was lost in the Sun's glare. The ancient Egyptians believed that when Sirius rose with the Sun, it added scorching heat to that of the Sun and made the summer air even hotter. (The name *Sirius* means "scorching" in Greek.)

The heat of the Dog Star was believed to drive dogs mad during this time. For these reasons, the hottest days were known as "the Dog Days," when bright Sirius was believed to multiply the Sun's heat. From ancient times to this very day, we still commonly speak of "the Dog Days of Summer."

Sunne {riseth / falleth} {houre} 7.mi.34 / 4.mi.26				Psalmes.	¶ Morning Prayer.		¶ Euening Prayer.	
					1. Lesson.	2. Lesson.	1. Lesson.	2. Lesson.
b	1	g	Kalend.	Circumcif. of Mary.	i	Gen.rij.	Luke rij.	Gen. riij.	Rom.i.
	2	A	bi ₰o.		ii	riiij	riiii	rb	ii
rij	3	b	b ₰o.	Martin.	iij	rbj	rb	rbij	iij
ij	4	c	iiii ₰o.		iiij	rbiij	rbi	rir	iiii
	5	d	iii ₰o.		b	rr	ruii		Coloſ.i.
r	6	e	prid.₰o.	Dog dayes.	bi	rrij	rbiij	rriii	ii
rbiij	7	f	Nonas.		bii	rriiij	rir	rrb	iiii

Calendar Page for July – King James Bible (A.D. 1611)
Indicating "Dog Days" on July 6

Who knoweth not, that when the Dog Star ariseth, the heat of the Sun is fiery and burning?
The effects of which star are felt exceeding much upon the Earth. As for dogs,
no man doubteth verily, but all the time the canicular days they are
most ready to run mad. –Pliny the Elder (circa A.D. 70)

In ancient Egypt, the Dog Days ran throughout late July and early August. The hot Dog Days ended with the annual flood of the Nile, which brought much-needed water to the crops parched from the summer heat. Each year, at just the right time, the Nile would rise, flooding the fields and saving the crops from the summer heat.

Toward the summer, the Nile waxeth and overfloweth the champaign, unique in all the landscape, river sole of the Aegyptians. In mid-season heats, often and oft he waters Aegypt o'er. – Lucretius (circa 50 B.C.)

In a providential circumstance, the annual flood of the Nile would always occur *just after* the heliacal rising of Sirius, when the Dog Star would first appear in the morning sky before the sunrise. Toward the end of the Dog Days, the Egyptians would intently watch Orion rising in the morning sky before sunrise, waiting for the first morning when Orion's Dog could be seen. Finally one morning, Sirius would be seen emerging from the Sun's glare. The Egyptians would then know the flood time was at hand, and the crops would be saved for another year.

For this reason, Sirius was a special star to the Egyptians. The first sighting of the morning rising of Sirius was celebrated in Egypt as the *Tep Renpit*, "The Feast of the Opening of the Year," the first day of the Egyptian new year.

Immortal Ptolemy and Queen Bernice, two divine benefactors in Upper and Lower Egypt, masters of the length of Egypt, proclaim the day that mighty Sirius comes forth as the Feast of the Opening of the Year, as named in the Great Book of the Season of Life... In this month is the time for gathering all the growing things, and the rising of the Nile. – From the Egyptian *Decree of Canopus* (238 B.C.)

The Egyptians discovered that there were *365 days* between heliacal risings of Sirius. The Egyptians also discovered that every four years, the heliacal risings of Sirius would occur after *366 days*. So the annual cycle of Sirius (and thus the "tropical year" of the Sun) was found to be 365¼ days. In this way, the Egyptians

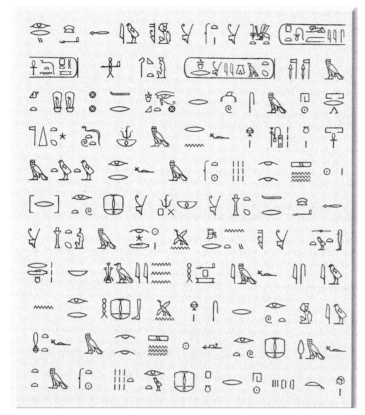

Hieroglyphics from the "Decree of Canopus"

developed the first calendar based on the Sun's annual cycle instead of the monthly cycles of the Moon's phases, as had been used in Greece, Mesopotamia and elsewhere in the ancient world.

The rising of Sirius with the Sun changes to another day every four years.
— "The Decree of Canopus"

Unlike the luni-solar calendar used by the Greeks and others, the Egyptians divided a 365-day solar year into 12 "months" of 30 days, each of which only approximately equaled a lunar month. The Egyptians added 5 holidays, intercalated at the end of the year, and a sixth day every 4 years.

The Egyptians by their study of Astronomy discovered the solar year and were the first to divide it into twelve parts and in my opinion their method of calculation is better than the Greeks; for the Greeks, to make the seasons work out properly, intercalate a whole month every other year, while the Egyptians make the year consist of twelve months of thirty days each and every year intercalate five additional days, and so complete the regular circle of the seasons. — Herodotus (circa 400 B.C.)

In later centuries, the Egyptian solar calendar was adopted as the official Roman calendar. This same solar calendar was maintained throughout the Middle Ages. A modified version of the same Egyptian/Roman calendar is still used in the modern world today. The Roman calendar has been through many changes since it was first established.

The Roman Calendar

The Roman calendar was originally developed by the legendary Romulus, who is said to have founded Rome in 753 B.C. The calendar of Romulus was very crude, having only 10 months and only 298 days. Intercalary months were added each year. The Roman calendar was improved by Romulus' successor, Numa Pompilius, who installed a lunar calendar and added two new months to the beginning of Romulus's year. The first day of each Roman month was called *the Kalends*. It is from this name that we get the term *calendar*.

THE ORIGINAL ROMAN MONTHS

MARTIUS - dedicated to Mars, god of war
APRILIS - "to open" - the month when buds opened
MAIUS - dedicated to Maia, a fertility goddess
JUNIUS - dedicated to Juno, the queen of the Roman pantheon
QUINTILIS - the fifth month (from the Latin *quinque*, which means "five")
SEXTILIS - the sixth month (from the Latin *sex*, which means "six")
SEPTEMBRIS - the seventh month (from the Latin *septem*, which means "seven")
OCTOBRIS - the eighth month (from the Latin *octo*, which means "eight")
NOVEMBRIS - the ninth month (from the Latin *novem*, which means "nine")
DECEMBRIS - the tenth month (from the Latin *decem*, which means "ten")

NUMA'S ADDITIONAL MONTHS

JANUARIUS - dedicated to Janus, the two faced god of beginnings
FEBRUARIUS - "Februa," a feast of purification observed in that month

The Julian Calendar

The old Roman lunar calendar was not very accurate and was frequently tampered with by politicians to advance their own political agendas. The Roman calendar had become quite a mess and was worthless as a tool for predicting the seasons. During the first century B.C., Gaius Julius Caesar seized power over Rome and instituted a policy of reforms intended to root out political corruption. This policy included calendar reform.

Falling in love with the Egyptian princess Cleopatra, Caesar became fascinated with Egypt and its culture. Upon consulting with Sosigenes, an Egyptian astronomer, Caesar discarded the Roman lunar calendar and installed a solar calendar in Rome after the fashion of the Egyptian calendar.

The Dictator Caesar... to which was entrusted the duty of regulating the year in conformity with the Sun's revolution, under the auspices of Sosigenes, an astronomer of considerable learning and skill. — Pliny (circa A.D. 50)

Caesar's new solar calendar was 365 days in length and included a "leap year" of 366 days every fourth year, in order to correct for the inequality of the tropical year. Caesar's calendar, the **Julian calendar**, restored order to the seasonal year.

Then turning his attention to the reorganization of the state, he reformed the calendar, which the negligence of the pontiffs had long since so disordered, through their privilege of adding months or days at pleasure, that the harvest festivals did not come in Summer nor those of the vintage in the Autumn; and he adjusted the year to the Sun's course by making it consist of three hundred and sixty-five days, abolishing the intercalary month, and adding one day every fourth year. – Suetonius (circa A.D. 120)

The lengths of the months were changed so that they no longer corresponded to the cycle of lunar phases but merely served to divide the year into twelve parts. By converting to a purely solar calendar, the seasons arrived on the same dates every year. Because of the intercalary day for "leap year," the vernal equinox occurs each year on March 20 or 21, the summer solstice on June 20 or 21, the autumnal equinox on September 22 or 23, and the winter solstice on December 20 or 21.

The Julian calendar was a tremendous innovation and was enforced over the entire Roman empire. To commemorate his achievement, the month *Quintilis* was renamed *Julius* (or July) in Caesar's honor. The first Roman emperor, *Caesar Augustus*, further modified the Julian calendar to its final form, and renamed the month *Sextilis* after himself, *Augustus* (or August).

Passover and Easter

The most important feast in Christianity is **Easter**, in which faithful Christians celebrate Christ's resurrection. The Easter celebration is based on the Jewish celebration of the **Passover**. We read in the book of Exodus how the LORD used Moses to lead the Israelites out of Egypt. In Exodus 12, the LORD sent the final plague, smiting the firstborn of all Egypt. The Israelites were saved by sacrificing a lamb and covering their doorframes with its blood, so that the LORD would "pass over" the house and not smite the firstborn of Israel. The LORD commanded that the Israelites remember the Passover in a seven-day "Feast of Unleavened Bread," which begins on the Full Moon (i.e. the fourteenth day) of the first month of the seasonal year.

In the first month, on the fourteenth day of the month at even, ye shall eat unleavened bread,
until the one and twentieth day of the month at even. –Exodus 12:18

In the lunar calendar, the New Moon is the first day of the new month. The Full Moon is at midmonth, the fourteenth day of the month. So Israel was instructed to celebrate the Passover on the Full Moon of the first month, called *Abib* (אָבִיב) in the books of Moses.

Observe the month of Abib, and keep the passover unto the LORD thy God: for in the month
of Abib the LORD thy God brought thee forth out of Egypt by night. –Deuteronomy 16:1

The word "Abib" means "sprouting" or "budding" and is the first month of spring, falling among our months of March and April. Abib is the only month of the year named by the LORD in the books of Moses.

However, the modern Jewish calendar has a common origin with the Babylonian calendar. In addition to using the 19-year cycle, the modern Jewish calendar uses months with names nearly identical to the Babylonian names. The books of Nehemiah, Ezra, and Esther (which record events after the Babylonian exile) use the month names *Sivan, Elul, Kislev, Tevet,* and *Adar,* nearly the same as their Babylonian counterparts.

Most notable in Nehemiah 2:1 and Esther 3:7 is the Babylonian month *Nisan* (ניסן), the first month of spring, which corresponds to the Mosaic month of Abib. In the modern Jewish calendar, Passover occurs on the fourteenth day of Nisan. The Jewish historian Flavius Josephus gives us an astronomical reference for the month of Nisan.

Hebrew	*Babylonian*
Nisan	*Nisanu*
Iyar	*Ayaru*
Sivan	*Simanu*
Tammuz	*Dusuzu*
Av	*Abu*
Elul	*Ululu*
Tishrei	*Tashritu*
Marheshvan	*Arahsamna*
Kislev	*Kislimu*
Tevet	*Tebetu*
Shevat	*Shabatu*
Adar 1	*Adaru (intercalary)*
Adar 2	*Adaru*

In the month of Xanthicus, which is by us called "Nisan," and is the beginning of our year, on
the fourteenth day of the lunar month, when the Sun is in Aries (for in this month it was
that we were delivered from bondage under the Egyptians) the law ordained that we
should every year slay the sacrifice which I before told you we slew when we came
out of Egypt, and which was called the Passover. –Josephus (circa A.D. 100)

In the time of Josephus, the Sun was in the constellation Aries at the time of the vernal equinox, the first day of spring in the Northern Hemisphere. Thus, in the traditional Jewish observance, the Passover feast begins with the Full Moon during the month of the equinox. As noted in Chapter 3, Moses would have led the Israelites out of Egypt under the light of the Full Moon, and the Full Moon thus would have shone down on Jesus and His disciples in the Garden of Gethsemane.

The early church celebrated Passover in a similar manner to Jewish observances, though the customs changed over time. But our Christian Easter observance is approximately based on the Hebrew Passover observance. For example, liturgical

*Jesus in the Garden of Gethsemane
- Gustave Dore' - A.D. 1866*

churches observe an extended Easter celebration, including a solemn, penitent "Holy Week" observance leading up to Easter, and a celebratory "Easter Week" following Easter Sunday, similar to the seven-day Feast of Unleavened Bread.

Easter was the first day, in the Old Covenant, when the moon was fourteen days old, and the seven days following were termed dies azymorum. This excellent custom is very delightfully observed among Christian people. Lo, they anticipate the first day with great honour, and carefully observe the age of the Moon from fifteen to twenty-one days old, and spiritually thrust away from them the devastating Devil, as the venerable apostle instructs us: "We must keep the feast not with the leaven of malice and wickedness, but with the unleavened bread of sincerity and truth." – Byrhtferth's Manual (A.D. 1011)

Christianity arose in the Roman empire, and like other Romans, the early Christians used the civil calendar of Julius Caesar for their common, day-to-day timekeeping purposes. In time, the early church developed a church calendar that combined elements of the Jewish lunar calendar with the solar calendar of Rome for predicting the times of different annual religious feasts.

Movable feasts were based on Jewish feasts, such as Easter and Pentecost. The movable feasts were determined by both lunar and solar calculations and landed on different dates each year. *Fixed feasts* such as Christmas were based strictly on the solar calendar and landed on the same date each year.

Easter – Pagan Origins?

The Hebrew word for "Passover" is *pesach* (פסח), which is translated as *pascha* (πασχα) in Greek. However, in the English language, the feast of Christ's resurrection is commonly called *Easter*. Even in the King James Bible, in Acts 12:4, the word *pascha* is translated as Easter. But in old-fashioned English writings, it's not uncommon to see the Easter feast called **The Pasch** (pronounced "pask"). Jesus is often figuratively referred to as "The Paschal Lamb."

Some today argue that Easter is really a pagan holiday, with bunnies and eggs symbolizing pagan fertility rites instead of the resurrection of Jesus. Entire books have been written to show that the name *Easter* is derived from the name of the Babylonian fertility goddess *Ishtar* or *Astarte*. Certainly eggs and bunnies are not of Biblical origin, but the name issue is mostly a matter of the semantics of the English language, since other European languages paint a different picture.

Easter = *The Pasch*	
Spanish	= Pascua
Italian	= Pasqua
French	= Paque
Russian	= Pascha
Swedish	= Pask
Norwegian	= Paske
Dutch	= Pasen

The name *Easter* is commonly believed to be derived from *Eostre*, the name of an ancient Anglo-Saxon goddess associated with a springtime festival. Our only source of information for this goddess and her supposed feast is this short passage from the Venerable Bede, an eighth century Anglo-Saxon Christian, whose book *On the Reckoning of Time* was the standard medieval work on the classical astronomy of calendar methods.

"Eastermonth," by which name the Paschal month has been called, was formerly called after the goddess Eostre, in whose name a feast was celebrated. Now the Paschal time has this same name, since they are accustomed to calling the joys of the new holiday after the ancient observance. – Bede (circa A.D. 700)

The German word for the Pasch is *Ostern,* and since the Anglo-Saxons were originally a Germanic tribe, these words are clearly related. The German word for *east* is *ost*, and other related words include the name of the nation of Austria, or *Osterreich*, "the Eastern Kingdom."

Old habits apparently die hard in the English and German languages, though there is no historical evidence connecting the Germanic *Eostre* to the Babylonian *Ishtar*, other than a similarity in the names. Nonetheless, it's pretty clear that the majority of traditionally Christian nations use the name *Pascha* as the proper name for the feast of Christ's resurrection, rather than a name of pagan origin.

Changing Customs

In the early centuries of the church, Christians kept the Pasch in the same manner as the Jews, beginning on the fourteenth of Nisan. But as time went by, the Christian church developed distinctive observances that differed from Jewish practices.

In the church at Rome, it became customary to celebrate the Pasch on the Sunday following 14 Nisan, in order to commemorate Jesus' rising on the first day of the week. This became a controversy in the late second century. Victor I, the bishop of Rome, argued that the churches of Asia Minor should follow the Roman practice, rather than celebrate the Passover on 14 Nisan, following the Biblical Jewish tradition. Some believed it was embarrassing to have some Christians fasting and praying in anticipation of Easter while others were feasting and celebrating its arrival.

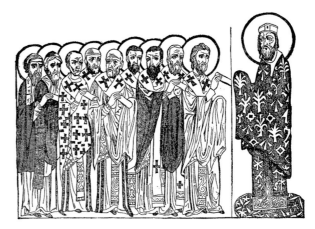

The Easter controversy was ultimately resolved in A.D. 325 at the *Council of Nicaea*. After affirming the doctrine of the Trinity, the assembled bishops decided that Easter would be celebrated on the first Sunday following the first Full Moon after the vernal equinox, March 21.

Council of Nicaea, A.D. 325
(From an Ancient Greek Manuscript)

We further proclaim to you the good news of the agreement concerning the holy Easter....all our brethren in the east who formerly followed the custom of the Jews are henceforth to celebrate the said most sacred feast of Easter at the same time as the Romans.
– The synodical letter of the Nicene council (A.D. 325)

Since the early centuries, the Christian churches used the official Julian civil calendar of Rome to calculate the date of the Pasch. Because of the leap years, it was not always easy to know the precise date of the equinox, and so calendar tables were prepared years in advance. In the Roman method of calculating Easter, the Paschal Full Moon must land on or after the vernal equinox.

Wherefore, the beginning of the month should be observed according to this rule, that the fourteenth of the Paschal Moon never precedes the Equinox, but is properly on the Equinox itself - that is, on March 21 - or when it has crossed over.
– The Venerable Bede (circa A.D. 700)

The Error in the Calendar

The Venerable Bede is known for many things, particularly his promotion of the *Christian era,* the method of counting the years since Christ's birth according to *Anno Domini (A.D.) – The Year of Our Lord.* Like most everyone else in ancient and medieval times, Bede accepted Caesar's length of the solar year as 365 days with an extra day added during "leap year" every four years.

The year of the Sun is when it returns to its place in the stars, completing 365 days and 6 hours, that is, one quarter of a total day. – Bede

However, even in ancient times it was known that this value of the solar year was not precisely accurate. A shortfall in the tropical year was discovered in about 200 B.C. by the Greek-Egyptian astronomer Hipparchus. Studying centuries of astronomical data, Hipparchus calculated that the year was short by about 1/300 of a day, or 4 minutes, 48 seconds. Thus, even in Caesar's time, it was known that 365¼ days was not an accurate value for the year.

I have also discussed the length of the year in one book, in which I prove that the solar year – that is, the length of time in which the Sun passes from a solstice to the same solstice again, or from an equinox to the same equinox – contains 365 1/4 days, less, very nearly, 1/300 of a day and night, and not the exact 1/4 which the mathematicians suppose it to have in addition to the said whole number of days.

– Hipparchus, quoted by Ptolemy (circa A.D. 150)

However, neither Julius Caesar nor the Venerable Bede accounted for any shortfall, and neither realized that in fact the solar year was precisely *365 days, 5 hours, 48 minutes and 42 seconds.* As a result, the time from one vernal equinox to the next was overestimated by *11 minutes and 18 seconds.* While this is only a tiny amount, over centuries of time, it added up. This minor annual discrepancy amounts to about three extra days every 400 years. In the time of Caesar, the vernal equinox occurred on March 24. By the time of the Council of Nicaea, the equinox was arriving on March 21. By A.D. 700, the time of Bede, the equinox landed on March 18.

Throughout the medieval period, the equinox was arriving earlier and earlier. Consequently, the date of Easter was arriving earlier. Given enough centuries, Easter would regress backward through the calendar towards Christmas!

Calendar Reform

By the 1500s the Julian calendar had slipped ten days from the Council of Nicaea, and the equinox was arriving on March 11. Calendar reform became a topic for discussion among church authorities, in part because the nature of the problem was poorly understood. The single largest obstacle in calendar reform was that the exact length of the year was not precisely known. Hipparchus' year was known from the works of Ptolemy, but it was understood that this value was not accurate enough.

Many scholars turned their study to the heavens, in order to perfect their knowledge of the Sun's interval. Kopernik, whose work placed the Sun at the center of the Earth's orbit, was inspired by the calendar reform effort.

> *When the Lateran Council was considering the question of reforming the Ecclesiastical Calendar, no decision was reached, for the sole reason that the magnitude of the year and the months and the movements of Sun and Moon had not yet been measured with sufficient accuracy.* – Mikolaj Kopernik (A.D. 1543)

The final solution was adopted forty years later in 1582 with the adoption of the **Gregorian calendar**. Upon consulting with the learned astronomers of the time, *Pope Gregory XIII* issued a proclamation that restored the vernal equinox to March 21.

> *So that the Vernal Equinox, which the Fathers of the Council of Nicaea fixed to March 21, be likewise restored, we instruct and order that ten days be taken away from the month of October of the year 1582, including the 5th through the 14th; and the day following the 4th, in which we celebrate the Feast of St. Francis, we appoint to be the 15th of October.* – Gregory XIII (A.D. 1582)

In this way, the Equinox once again arrived on March 21, as it had in A.D. 325. To accommodate future drift in the calendar, Gregory established that the intercalary day February 29 would be omitted from century years, except once every four centuries.

> *Thereafter, so the Equinox does not recede from March 21 in the future, we also establish that a leap year every fourth year must be continued (as is customary), except in century years. In this way, the years 1700, 1800 and 1900 will not be leap years. The Year 2000 will be a leap year with an intercalated day, February 29, as is our customary habit, and continuously the same order of intermittent intercalated leap year days, every 400 years, will be perpetually maintained.* – Gregory XIII

And so Gregory established that three out of four centennial years would *not* be leap years. In this way, three days are dropped from every 400 years, thereby maintaining the predictable order of Easter and the seasons for millennia into the future. The Gregorian method is accurate to within *one day every 3300 years*. Should the LORD tarry, people in the Year A.D. 4900 will have to decide how to handle this day!

Remarkably, Gregory XIII looked ahead from the medieval period to our generation in order to establish that the year 2000 would be the first centennial leap year in 400 years. Sadly, our generation is so uninformed about Classical Astronomy that February 29, 2000 came and went with little notice, in the media or otherwise.

The reformed Gregorian calendar was immediately adopted in October, 1582 throughout the Roman Catholic nations of Europe. But the Protestant and Eastern Orthodox nations resisted this "popish innovation." For a century and a half thereafter, the nations of Europe maintained an awkward system of keeping two dates for every notable event, one in the "Old Style" of the Julian calendar, and another in the "New Style" of the Gregorian calendar. For example, George Washington's birthday is sometimes given as "February 11, 1732 O.S., February 22, 1732 N.S."

Over time, the Protestant nations gradually accepted the Gregorian calendar. In 1752, England finally adopted the New Style, and its American colonies followed at the same time.

> *The King and Parliament have thought fit to alter our Year, by taking eleven days out of September, 1752, and directing us to begin our Account for the future on the first of January... wishing withal, according to ancient Custom, that this New Year (which is indeed a New Year, such an one as we never saw before, and shall never see again) may be a happy Year to all my kind Readers.*
> – *Poor Richard's Almanack* by "Richard Saunders," a.k.a. Benjamin Franklin (A.D. 1752)

Nowadays, the Gregorian calendar has become the civil calendar that regulates the affairs of the entire secular world, including nations far and wide that have no historical Christian heritage.

The Eastern Orthodox church still retains the Julian calendar as the basis of the church calendar, preserving the method established at Nicaea. By the twenty-first century, the seasons have slipped thirteen days from the time of Nicaea. So the vernal equinox is now arriving on March 8, O.S. The Eastern church celebrates Christmas on December 25 as reckoned by the Julian calendar, which is January 7 on the Gregorian calendar. So ironically, 1700 years after the Council of Nicaea established a common celebration of the Pasch, Christendom is still divided over when this holiday should be celebrated.

The LORD's Timekeepers Abandoned

For centuries, it was sufficient to observe the cycles of the Sun and Moon to measure the days of the Pasch. But in our high-tech modern era, not even the simple cycle of *the Day* is exact enough for timekeeping. Using sophisticated measuring devices, it has been discovered that the Earth's rotation is not constant. Sometimes the Earth rotates fast and other times slow, by tiny fractions of a second. No one knows for sure why this happens. Some scientists believe that molten rock at the Earth's core "sloshes around" and that this affects our world's rotation.

An Old German Woodcut (A.D. 1687)

The Moon is even worse than the Earth as a timekeeper. The Moon is caught in a gravitational tug-of-war between the Earth and the Sun. As a result, the gravities of these bodies are constantly altering the Moon's orbit, expanding and contracting it, and in the process speeding up the lunar month and later slowing it down. The 29½ day lunar month is only an average, since any particular lunar cycle can be as much as *five and a half hours* longer or shorter than the average.

Unlike the Earth's daily rotation, the tropical year is a very accurate, predictable interval. But it is too long and must be divided into shorter, more convenient units. Atoms vibrate at a very constant rate which can be precisely measured, so today, we use *atomic time,* in which these atomic vibrations are counted, giving us an extremely precise measure of time, accurate to within *a billionth of a second!*

In our modern technological era, the *second* is our fundamental unit of time, and is measured by 9,192,631,770 vibrations of a Cesium atom. Our modern year is counted as a few hundred *quadrillion* of these atomic vibrations, as recorded by a series of "atomic clocks," which in United States are maintained by the U.S. Naval Observatory and the National Institute of Standards and Technology.

Over a period of time, the orbit of the Moon causes the rotation of the Earth to slow down slightly, causing the cycle of the day to drift slightly from true atomic time. When this error adds up to a full second, the professional timekeepers intercalate a *leap second*, which keeps our sloppy natural world in line with the orderly rhythm of our technological, machine-driven culture.

For most of history, humanity has taken its time from the stars, and the natural cycles of the heavens have allowed us to measure the days of our lives and the years of human history. In our modern machine era, things are the other way around. The cycles of the heavens are now regulated and defined by our human creations, the clocks. Instead of the heavens measuring human time, the humans are measuring celestial time!

Nowadays, precision clocks and a professional time service provides us the time of day, accurate to an infinitesimally small fraction of a second. We no longer rely on the Sun, Moon, and stars to tell us the time of day or the times of planting and harvesting. In so many ways, our culture has built a comfortable wall of technology, separating us from the LORD's natural creation. Many people are content to live behind this wall and never glance up at the sky above.

"The New Jerusalem" - Gustave Dore' - A.D. 1866

In this way, everything written in this book has become *irrelevant*. We no longer need the heavenly bodies for keeping time. The chore of observing a sundial and the celestial bodies themselves has been replaced by a quick glance at the clocks and calendars that hang on our walls. Besides, the Sun and Moon and stars are only for this life and will not exist in God's Holy City.

And the city had no need of the Sun, neither of the Moon, to shine in it: for the glory of God did lighten it, and the Lamb is the light thereof. –Revelation 21:23

However, as long as people still speak of *days, months,* and *years,* these lessons will *not* be irrelevant. Our modern technology has freed us to observe the heavens just because *we want to*...because the Creation is *beautiful* and *wondrous* and has much to teach us.

Whether you live under the bright glittering stars of the country or under the feeble stars of the city, you can still enjoy the wonders of the starry sky and the phenomena of the seasons. The celestial sky is a remarkable aspect of nature that we can all behold. The best part is, the stars are a sight we can appreciate *for free!* There's no charge for marveling at the starry sky, and the sky can never be taken away.

Let them be for signs, and for seasons, and for days, and years.

Don't stop with this book. Add experience to your study of the stars. Make it your custom to practice the ancient *skycraft.* The depictions of the sky shown in this book are crude imitations compared to the awesome majesty of the LORD's true sky. All of the many cycles that we have seen in our story can be observed and verified without special equipment. So observe the cycles of the heavens – the *Signs & Seasons* of the lights in the sky above – and discover these precious things for yourself.

They that be wise shall shine as the brightenss of the firmament; and they that turn many to righteousness as the stars for ever and ever. –Daniel 12:3

Field Activities

Mastering Your Knowledge and Understanding of the Sky through Practical Observation

It is the glory of God to conceal a thing: but the honour of kings is to search out a matter. –Proverbs 25:2

 Signs & Seasons

Field Activities

With many things in life, we learn by doing, and visual astronomy is no exception. You could read this book and perhaps understand the concepts *in theory*, but without actually observing the sky, you will never master the subject *in practice*. You can only get a limited understanding from reading *Signs & Seasons*, since it only shows flat pictures, unlike the real sky, which is three-dimensional and visible in all directions. So this book is most useful as a guide to learning to observe the sky.

As stated over a century ago by noted astronomer Asaph Hall (quoted in the introduction):

Elementary astronomy should be taught in the high schools and preparatory schools, as well as in the colleges. Preparatory work in it ought to be accepted for admission to college.

The field activities in this book are intended to assist high school homeschoolers in recording work hours that will establish high school credit for creating a transcript. However, these activities can also be adapted as "unit study" work for younger students under a parent's supervision.

Creating a Field Journal
To this end, instructions are provided for each chapter to help you create a *field journal* for recording observations, including the *time and date*. The *amount of time* spent on each activity should also be recorded. The field journal should be a small 3-ring binder for keeping loose-leaf paper so that pages can be added and rearranged. Some entries can be listed by topic, and others can be listed by date, for making daily, weekly, or monthly journal entries.

Types of Activities
* *Sketching* – In some activities, you will make sketches of the Sun, Moon, and stars. Sketching forces you to closely examine the illustrations in the book and the appearances of the sky. This reinforces a deeper understanding of the subject matter. Don't worry if you're not the greatest artist! Your field journal is primarily your own tool for learning the sky.

* *Manipulative Activities* – some hands-on activities require the use of a typical rotating 12-inch world globe. If you don't own one, these are often found at public libraries. Also, some activities involve creating useful tools from simple cardboard, such as *volvelles*, traditional instruments for depicting the motions in the sky.

Completion of Activities
These activities should be self-guided. Do as many of the activities as you like. Do not worry if you cannot complete them all. These activities should be *fun!* Certain activities involve constellations, and not all are visible at convenient times of the night or at every time of year. As always, most of the outdoor activities require clear skies, which are not always available in every climate during every season of the year. But the more activities you complete, the more you have to record in your journal for greater high school credit. Consult the suitable sources for high school credit standards in your area.

You can also record any other interesting observations, such as meteors or halos around the Sun or Moon. You can make up your own activities and record those as well. Feel free to expand your study beyond *Signs & Seasons*. For example, you can learn about "deep sky" objects and study the sky with a telescope, or you can visit a local planetarium, observatory, or astronomy club. The more you study the sky, the more you will learn and understand. After many years of study, the author is still learning new things about the sky!

Field Activities
Chapter 1 - The Light He Called Day

Create a Backyard Compass
Materials: Sticks, a tape measure, and five paving stones from a garden supply center.

This is a very important activity, and your backyard compass will be used throughout the field activities. You will make a compass that is big enough to stand on, as shown in the book. This will help you find direction and learn to orient yourself as you learn the signs in the sky.

The first thing you need to do is find "high noon," the time of day when the Sun is highest in the sky and the shadows are the shortest. As Pliny the Elder instructed in A.D. 70:

After observing the quarter in which the Sun rises on any given day, at the sixth hour of the day (i.e. at noon) take your position in such a manner as to have the point of the Sun's rising on your left; you will then have the south directly facing you, and the north at your back: a line drawn through a field in this direction is called the "cardinal" line.... It will be the sixth hour of the day, at the moment when the shadow straight before him is the shortest. Through the middle of this shadow, taken lengthwise, a furrow must be traced in the ground with a hoe, or else a line drawn with ashes, some twenty feet in length.

So here's what to do:

*   Pick a site in your backyard away from the house and other buildings, with a wide open view in as many directions as possible. (Get your parent's permission before beginning!)

*   Pound a stick in the ground about one foot long. Be sure the stick is placed very straight into the ground.

*   On a sunny day, observe the shadows from between about 10:00 A.M. and 2:00 P.M. (since high noon can occur at very different times depending on the season and your location.)

*   Every 20-30 minutes, place a short twig into the ground at the end of the stick's shadow.

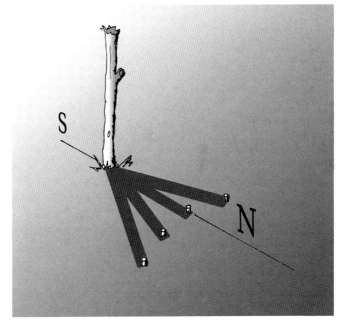

*   After the time is up, use a ruler or tape to measure the distance between each twig and the stick. The shortest distance is your *cardinal line* that runs from north to south!

*   Carefully extend your cardinal line 10 feet (3 meters) to the north and to the south from your stick. Place paving stones at each end point. These are the north and south points of your compass.

*   Remove the stick and place a paving stone in its place. This is your central *standing stone.*

* From your standing stone, measure a line perpendicular to your cardinal line, another 10 feet (3 meters) on either side. Check carefully to make sure your lines are even. Place paving stones at these ends. These are the east and west points of your compass.

* Recheck your compass over the next two or three days to make sure that the shadows really are shortest in the direction of your cardinal line.

* When your compass is accurate, you can now stand on your standing stone and look at each direction of the compass, day or night and when it's cloudy!

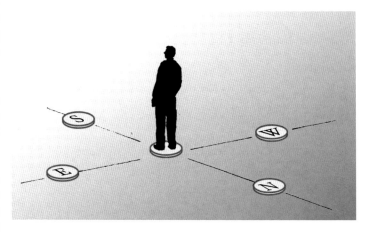

* You can write the names of the directions on your compass points – N-E-W-S. This will help every member of the family find direction. Also, you can dig out under your stones to set them into the earth to make sure the lawn mower won't hit them.

Backyard Compass Activities

Sunrise, Sunset and Noon
While standing in your backyard compass, observe the directions of sunrise, noon, and sunset over a period of several days. Record these results in your field journal.

Find the times of sunrise and sunset from your local newspaper or the Internet. Try the U.S. Naval Observatory *Complete Sun and Moon Data for One Day* Web page:

http://aa.usno.navy.mil/data/docs/RS_OneDay.html

Confirm – Does the Sun always rise due east and set due west? It only does on the first days of spring and fall (March 21 and September 23). From March 21 to September 23, the Sun rises and sets towards the north. From September 23 to March 21, the Sun rises and sets towards the south (more about this in later chapters). In your journal, sketch the views you observe. Include a horizon with trees and buildings, and include the initial of the direction of the compass point. *Remember! Never stare directly at the Sun!*

Noon Shadows (on a separate page in your journal)
What direction does your shadow point when it is 12:00 P.M. on the clock? What is the time on the clock when your shadow is shortest and points toward the north? Is it daylight savings time? How might that affect the difference between clock time and the Sun's shadows? Draw a sketch of how your compass looks with shadows and also include the time. Repeat these measurements at least once a week for a period of three months. Does the time difference between the clock and the shadows change over the months?

Is your neighborhood "astronomically aligned"?
Look at a map of your community and find the compass. Are the streets in your community laid out along the compass? Confirm the direction of your street on the map with your own observations. Stand on your sidewalk or driveway around the time of high noon, when the shadows are shortest. Measure your own shadow or the shadow of a family member to find when

the shadows are shortest. Do the shortest shadows line up with your driveway or sidewalk? If so, you can make a "backyard compass" on your driveway with sidewalk chalk! (Again, ask permission first!)

Compare the times of your shortest shadows on your driveway or sidewalk and your backyard compass. Are they the same? (If not, one or the other is wrong!)

Use sidewalks and driveways to sight the directions of rising, setting and noon passage. Walk around some other astronomically aligned streets in your community at these times, especially ones that have clear views of the horizon. Record your results. Always remember not to stare at the Sun!

Exposures
Notice which rooms in your house receive the morning Sun, noon Sun, and evening Sun. Into which rooms does the noon Sun never directly shine? Record your results. Learn about which outdoor plants do best in different exposures. Go outside your house and notice the different plants growing on different sides of the house. Ask a parent, relative, or neighbor who enjoys gardening, or visit a nursery where plants are sold. In which exposure should you put plants that like full sunlight? Partial sunlight? Shade?

As you travel with family to stores and other places, note the time of day and the direction of the Sun. Track your direction based on the Sun's position at that time. Note how your direction of travel changes with left and right turns. When you arrive at your destination, determine which overall directions you traveled from home, e.g., southeast, northwest, etc. When you get home, confirm this with a map of your community. Do this for several trips over a period of days or weeks and record your results. Learn the general directions to at least 10 familiar places. Include the nearest town, your regular shopping center, your church, grandparents' house, 3 neighbors (in different directions), and 3 friends (in different directions). Note the exposures of these places, e.g. the front entrance, large windows, etc.

Horizon Activity
Can you see the horizon from your house? If not, visit an open area, e.g., a field or other place with few buildings or trees. If you live near water, visit the shoreline. Estimate the distance to the farthest objects (i.e., hundreds of feet or more than a mile.) Can you see the actual edge of the Earth, or is the view blocked by buildings or trees? Imagine the horizon as a big circle with you at the center. If you are near a hill or have access to a window in a tall building, notice that a more distant horizon can be seen than when standing on the ground.

Twilight Activity
As day changes to night, our ability to see color changes. The retinas in our eyes include rods and cones. During the bright daylight, our cones help us see color and also read words on paper. At night, our rods help us see in darkness, but the rods cannot distinguish color or enable us to read.

Record the time of sunset. During early twilight, note the bright colors in the sky and of ground objects. Keep some colored objects with you. As twilight deepens, record the times when it becomes difficult to read and when it becomes difficult to distinguish colors. Also, record the times when the first stars can be seen. Record a later time when you notice several stars that can be seen. Record a time when the sky begins to look starry but a patch of twilight glow can still be seen on the sunset horizon. Finally, record a time when no twilight can be seen. How do the times of twilight compare with the changes from day vision to night vision?

Sketching Activities

Earth's Rotation
Sketch a picture of the Earth. Include a compass (as shown in the chapter) and also familiar continents. Show the Earth's axis and include an arrow showing the direction of the Earth's rotation.

Sun's Daily Motion
Draw an oval shape to show the horizon, wide enough to span a page – at least 6 inches. Include compass points. Show the proper position of the Sun at sunrise, midmorning, noon, afternoon, and sunset. Sketch arrows showing the motion of the Sun. Add a person in the center of the compass, and show the shadows for each position of the Sun. Indicate the direction of the Sun's shadow over course of the day. Confirm this motion with your backyard compass.

Sketch a cartoon panel of the horizon with a tree line and other foreground objects. Show the sunrise and an arrow with the direction in the sky of the Sun's motion. Draw a similar panel showing the direction of the afternoon Sun, moving toward the sunset. Confirm with daytime observations of the Sun's position.

Globe Activities
Use a 12-inch rotating Earth globe, preferably one from the Cram Company. Place the globe in a dark room with light shining in from the next room, preferably a small light. Show the proper rotation of the Earth. Note the sunrise terminator and the sunset terminator as the globe turns. Make a small "stickman" – a cut-out of a person – and tape it to the globe over your own location. Simulate sunrise, noon, and sunset.

When it is night over North America, where in the world is it daytime?   When it is sunrise over your city, where is it sunset? Do this for several famous cities in the world and record your results.

For the Earth's rotation, if you're facing a globe so that north is "up," which direction would be the correct direction of rotation – right or left? Is there anything familiar from television or movies that correctly shows the rotation of the earth?

Here's an outside activity, to be done after dark with at least two people. Hold a bright flashlight several feet away from the globe to simulate the Sun.

To simulate the geocentric theory, one person holds the flashlight and walks around the globe in a circle toward the west to simulate the daytime motion of the Sun. The other person finds your home town on the globe and notes the movement of the nighttime shadow behind the Earth as the Sun moves toward the west. Note the sunrise (where your home first enters the light) and the sunset (where your home first leaves the shadow).

To simulate the heliocentric theory, one person holds the flashlight steady and the other person rotates the globe toward the east. Note the movement of your home as the Earth rotates toward the west. Note the sunrise (where your home first enters the light) and the sunset (where your home first leaves the shadow).

For a sunrise, if north is up, which side of the Earth is in daylight (left or right?) Which side is in night? For sunset, if north is up, which side of the Earth is in daylight (left or right?) Which side is in night?

Volvelle Activity

Make a volvelle to illustrate the daily motion of the Sun.
Materials: Cardstock (manila file folders work well), a compass, pencil, string, brass fasteners (from an office supply store)

Use a compass to draw a 9-inch (22cm) diameter circle on the cardstock. Draw another circle 8½ inches (21 cm) in diameter. Cut out the circles. On both circles, draw a line in pencil through the center to the edges and draw another line perpendicular through the center. Carefully punch holes in the middle and insert a brass fastener.

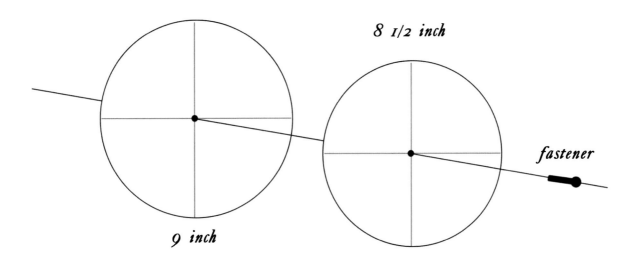

Use the remaining cardstock to create a horizon that extends from the edges across the center. Trim the edges of the horizon and tape them to the edges of the 9-inch circle so that the horizon is lined up with one of the lines on this circle and the other line is vertical. On the horizon, draw a tree line and buildings or other details and label the left side *East* and the right side *West*.

On the edge of the 8½-inch circle, at the end of one of the intersecting lines, draw a small Sun about ¼ inch wide. On the top edge of the 9-inch circle, at the top end of the vertical line, write *Noon*. At the bottom end of the vertical line, along the bottom edge of the circle, write *Midnight*.

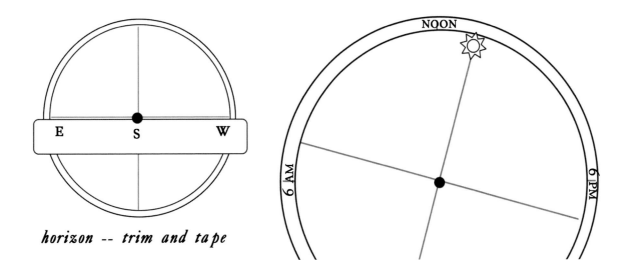

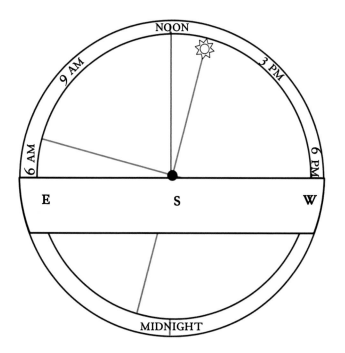

Along the edge by the eastern horizon write 6 AM, and at the western horizon write 6 PM. On the edge of the circle at the midpoints between the lines, indicate 9 AM, 3 PM, 9 PM and 3 AM. Divide the spaces between each of these into thirds to fill in the rest of the hours in a 24-hour day. Tie a string around the brass fastener, loop it over the noon mark, and tape the other end to the back of the 9-inch circle to make a meridian. You can now depict the Sun's passage for each hour of the day and night. (We'll modify this volvelle in later chapters to show the monthly cycle of the Moon.)

How many hours does it take for the Sun to move through ¼ of its volvelle circle? How many hours to turn through a complete circle?

Historical Timeline Activity

As you can see from the historical authors quoted throughout this book, Classical Astronomy has been understood and practiced throughout history. Create a timeline of these historical authors, showing the centuries in which they lived. Start with the Prologue and add to your timeline with each chapter. Learn more about these authors and create journal entries about them. Include their locations, their positions of authority (if any), and their significance in western history and literature. Consult books and curricula from your family's library, as well as encyclopedias and the Internet. A biographical index of these authors is included in the Appendix, and some of their major works are cited in the Bibliography.

Field Activities
Chapter 2 – The Darkness He Called Night

In this section, some activities might require you to observe the sky late at night or early in the morning before sunrise. Have your parents accompany you or at least get their permission to be outside during these hours. It might be a good idea to schedule a family activity around a number of these observations, or to do them while on a campout under dark skies away from city lights.

N.B. – If you live on an astronomically aligned street, for backyard compass activities, repeat the activities from your street, sidewalk, and driveway.

Spherical Sky Activity
Observe a dark sky, preferably away from city lights and in a wide open area. Determine if the stars on the horizon look any closer or farther away than stars near the zenith. Imagine a spherical appearance to the sky, as though the starry sky formed a dome overhead.

In your field journal, draw a circle with a center, using a compass. Measure the distance from the center to the circle from 6 different directions. Is it the same or different? When drawing with a compass, does the distance change between the compass point and the pencil tip?

Northern Constellations Activity
Find the Big Dipper in the night sky. Use the "pointer" stars on the bowl of the Big Dipper to find Polaris. (This star is about as bright as the Dipper's stars but can look faint as seen from the city.) If the Big Dipper is not high overhead, find Cassiopeia on the other side of Polaris from the Big Dipper. Make sketches in your field journal of these constellations as they appear in the sky. Record the date and time.

Stand in your backyard compass at night. Face toward the north and then look up. Can you find Polaris? Note again the position of the Big Dipper. Is the Dipper to the east or to the west of Polaris?

Over a number of nights, practice finding the North Star from the Big Dipper. Look from different places other than home. In your journal, record the dates and times and the locations. Learn to use Polaris to find your direction at night. Make it a habit to find Polaris when you travel to different places after dark, including your regular places around your town (church, shopping, homes of friends and family, etc.) and if you travel long distances. For the 10 locations you observed in Chapter 1, visit them after dark. Find the North Star and use it to observe which side of the building faces north. Record your results and compare with the exposures you recorded in that activity.

Orion Activity
Learn to find the constellation Orion.
Since Orion is best seen when it's high in the sky above the south, find Orion during your current season. In the autumn, look in the early morning before sunrise. In early winter, Orion can best be found before midnight. In the early spring, look for Orion in the early evening, after sunset. Orion cannot be seen at all during the summer. (See the Appendix for a monthly list of the visibility of Orion.) In your journal, practice sketching Orion as you see him in the sky.

Rotation around Polaris Activity
Observe the rotation of the Dippers and Cassiopeia.
First Night – Observe these constellations in the evening after nightfall and again at midnight.
Second Night – Observe them in the evening after nightfall and again in the morning before sunrise.

For each night, sketch the positions of these constellations at each time. Record the date and times and indicate the number of hours elapsed between observations. From your observations, estimate how many hours it would take for the northern constellations to complete one-quarter of a turn around Polaris. How many hours for a half turn? How many hours would it take to complete a full turn around Polaris? If the Dipper is west of Polaris, how long will it take until Orion can be seen at the meridian?

Cardinal Line Activity

Just as you found a cardinal line from the Sun in the last chapter, you can also find a cardinal line from Polaris. Starting from the cardinal line of your backyard compass, take two sticks of uneven length and pound the longer one into the ground. Lying close to the ground, sight Polaris over the top of the stick. Take the shorter stick and hold it away from the longer stick. Find a place for the shorter stick where Polaris can be sighted over the tops of both of the sticks. Pound the shorter stick into the ground and confirm that Polaris can still be seen over the tops of both sticks. A line between the two sticks is a cardinal line that extends from north to south. Confirm that this cardinal line agrees with your compass's cardinal line.

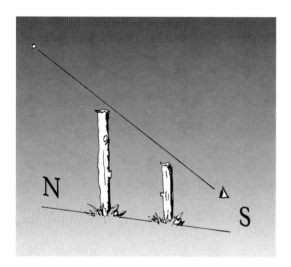

Globe Activity

Use the globe to demonstrate the rotation of the northern constellations.
Sketch the Big Dipper and Cassiopeia onto cardboard. Place a dowel rod or a bar or pipe through the location of Polaris. Line up the dowel rod with the axis of your 12-inch globe, with the cut-out stickman taped to the globe along the equator. Turn the dowel rod to rotate the constellations counterclockwise, sighting them from along the edge of the globe from behind the stickman. Then hold the dowel rod still and turn the globe toward the east, still sighting from behind the stickman. Compare how the rotation of the globe causes a shift in the apparent positions of the constellations.

Northern Stars Volvelle

Make a volvelle to illustrate the daily rotation of the northern stars.
As in Chapter 1, draw and cut 8½- and 9-inch circles (21 and 22 cm), with intersecting perpendicular lines through the centers of each. Carefully punch holes in the middle and insert a brass fastener.

On the 8½-inch circle, use your compass to draw a 5-inch circle (13 cm) to represent the circumpolar circle. Along the circumpolar circle and one of the intersecting lines, sketch the

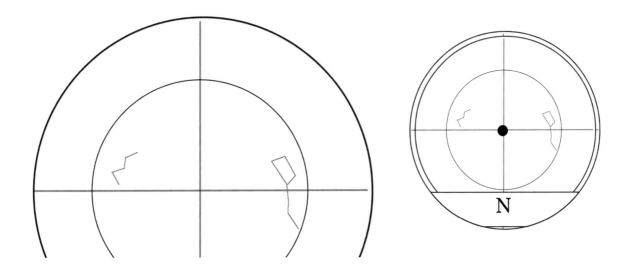

Dippers and Cassiopeia as they appear in Chapter 2 and as shown above. (Make them small, so that the Big Dipper is not more than 2 inches [5 cm] long.)

Use the remaining cardstock to create a horizon below the center of the volvelle, touching the bottom edge of the circumpolar circle. Trim and tape the edges to the edges of the 9-inch circle, and decorate the horizon as you wish (treeline, etc.). Add an *N* for north on the horizon, under the brass fastener (which takes the place of Polaris). Loop some string around the brass fastener and over the top to simulate the meridian. Tape the end of the string onto the back.

Rotate the constellation circle counterclockwise to simulate the rotation of the northern constellations. In later chapters, you will add information to this volvelle that will assist you in finding the orientation of the northern constellations for any time of day, every month of the year!

Meridian Activity

While standing in your backyard compass, look straight up overhead to the zenith. Turn to look over at the North Star and then down to the northern horizon. Follow the line back to the zenith and down to the southern horizon. Imagine the *meridian* as a half-circle spanning the sky through these points. Repeat this experiment facing in each direction of your backyard compass. Record your results and any other interesting observations.

On any given night, locate the Big Dipper and Cassiopeia with respect to the North Star. Is either at the meridian? Are they east or west of the meridian? Record your observation results with date and time. Using your volvelle and the results from the observations above, estimate how long before either the Dipper or Cassiopeia reaches the meridian on that night (i.e., a quarter turn? more or less? half turn? etc.). If one of these constellations will be visible at the meridian before sunrise, confirm your estimate by going outside to observe. Record your date and time and sketch your observation.

Observe the stars near the meridian. Observe bright stars in the skies to the east and west of the meridian. Come back in an hour – are the stars that were near the meridian more toward the east or west? Are they higher or lower in the sky? Are the stars in the eastern sky higher? Are the stars in the western sky lower? Have any moved along the meridian? Check in another hour and compare the results. Sketch any prominent stars and record the dates and times of each observation.

Repeat these observations over several days, checking the sky at different times of the night. Day 1 – check the sky in the early evening, day 2 – before midnight, day 3 -- at midnight, etc. Sketch your observations and try to notice if you can observe any of the same stars. You might be able to use this information in later chapters.

Record what you've observed. Record the general directions of these stars from your backyard compass and whether they are high or low in the sky. Record the dates and times of your observations.

Circumpolar Circle Activity
While observing the Big Dipper or Cassiopeia near the meridian, determine whether the opposite constellation is within your local circumpolar circle and whether it can be seen among the trees or at all even when at lower meridian, below the North Star.

Note – the circumpolar circles change with latitude. The Dippers and Cassiopeia can be seen at all times from latitude 40 degrees north and points north. 40°N is near the cities of New York, Boston, Philadelphia, Cleveland, Chicago, Denver, and San Francisco. New England, the northern Plains States, the Pacific Northwest, Canada, Britain, and Alaska are all farther north.

However, in the southern United States, especially points south of 30°N such as Florida, south Texas, and southern California – the circumpolar circles are smaller, and the Big Dipper and Cassiopeia actually set before reaching the lower meridian!

Direction Activity
Use a pizza box or another piece of cardboard to make a "reverse" compass to represent the sky, as shown on page 50, with east to the left and west to the right. Stand in your backyard compass while holding the reverse compass and facing the south. Note that both compasses point toward the same horizons – north, east, west, and south.

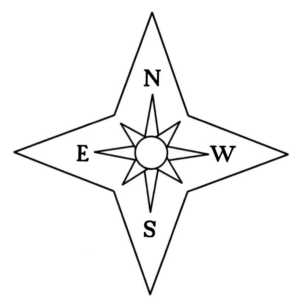

Hold your reverse compass overhead, at the zenith. Note that it still points north i.e. toward the North Star. Lean further backward, holding your reversed compass along the meridian until it approaches the North Star. Note that "north" is the direction along the meridian *toward* Polaris, and "south" is the direction along the meridian *away from* Polaris. Become familiar with the concept of the sky being divided by the meridian into two halves – an eastern rising half and a western setting half.

Celestial Equator Activities
Make a Celestial Globe.
Obtain a styrofoam ball from a craft store, preferably 5 or 6 inches (15 cm) or larger. Draw 2 dots on opposite sides to represent the poles. Draw a circle between the poles at an equal distance from each. If the ball already has "poles" and an "equator" from the molding process, use these, and draw over those features with a marker. This shows that the celestial equator in the sky is similar to the terrestrial equator on the earth – a circle that is exactly centered between the two poles. You'll add features to this celestial globe in later chapters.

Find the equator from Orion
Find Orion at meridian. Look at the right hour for the season (fall mornings, winter midnight, evenings of early spring. See the Appendix for a monthly list.) From your backyard compass, note the height in the sky of Orion's belt near the meridian as compared to objects on the ground – trees, buildings, telephone poles, etc. Use this to determine the location in the sky of the celestial equator when Orion is not visible.

Look due east in your backyard compass. Turn your eyes from the eastern horizon, up through Orion's belt, and follow toward the due west point on the horizon. Turn and look at Polaris. Imagine the celestial equator as a circle that is exactly in the middle of the starry sky between the poles. In your field journal, draw a circle representing the celestial sphere and an ellipse to represent the horizon. Draw dots for the celestial poles and an oblique circle that represents the celestial equator.

From your backyard compass, observe Orion after rising or before setting (depending on the season and time of day). Confirm that it rises due east and sets due west. Sketch Orion in your notebook with the time and date of the observation.

Orion Volvelle
Make a volvelle to illustrate Orion on the Celestial Equator
As done in Chapter 1, draw and cut 8½- and 9-inch circles (21 and 22 cm), with intersecting perpendicular lines through the centers of each. Carefully punch holes in the middle and insert a brass fastener.

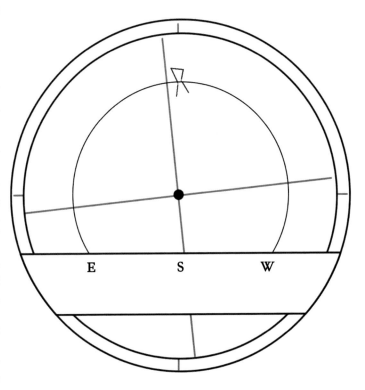

On the 8½-inch circle, use your compass to draw a 6-inch circle (15 cm) around the center to represent the celestial equator. To the right of one of the intersecting lines, sketch Orion with his belt along the equator (draw Orion small – about ¾ inch (1.5 cm) long. Use the remaining cardstock to create a horizon through the center of the volvelle. Write an *S* for south on the horizon under the brass fastener. Write *E* on the left and *W* on the right where the equator crosses the horizon. Loop some string around the brass fastener and over the top to simulate the meridian. Tape the end of the string onto the back.

Rotate the constellation circle clockwise to simulate the daily rotation of Orion along the celestial equator. In later chapters, you will add information to this volvelle that will assist you in understanding the passage of the seasons!

Field Activities
Chapter 3 – The Cycle of the Moon

Moon Phases – First Month

Use a wall calendar, newspaper, or other reference to find out the date of the next New Moon. Over the next couple of nights, look for a thin crescent Moon in the western sky during evening twilight after sunset. Record in your field journal the date and time of the first sighting of the waxing Moon. Sketch the appearance of the Moon, noting how thick it is, how far it is above the horizon, and how far away from the place of the sunset. Note the direction on the compass and include ground objects such trees, buildings, and telephone poles for reference points. To get a nice, uniform circle, draw circles with a template or trace a round object such as a coin. Draw the curve of the Moon's terminator each night, and color in the dark side of the Moon.

Clear skies permitting, observe at the same time the next day. Note how far the Moon has traveled across the sky in only a single day. Sketch your observations and record the date and time. You can use a single large panel to sketch the Moon's changing position and appearance over a period of days. Repeat the above for waxing crescent, First Quarter, and waxing gibbous phases, through the Full Moon. Be sure to indicate relative direction as seen from your backyard compass.

Label your picture to indicate the phase of the Moon, i.e. waxing or waning, crescent, half, gibbous, or full, and indicate the nights of the Moon's quarters – New Moon, First Quarter, Full Moon, Last Quarter. Also, draw a "celestial" picture of the Moon in orbit around the Earth and correlate the Moon's orbital position with the phases you see in the sky.

Each night note the position of the Moon one hour after your first observation. Also check in the next hour and as often as you like. Sketch and record your observations. Include comments about the weather. Was there a clear sky? Hazy? Any clouds?

After the Full Moon, note the risings of the waning gibbous Moon. Record the time after dark when you first see the Moon. Sketch its appearance, including height above the horizon and direction as seen from your backyard compass. Repeat the above for several days afterwards, until the Moon is rising too late to be seen before bedtime.

Starting in the waning gibbous phases, get up around sunrise and look for the Moon in the morning sky. Record the times and sketch the appearance of the waning Moon, including direction and height above the horizon. Note how far across the sky the Moon has traveled since the evening before.

Observing in the morning sky, repeat the above through the waning phases – waning gibbous, Last Quarter, waning crescent, until the next New Moon.

During thin crescent phases – observe the Earthshine.
In early waxing crescent phase, notice and record changes in earthshine each evening at it waxes from a thin crescent to a half-moon. Sketch what you see, including date and time. In waning crescent phases, in morning twilight, notice and record changes in earthshine as the Moon wanes from a half moon to a thin crescent. Sketch what you see, including date and time.

Observe Moon Shadows.
Also note the evening when you can first see shadows cast by the Moon's light. This will depend on the clarity of the atmosphere and amount of ground lighting in your area. Also, notice that the fainter stars become harder to see as the thin crescent Moon waxes and grows brighter.

During the thick gibbous and full phases – observe the Man in the Moon.
Sketch the Moon with the *maria* (dark features). Can you spot the Man in the Moon? These features are easiest to see in bright twilight or when a gibbous or Full Moon is rising orange, low in the evening sky. Notice how the face on the Moon is revealed as the phases increase and decrease. Using other resources, learn the names of the "seas" on the Moon, and correlate them with the features of the Moon's face.

At the Movies....
Next Easter, if you see the movie *The Ten Commandments*, note that the plague of the firstborn is incorrectly shown occurring during a waning crescent, not a Full Moon as it should be on the night of Passover. However, *The Passion of the Christ* accurately shows Jesus in the Garden of Gethsemane under a Full Moon.

Moon Phases – Second Month

Observe and record the risings and settings of the Moon, and note how these change with each phase. To find the Moon's rising and setting times, consult the weather section of your local paper, where such information can usually be found. Record this information each day for a month as a table in your journal. If your family doesn't get the paper, use the U.S. Naval Observatory *Complete Sun and Moon Data for One Day* Web page:

http://aa.usno.navy.mil/data/docs/RS_OneDay.html

Subtract each day's rising and setting times from the days before or after to measure the exact difference in rising from day to day. Record these in a separate column in your journal. How close are these differences to 48 minutes? (Remember, 48 minutes is only an average.)

Weather permitting, try to observe the Moon rising or setting at these times. If you don't have a clear horizon, look an hour or so after moonrise or before moonset. Be sure to look during the daytime, since the Moon is usually easy to see in the bright daytime sky. Record and sketch your observations.

Things to Keep in Mind
The Moon will often rise at a certain time and set at a time after midnight the next day. Be sure to keep your rising and setting times together for each *lunar day* – one complete interval of the Moon above and below the horizon. The papers publish only the rising and setting times of the Moon that occur on that particular date. This can be misleading since the moonset of the previous lunar day can be shown at an earlier time than the moonrise of the next lunar day. Be sure to compare your rising and setting data from the days in the newspaper or on the web.

Also, there will be days in each lunar month when the Moon does not rise and set. Because the Moon rises about 48 minutes later each day, the Moon's daily cycle between risings is longer than 24 hours. There are times when it rises or sets shortly *before midnight* on one day and does not rise or set again until *after midnight* the next day!

Using a wall calendar, note the dates of the Moon's quarters. Confirm with observations and record the results. Count the number of days between quarters and confirm the length of the lunar month.

Moon Phases – Third Month

Moonfinding – Observe the Moon each day as it crosses the meridian.
For this month, keep a chart of the moonrise and moonset in columns, along with columns for sunrise and sunset for a month (with each date as a row). Include a column to indicate the

principal phases (e.g. waxing crescent, waxing gibbous, etc.) and quarters. Count the number of hours between moonrise and moonset. Divide that number of hours by two, and add that to the moonrise time. This will be the time when the moon transits the meridian. Record these transit times in a separate column on your chart. (N.B. – Be careful. For a date when the moonset is before the moonrise, count that moonset with the previous day's moonrise.)

Standing in your backyard compass, look for the Moon at the meridian at the calculated times. Spend time looking if the Moon is not easily visible. In the crescent phases, when the Moon crosses the meridian during the day, try standing in shadows of a building to block the glare of the Sun. *Never look directly at the Sun!!!* In the gibbous phases, observe the rising Moon a couple of times at hours before it reaches the meridian.

Globe Activity
Demonstrate the Moon's orbital motion and its phases.
Using your 12-inch globe, take a softball to represent the Moon. In your backyard, place the softball 30 feet (9 meters) away from the globe. This accurately shows the proportional distance between the Earth and the Moon. In your backyard, pound a stick near the "Earth," and loop 30 feet of rope around the stake. If working on pavement, use chalk to trace a circle with a 30-foot radius.

Place a basketball or beach ball somewhere very far away to represent the position of the Sun. Following the end of the rope, walk the "Moon" around the Earth to different positions, counterclockwise around the globe, to represent its orbital motion. Leaning over the Earth, sight along its edge as it rotates to observe the rising and setting of the Sun with respect to the Moon's position.

At nighttime, allow a distant light (a porch light, street light, portable gas lamp, etc.) to shine on the globe and softball. Observe the terminators on the globe and softball. Looking from the globe, as the Moon moves around its orbital circle, notice the changes in the terminator. Note the position of the Moon in its orbit when the quarters, crescent phases, and gibbous phases are observed. Record all the above results.

Volvelle Activity
Modify your Sun volvelle from Chapter 1 to include Moon phases.
On your 8½-inch Sun wheel, draw circle about 7¾ inches (about 20 cm) in diameter. At the place where this circle crosses the intersecting line near the Sun, draw a small black circle, about ¼ inch (about ½ cm) wide to indicate the New Moon. (Use pencil in case you make a mistake.) On the opposite point where the line crosses the circle, draw a white circle to indicate the Full Moon.

Face the wheel with the New Moon on the right and the Full Moon on the left. On the top of the other intersecting line, where it crosses the circle, add a First Quarter circle, with the white side facing toward the Sun. Flip the circle over and add a Last Quarter circle at the opposite end, also with a white side facing the Sun.

Add 6 more small circles between each of the quarters to indicate the phases. This shows the phases for 28 days, close but not exactly the length of the lunar month. Draw a progression of crescent or gibbous phases onto the circles. The crescent phases are between the half-moons and the Sun, and gibbous phases are between the half-moons and the Full Moon. (Don't worry if the phases aren't perfect!) Underneath each moon, write a small number to indicate the age of the Moon after the New Moon. The First Quarter is 7 days, the Full Moon is 14 days, and the Last Quarter is 21 days. Label each moon in between.

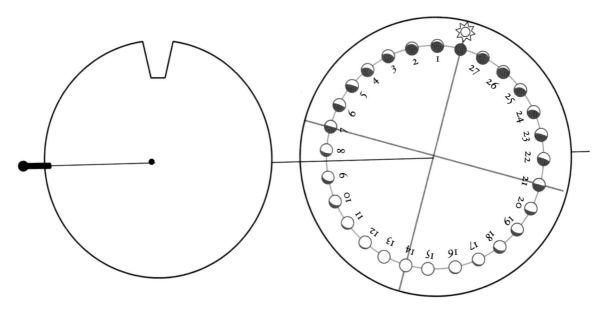

Make a window wheel. Cut out another circle 8 inches (20 cm) in diameter. Along one edge, cut out a notch about ¾ inch wide and ¾ inch deep (about 2 cm each). Assemble the wheels with the window wheel on top. If made properly, the window wheel should reveal a selected Moon phase (and age) and hide all the others. Deepen the notch if needed.

Volvelle Activities

* Turn the window wheel to the New Moon. Set the movable wheels so that the Sun and New Moon are at 6:00 A.M. Turn the wheels together to show how the New Moon rises, transits, and sets with the Sun.

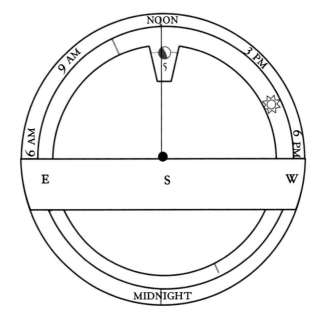

* Turn the window wheel to reveal the first waxing crescent phase. Turn the wheels together to show how the waxing crescent rises, transits, and sets *after* the Sun. Repeat for all the waxing crescent phases, observing that the Moon follows the Sun by a greater amount each day.

* Tell time by the Sun on the volvelle. If you dial in a First Quarter Moon, notice that when the Sun is at 6:00 P.M., the Moon is at the meridian. For each phase, you can approximately determine the Moon's transit times by aligning the Moon with the meridian and reading the time on the outer wheel that is aligned with the Sun. Compare with the calculated times from the above section.

* Turn the window wheel to each phase and repeat the above. Rotate your Sun and Moon volvelle to find the approximate times of the Moon's risings, transits, and settings.

* Remember to take into account standard time and daylight savings (explained in Chapter 5). On your horizon portion, write *Tell the Time of Day from the Position of the Sun. From March through November, add an hour for Daylight Savings.*

Field Activities – Chapter 4
The Tabernacle for the Sun

Please note:

*In this section, you will begin to learn the constellations. There is an Appendix of constellation tables that will help you learn the best times to find the constellations and the bright stars. However, there is one point that needs to be emphasized – **learning the constellations requires WORK**. You won't learn anything if you poke your head out for one minute and then give up. And you can't learn all the constellations in just one night.*

As you work at learning the constellations, you will make mistakes and get confused. You might learn some one night and be unable to find them the next night. You might forget everything you learn and need to start over. It might be quite frustrating. This is all a normal part of the process. Also, the bright planets can add to the confusion, since they are brighter than the stars, and can mess up the appearance of the constellations until you learn the patterns.

*Learning the sky requires **persistent** and **regular** effort. You might need to spend at least 15-30 minutes on clear nights over a period of weeks and months. It will probably take you at least a whole year to learn the entire sky, to observe a complete annual cycle of constellations.*

However, if you do learn the sky, the benefits are great. Once you learn the stars, you will know them for the rest of your life. You can learn to tell time and navigate by the stars. You can see the same stars from anywhere in the world. They will make your travel experiences richer and more interesting, and be a familiar sight while abroad. As everything in your life changes over the years, the stars won't. They will be the same as they've always been through all history.

Visibility of the Night Sky

Most of the star scenes in *Signs & Seasons* depict a fully dark night sky, as God created it, as can be seen from rural areas. However, your ability to see all these stars depends on the weather and also if you live in a city with a lot of street lighting.

Some constellations won't be visible at all from brightly-lit urban areas. However, it might actually be easier to pick out the brighter constellations from a city sky with fewer stars. On a clear night under an unspoiled rural sky, more stars are visible. It can be hard to pick out constellations because so many stars appear so bright.

Wherever you are, not many stars can be seen under moonlight, since the glare of this natural light pollution hides the dimmer stars. When the Moon is waxing, you can best find the constellations after the Moon has set. During the waning Moon, the skies are darkest in the evening, before the Moon rises.

Even from a dark sky location, not many stars can be seen if the weather is hazy, and obviously none can be seen if it's cloudy. The clearest night skies are on days with low humidity, when Sun shadows are very dark. Grey, fuzzy Sun shadows always mean hazy skies.

Note: If you have difficulty finding the zodiac constellations, feel free to combine these activities with the constellation observing activities in Chapter 6.

Sketching Activities
Sketch the zodiac constellations
Referring to the constellation tables in the Appendix, find the zodiac constellations visible for the early evening hours for your current month. Also find the constellations visible at midnight and in the morning before sunrise. Sketch the "connect-the-dot" patterns shown in Chapter 4 for these zodiac constellations. It would be much easier to find the constellations if you could see those connecting lines! But the constellation patterns are generally formed from the brightest stars visible in each part of the sky. Once you learn to recognize those patterns, it's easier to visualize the connections between the stars that form the patterns.

Sketch a flat map of the zodiac
Take an entire sheet of graph paper turned sideways (i.e. the "long way"). Draw a horizontal line in the middle of the page for the equator. Draw 5 equally-spaced vertical lines, representing the solstices and equinoxes. The second vertical line from the right represents the summer solstice. On this line, place a mark about 1 inch (2½ cm) above the equator. The fourth vertical line represents the winter solstice. On this line, place a mark about 1 inch (2½ cm) below the equator.

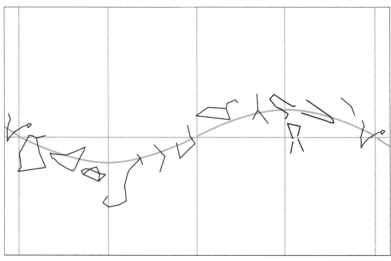

Starting at the vernal equinox (where the first line on the right crosses the equator), draw a "wave" through the vernal equinox to the summer solstice, and over the autumnal equinox to the winter solstice, and back to the vernal equinox, to connect the north and south extremes to the equator crossings. This wave represents the ecliptic.

At the solstice and equinox points, add small star patterns for each zodiac constellation as shown in Chapter 4. Fill in the rest of the zodiac constellations between the seasonal points. Also include Orion as shown, with his belt along the celestial equator. You'll use this map in later activity sections.

Observing the Constellations
Observing Orion
Referring to Table I in the Appendix, find the best time for viewing Orion in your current month (in all seasons except Summer). Upon finding Orion, find Gemini and Taurus, as shown in Chapter 4. Sketch the constellations as they appear in the sky. Record the date and time.

Observing the zodiac
Evening – Referring again to the constellation tables in the Appendix, find the zodiac constellation visible near the meridian in the evening for your date. If you can't find it, try again in a couple hours before bedtime. Record your results. How does the actual appearance of the constellation compare with your sketches? Can you see all the stars, or are the faint ones invisible? Have you spotted a planet? (Consult the planet tables in the Appendix for the current location of the planets.) Use your reverse compass to find your direction in the sky. Can you identify any zodiac constellations to the east or west of the meridian?

Midnight – Repeat the above for the zodiac constellation at the meridian at midnight. How does this compare to your observations of the sky in the early evening? Can you identify any other zodiac constellations rising or setting?

Morning – Observe the zodiac constellations at the meridian in the morning before sunrise. How does this compare to your observations at midnight? How has the sky changed over the night? Can you tell which zodiac constellations are higher or lower in the sky?

For observers in the city
Observe zodiac constellations from home as noted above, recording the date and time of your observations. Sketch the constellations as they appear under the city lights, including all the visible stars. Compare with the star patterns shown in the book. Indicate if any stars cannot be found from your home. Add comments about the brightness of the visible stars.

Follow up and observe the sky from a dark-sky location, perhaps during a campout or other trip to a rural location. Repeat the sketch activity and indicate if more stars are visible. Add comments about whether the stars appear brighter than in the city.

Identifying stars
Of the constellations you learned in Chapter 4, can you determine if any of the bright stars were observed in the meridian activity of Chapter 2? Record the star names and constellations.

Observing the celestial equator
Looking from your backyard compass or your "equator spot" from Chapter 2, observe Virgo in the sky. Note that these stars are nearly as high above the horizon as Orion. Also, observe the Water Jar in Aquarius and the Circlet in Pisces. Can you tell that these stars are about as high in the sky as Orion's belt?

Observing the northern sky
While observing the zodiac constellations, turn around and observe the positions of the Dippers and Cassiopeia. When Gemini is at the meridian, the Big Dipper is east of Polaris. When Leo is at the meridian, the Big Dipper is overhead, close to Leo (more in Chapter 6). When Scorpius and Sagittarius are near the meridian, the Big Dipper is west of Polaris. When Pisces and Aries are near the meridian, Cassiopeia is overhead.

Observing risings and settings of the zodiac
Once you become familiar with the constellations of the zodiac, try to observe them at their risings and settings. Northern constellations rise and set toward the north, and southern constellations rise and set to the south.

Modify your backyard compass
Add four more marker stones between the cardinal stones to indicate NE, NW, SE, and SW.

Find the positions of rising and setting constellations with respect to your backyard compass. Whichever constellation you can find at the meridian, look one-quarter of the way around the zodiac on either side to find the stars that are rising and setting. For example, if Gemini is at meridian, Pisces is setting due west and Virgo is rising due east. Also, if Virgo is at the meridian, Gemini is setting in the northwest and Sagittarius is rising in the southeast. Sketch the constellations you see and record the date and time.

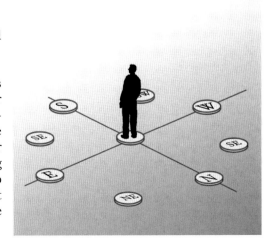

Research Activity

Learn about precession. Read up in encyclopedias and on the Internet. Record your findings in your journal. This subject will be treated in a later volume of this series.

Celestial Globe Activity

Using the celestial globe you created in Chapter 2, make a mark on the equator opposite Orion and two small marks at equal distances in between on the equator. Measure the distance one of the Poles to Orion, and find the midpoint. Find the distance between that midpoint and Orion, and place a dot at that point. Find the opposite mark on the equator from Orion, and at an equal distance below the equator, make another dot. Connect these dots above and below the equator to make a slanted circle around the globe, passing through the other marks on the equator between. This slanted circle will represent the ecliptic.

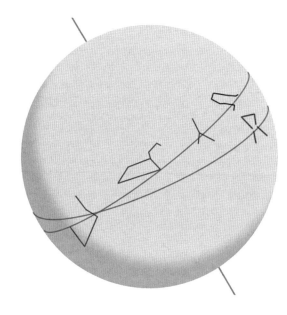

The extreme points of the slanted circle will represent the solstices, while the crossing points at the equator will represent the equinoxes. At the extreme points above Orion, draw a small figure of the star pattern for Gemini. At the opposite extreme point, draw the pattern for Sagittarius. At the intersecting point to the right of Gemini and Orion, draw the pattern for Pisces. And at the other intersecting point, draw Virgo. Fill in the other zodiac constellations in between.

Your celestial globe is an *inverted globe* of the sky. The actual sky appears to be *concave*, with the constellations on the *inside* of the sphere. But with this plan, we can place the constellations on the *convex exterior* of the sphere – an opposite arrangement to the real sky. We'll add more to our sphere in later chapters.

Volvelle Activity

Modify your Orion volvelle from Chapter 2 to include zodiac constellations.
On your moveable wheel, along the perpendicular line near Orion, make a mark about ¾ of an inch (2 cm) toward Orion from the center of the equator. Use this mark as the center of the ecliptic circle. Draw an off-center circle to represent the ecliptic, the same diameter as the equator, so that the outside of the circle passes over Orion.

The perpendicular lines represent the solstices and the equinoxes. On the circle above Orion, add the pattern for Gemini as it appears in the book. Turn the wheel around, and on the opposite side, draw the pattern for Sagittarius. Add Pisces and Virgo to the respective intersecting points for the equinoxes. As before, fill in the other constellations on the ecliptic, as shown in the book. Assemble your modified volvelle.

Using your volvelle
*   Rotate the constellation wheel, looking at where the ecliptic crosses the horizons. Notice how the Ecliptic moves to the north and south as the wheel turns.

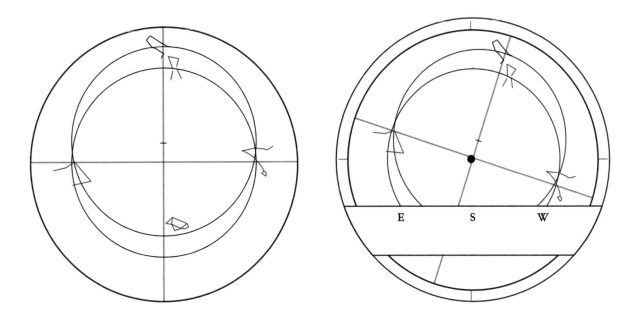

*   Look at the meridian as the wheel turns. Notice how the succeeding constellations are higher and lower as they cross the meridian, with Gemini at the highest and Sagittarius at the lowest.

*In the next chapter, we'll modify the volvelle to illustrate
the Sun's annual motion along the ecliptic.*

Field Activities
Chapter 5 – The Cycle of the Sun

Research Activity

Make a table of rising and setting times for the Sun for your hometown at about weekly intervals over one or more seasons or even a year. You can collect this information in advance from an almanack, such as *The Old Farmer's Almanac*, or from the U.S. Naval Observatory *Complete Sun and Moon Data* Web page:

http://aa.usno.navy.mil/data/docs/RS_OneDay.html

Include a column for the number of hours of daylight. Find this by counting the hours between sunrise and noon, and between noon and sunset. Include a column for the time of high noon, when the Sun reaches the meridian. Find this number by dividing the number of hours of daylight by two, and add that number of hours to the time of sunrise.

From your chart, notice the times of sunrise and sunset. In what months do these times change quickly from day to day? In what months do these times change slowly? Notice how there is little variation for a month before and after the solstices and how quickly the sunset times change for a month before and after the equinoxes. Make a bar graph showing sunrise and sunset times over the span of months.

Flat Map Activity

Make several photocopies of the flat map you created in Chapter 4. Draw small pictures of the Sun on your map as follows, or else get some small Sun stickers from a craft shop (these are usually readily available). Place a Sun on your map at the point of the vernal equinox in Pisces and label it March 21. Place another sticker at the summer solstice in Gemini, and label it June 21. Repeat for the autumnal equinox and the winter solstice. After the four seasonal points are in place, add Suns to each of the other zodiac constellations, and label each the 21st of the respective month. (For example, label the Sun near Aries April 21 and the Sun by Taurus May 21.) This roughly shows the apparent position of the Sun on the ecliptic during each month of the year.

Solar System Map

Make an overhead view of the solar system to show how the changing orbital position of the Earth results in the changes in the apparent position of the Sun against the background stars. On a full sheet paper, draw two perpendicular lines that intersect in the middle of the paper. Draw a large circle almost the size of the paper, centered on the intersecting point. This will represent the Ecliptic.

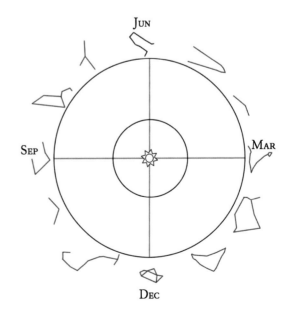

Draw the zodiac constellations around the circle, starting with the solstices and equinoxes and filling in from there. Behind each constellation, write the name of a month as follows: *Pisces – March, Gemini – June, Virgo – September, Sagittarius – December.* Fill in the other months.

In the middle, draw a small Sun. Around the Sun, draw a circle about 2 inches (5 cm) in diameter. This will represent the orbit of the Earth. Make photocopies of your completed map to be used for activities in this section and in later sections.

* Make a map to show each of the seasons. Label one of your copies *spring.* Draw the Earth on its orbit opposite the Sun from Pisces. Draw an arrow from the Earth to the Sun and extend it toward Pisces. This shows the Sun's apparent position on the ecliptic on the vernal equinox. Repeat for the months of April and May, and show the Earth's counterclockwise motion around the Sun. Repeat the above for all four seasons.

Observing Activities

Sunrise and Sunset

If you have a clear horizon to the east or west, observe the rising or setting of the Sun over the span of several months. (Find the times of sunrise and sunset from the research activity above or any weather news source, such as the newspaper, TV weather report, or a weather page on the Internet at Yahoo, MSN, AOL, or Weather.com.) Check about once a week, and record the date and time of sunrise or sunset. Standing in your backyard compass, record the direction of the sunrise or sunset with respect to the eight points of your compass.

Notice the seasonal changes in the direction of the sunrise and sunset. If you don't have a clear horizon, observe and record the first appearance of the Sun from behind ground objects. Be sure to not look directly at the Sun, but instead observe the shadows. Make a single sketch that shows the Sun's different rising or setting positions between the equinoxes. Note that the Sun's position changes rapidly around the equinoxes and slowly around the solstices. Compare these observations with the amount of daylight measured during these periods.

Exposures

Following the activity in Chapter 1, observe the changes in the direction of sunlight through your house windows over the seasons. Notice where the sunlight lands on the walls and floors in the rooms of your house. Pick a place (maybe where you work) and observe the position of the Sun's rays at the same time each day. Put a piece of masking tape along the edge of the sunlight to indicate the position of the rays. Write the date and time on the tape. Note the changes in the rays over a period of weeks and months.

Observing Equinoxes and Solstices

Note the rising and setting Sun between the equinox and its northern or southern extremes on the solstice. If you have access to a street having a clear horizon that runs east to west, watch the Sun rise and set over the ends of the street on the equinox. Also, in the days and weeks before and after the equinox, the Sun can be seen rising and setting to the north or south of these directions.

Observing Shadows

When the Sun rises and sets, observe and record the directions in which the shadows point, as seen from your backyard compass. During the spring and summer, note the time of day when the Sun passes above the due east and due west horizons, when the shadows point to the opposite horizon. Measure the lengths of shadows at these times as compared to the object. For example, measure the length of a stick or the height of a person, and divide the length of the shadow by the length of the object to find a percentage. For example, if the shadow is twice as long as the object, the percentage is 200%. Repeat this at least once a week for an entire season (or even a whole year). Keep a record of your results.

Finding Your Local High Noon

As we've seen, with our modern systems of standard time and daylight savings time, 12:00 P.M. as read from a clock is somewhat different from high noon, when the Sun is at the meridian and sundials read noon. But high noon isn't so hard to figure out.

Daylight savings time is from March to November, and high noon occurs sometime on or around 1:00 P.M., instead of 12:00 P.M. But because of standard time, *local noon* at most locations consistently varies by as much as a half-hour or more, depending on where you live in your time zone.

Within each time zone, standard time is taken from the local time of the time zone meridian. The time zone meridians are at longitudes 15 degrees apart. In the United States, the meridians are as follows:

> *75 degrees west – Eastern Standard Time*
> *90 degrees west – Central Standard Time*
> *105 degrees west – Mountain Standard Time*
> *120 degrees west – Pacific Standard Time*

You can find the correction for your local time to standard time by counting 4 minutes difference for each degree of longitude your hometown is from your time zone meridian. If you live in the western part of your time zone, add 4 minutes for each degree from the meridian. If you live in the eastern part of your time zone, subtract 4 minutes for each degree from the meridian. For example, Cleveland, Ohio is at a longitude of about 82 degrees, 7 degrees west of the eastern time zone meridian. So the Sun reaches high noon in Cleveland at about 12:28 P.M., or about 1:28 P.M. during daylight savings.

(There is still another correction for "sundial time" called *the equation of time*, which can vary the time of high noon by as much as another 20 minutes. We'll learn more about this in a later volume of this series.)

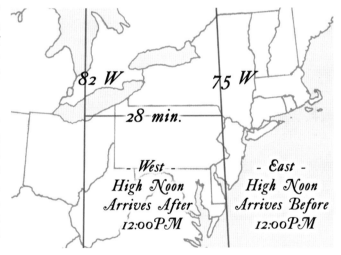

*   Using a map, find your longitude. Do you live east or west from your time zone meridian? Find the correction for your local time to Standard Time as explained above. Using your backyard compass, confirm that the Sun reaches High Noon at more or less your calculated time.

*   Using a map, find the longitudes of several cities in your time zone. Calculate the local noon correction for these cities. For example, in the eastern time zone of the United States, compare: Bangor, Maine; Philadelphia, Pennsylvania; and Grand Rapids, Michigan.

Noon Shadow Activity

Measure the changes in the lengths of the noon shadows over the span of several seasons or between solstices. Find the precise time of high noon for your location, when the shadows point north. Take into account daylight savings and your time zone correction, as explained in the previous section.

At high noon, measure the lengths of the noon shadows. Measure a stick and its shadow, or for more fun, use a tape measure to measure the heights of members of the family and their shadows. Divide the length of the shadow by the length of the object casting the shadow to get a percentage of the shadow length (as discussed above).

On the Summer Solstice, the Noon shadows are their shortest. On the winter solstice, noon shadows are their longest. On the equinox, the Sun is just as high in the sky as Orion's Belt, the Water Jar in Aquarius, or the Circlet in Pisces. Repeat these shadow measurements at weekly intervals over the course of at least two seasons or from solstice to solstice. Make a table that shows the percentage of shadow lengths and also the clock time of high noon.

Lag of the Seasons Activity
Keep a temperature record over the span of the seasons.
Record daily high and low temperatures over the course of the summer or winter season. Read the temperatures from a home thermometer, or else collect the official local temperature data from the newspaper or television news. Make a bar graph that shows daytime temperatures over your period of measurement. Note when the warmest and coolest periods were as compared with the solstices and equinoxes.

Globe Activities
Heliocentric Globe Activity
On manila folders, draw the pattern of each zodiac constellation as shown in Chapters 4 and 5. Make these constellation signs so the up end of each constellation is toward the fold. Set up these folders outdoors in a big circle, at least 30 feet (or 9 m) in diameter. Start with setting up the solstices and equinoxes at the quarter points. Set up the other constellations in between.

Put a lamp in the center of the circle. Use a work light with an extension cord or a portable gas lantern, etc. Set up your globe opposite the "Sun" from the sign for Gemini. Set the axis of the globe so that it "leans" toward the Sun and Gemini. (Twelve-inch world globes typically have a stand that is inclined just like the Earth's axis.)

With the North Pole of the globe inclined toward the Sun and Gemini, note the terminator on the globe. The North Pole is in full light, and most of the Northern Hemisphere is in the light. Note that the entire South Pole and most of the Southern Hemisphere is in darkness.

Move the "Earth" counterclockwise around the "Sun" to autumn, keeping the globe's axis pointed in the same general direction so that the lamp is aligned with the sign for Virgo. Repeat the above observations. Repeat for each season. Demonstrate this for friends or family members to help them understand Classical Astronomy.

Geocentric Globe Activity
Using the globe and the light, demonstrate why the Sun appears higher in the sky in the summer than in winter. Set up your constellation signs at different heights, outside in a big circle. Maybe Gemini can be set on a step ladder, Sagittarius on the ground, and the equinoxes on chairs at a height in between the extremes.

Set the globe on a chair in the middle of the circle, with the globe axis pointed straight up. Move your lamp in front of these constellations. Put your paper stickman on the globe at your location. Note the variations in the orientation of the terminator on the globe with the Sun at these different heights, over the seasons. As above, show this to other people to help them understand why the Sun appears to rise and fall over the seasons.

Celestial Globe Activity

Use your celestial globe from previous chapters and the Sun stickers as in the previous activity. Place Suns on each of the equinoxes and the solstices and other points in between. Place your fingers at the poles of your globe and rotate it. Notice how the rotation of the Sun varies at each of the seasonal points.

Volvelle Activity

Modify your Orion and zodiac volvelle to illustrate the Sun's motion along the ecliptic.

Add hours to the outer circle of your volvelle. At the top of the outer circle, write *noon*. On the left side, write *6:00 A.M.*, and on the right side, write *6:00 P.M.* Write *midnight* on the bottom. Add the other hours at equally-spaced positions in between.

On the rotatable constellation wheel, write *June* at the top, along the intersecting line above Gemini. Write *March* on the right side of the other intersecting line, above Pisces. Write *September* on the left side of that line, above Virgo. Write *December* above Sagittarius on the opposite side of the first intersecting line, opposite Gemini. Fill in all the other months, writing them above the constellations drawn on the wheel. You can also split the months into weeks by dividing each month into four sections. Since your intersecting ines represent the solstices and equinoxes, make sure that you have only one "week" to the left of the intersecting line, and three to the right.

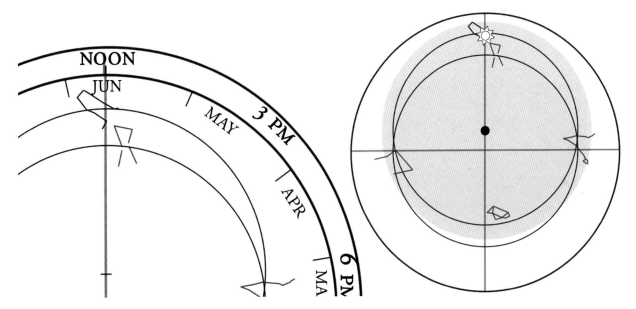

Obtain a stiff sheet of acetate transparency material, like the type used for writing words to be shown on an overhead projector. (Perhaps your church has some extra sheets.) Cut out a transparent circle about 6½ inches (16 cm) in diameter. Draw a small circle to represent the Sun, about ¼ inch (about ½ cm) from the edge. Use another brass fastener to affix the center of this transparency to the center of the zodiac circle on your inner wheel. If you can't get a sheet of transparency material, use the Sun stickers from the other activities.

As with your Sun and Moon volvelle, you must remember to take into account standard time and Daylight Savings. On the horizon portion of your Orion and Zodiac volvelle, write *Tell the Time of Day from the Position of the Sun. From March through November, add an hour for Daylight Savings.* Also write on your volvelle the correction for local time calculated in the previous activity.

*   Rotate the clear circle (or add a sticker) so that the Sun is aligned with the month of March (i.e. the vernal equinox). Turn the clear circle together with the inner wheel to show how the Sun rises and sets on the vernal equinox. If your horizon is made correctly, it will show the Sun rising due east and setting due west.

*   Turn the clear circle to the next month, April (or move the sticker to that spot). Repeat the above. Notice how the Sun rises and sets farther to the north. Repeat for each month of the year. Notice how the rising and setting varies to the north and south over the seasons. Notice how the Sun is progressively higher and lower at the meridian with each month of the year.

*   As you rotate the Sun through the hours, note the progression of zodiac constellations that cross the meridian during each hour. As you move the Sun into the nighttime hours, notice which constellations are visible at each hour of the night. Set the Sun to your current month. After dark, turn the inner wheel to the hour, look at the constellation at the volvelle meridian for that time, and confirm from your backyard compass whether that constellation is actually over the south. Use your volvelle in this way to find the constellations.

N.B.: Even though hours have been placed around the outer edge, your flat volvelle cannot be made to correctly imitate the spherical sky and will not give accurate hour readings. However, your volvelle will approximately illustrate the progression of the celestial bodies and many interesting aspects of the sky. Compare your volvelle readings with actual observations.

Field Activities
Chapter 6 - The Seasonal Skies

Sketching, Flat Map, and Celestial Globe Activities

Referring to the constellation illustrations shown in Chapter 6, sketch these constellations in your journal, naming any bright first magnitude stars. Become familiar with these star patterns. This will help you in finding the constellations in the sky.

Add these constellations to your celestial globe and your flat map, which you made in previous chapters. For your flat map, be sure to sketch them in with pencil. Once you have all the stars added in the way you like, draw over them in ink, so you can make clean photocopies (which will help in Chapter 7).

Solar System Map Activity

Using the solar system maps you made in the previous section to represent each season, draw arrows to the opposite directions from the Sun. Note the opposite constellations. For your current month, confirm from your observations whether this constellation rises in the evening after the Sun sets and reaches the meridian at midnight.

Find Your Limiting Magnitude

Determine the *limiting magnitude* of your local sky, the magnitude of the faintest star visible. Knowing your limiting magnitude will help you determine whether or not the faint constellations such as Pisces and Capricornus can be seen from locations in the city or suburbs. The Little Dipper is an excellent indicator, since the bowl and handle include faint stars of fourth and fifth magnitude. Consult the picture on page 120 for a guide. If you are in a rural location with the Milky Way overhead, your sky is magnitude 5 or better, and you should have no problem seeing the faint constellation stars.

Observing the Zodiac

In late evening twilight, observe the zodiac constellation in the western sky above the place of the sunset. Sketch what you see, recording the date, time, and direction. Does this confirm the Sun's position on the ecliptic for your current month?

Calculate the time of your local astronomical midnight. Count the hours and minutes between sunset and sunrise, divide by two, and subtract that number of hours from the time of sunrise. Go out and observe the sky at that time and note the zodiac constellation at the meridian. Confirm whether this constellation is directly opposite in the sky from the unseen place of the Sun.

Observe the zodiac constellation above the eastern horizon in early morning twilight before the sunrise. Sketch and record what you see. Does this also confirm the Sun's position on the ecliptic, as found in the evening and at midnight?

Continue to observe the western sky in late evening twilight at least once a week for a period of months. Notice how the zodiac constellations disappear into the sunset over a period of time. Similarly, observe the eastern sky before sunrise during the same period and observe the zodiac constellations emerging from the sunrise. Sketch your results, and record the times and dates of your observations.

Observing the First Magnitude Stars

Consulting the star map pictures in Chapter 6 and the table in the Appendix, find the first magnitude stars visible in the evening sky during the current season. Note the positions of these stars as compared to the zodiac constellations. Make a table of which zodiac constellations are directly north or south of these bright stars.

Referring to the zodiac table in the Appendix, find the times when these first magnitude stars are near the meridian during your current month. Go out at those times and observe these stars. Are any of the bright stars near the zenith? Identify the names of the stars and their constellations. Sketch and record your results.

Consulting the constellation patterns shown in Chapter 6, observe the sky using your reverse compass from Chapter 2. Determine which constellations are to the east and to the west of the meridian. Are any bright first magnitude stars visible in the eastern or western sky? Identify these stars and their constellations

Make a list of the constellations that can be seen in the evening. For each constellation, indicate the directions to the nearby constellations. For example, Orion is south of Gemini and northwest of Canis Major. Use your reverse compass from Chapter 2 to properly navigate around the sky.

Find Vega and Capella.
These bright stars lie quite far to the north, and at least one is always visible above the horizon from each state in the United States and the latitudes farther to the north. As a matter of fact, these stars are within the "always visible" circle as seen from the latitude of London and beyond! Vega and Capella can be found from their positions as compared to the Big Dipper and Cassiopeia. Learn to identify these stars and find their neighboring constellations. Sketch and record your results, including date and time.

Refer to the list of bright stars you observed in the meridian activity of Chapter 2. Can you now identify any of these bright stars? If so, record the star names and constellations. Otherwise, try to determine which stars they might be from the dates and times of their observations. Use your volvelle as modified below to help you make this determination.

Observing the Northern Sky

On one evening each week, observe the Big Dipper and Cassiopeia at the same time, e.g., 10:00 P.M. Once a month, sketch the orientation of these stars as they appear at that hour. Note the progression over the months.

Cassiopeia lies amidst the Milky Way at its northernmost extent and can help you visualize the connection between the summer and winter skies. Under a dark sky, if you can see the neighborhood of Orion, follow the Milky Way north past Capella to Cassiopeia and continue back again toward the horizon. Imagine the place of the Summer Triangle somewhere below the horizon. If the Summer Triangle is in the sky, follow the Milky Way past Vega to Cassiopeia and down to the northern horizon. Imagine Orion and friends invisibly below the northern horizon.

Observing Orion

Find the time for observing Orion in your current month. Note the position in the sky. Observe and sketch Orion once a week at the same time. Note the progression of Orion across the sky over a span of three months. Repeat this for two other constellations.

Visual Acuity Activity

Pleiades – Being able to count six stars in the Pleiades is a great test of eyesight. Sharp eyes can easily pick out all six. Nearsighted eyes may see the brighter stars clearly, but not all. To some eyes (like the author's!), the Pleiades look like a fuzzy blob. Observe the Pleiades with your whole family or other group of people. See how many Pleiades stars each person can count.

Mizar – Big Dipper – The star Mizar is at the bend in the handle of the Big Dipper. This star is a visual double star, and sharp eyes can easily spot two stars instead of one. However, those with nearsighted vision can only spot one star. Have your group spot Mizar and see who can find two stars or only one.

Use binoculars or a telescope to find *deep sky objects* such as galaxies and nebulae. Find the *Andromeda Galaxy* as shown in Chapter 6. Also, look for the famous *Orion Nebula* in the Sword of Orion. There is a prominent *globular cluster* in Hercules, to the south of the northwest star in the Keystone. To learn more about the deep sky, read *Sky & Telescope* magazine or visit a local amateur astronomy club. We'll learn more about the deep sky in a later volume of this series.

Globe Activity

This is a follow-up to the seasonal globe activity from chapter 5. Use your globe and your "geocentric" constellation setup to demonstrate the constellations visible in the evening, at midnight, and in the morning. Set your globe in the center with the zodiac constellation signs arranged around it in a circle. Place a lamp for the Sun in front of the constellation for the spring. Tape your stickman onto the globe to represent your location on the Earth.

* Turn the globe so that your stickman is on the sunset terminator. Note the constellation opposite the Sun. Note the constellation in between, representing the stars at the meridian in evening twilight.

* Turn the globe to the midnight position. Note that stickman is facing the constellation opposite the Sun, which corresponds to the stars at the meridian at midnight. Turn the globe so stickman is on the sunrise terminator. Note the arrangement of the constellations from this perspective.

* Repeat the above for each season. Repeat the activity using the softball to show the constellations of the moon's phases in each season.

Volvelle Activities

Add stars to your constellation volvelle

As space permits, add the first magnitude stars you learned in Chapter 6 to your Orion-Zodiac volvelle. Label these stars by name. Add the constellations you learned in this chapter. Don't worry if there's not enough room; the constellations need not be drawn to scale.

* You can use your volvelle to estimate when any of the stars will be near the meridian. Suppose you wish to find out when Leo will be near the meridian on a certain date. Turn your Sun to the desired week or day of the month. Then turn the Sun and the constellation wheel together until Leo is at the meridian. Note the hour of the day at which the Sun is pointed, and take daylight savings into account. Is the Sun still in the sky at that hour? If so, Leo cannot be seen at the meridian. But if the Sun is down, you can find Leo if you look at that hour!

* Using your volvelle, you can find any configuration of the sky for any time of the year. Look for 10 different constellations at various hours. Observe the constellations and record your results.

*   Turn your constellation wheel so that Orion is in the east. Turn the Sun to line up with different months around the dial. Observe the Sun's position and record the time of day when Orion is rising for each month of the year. Repeat the above for when Orion is at the meridian and western horizon. Compare your volvelle readings with the Orion table in the Appendix. Repeat these readings for any constellation.

*   Experiment with your volvelle to discover interesting information about the Sun and stars.

Add hours and months to your Northern Sky volvelle
Modify your northern sky volvelle to find any orientation of the Big Dipper and Cassiopeia for any hour of the day, any day of the year! On your fixed wheel, write 12 AM at the top, 12 PM at the bottom, 6 AM at the perpendicular position to the left, and 6 PM to the perpendicular to the right. Add in all the other hours in the spaces in between.

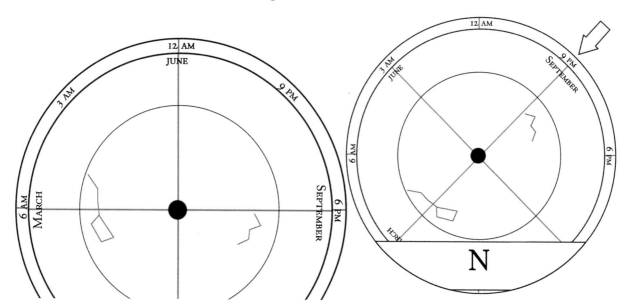

Along the end of your moveable wheel, at the end of the intersecting line through the Big Dipper, write *March*. At the opposite end of this line, through Cassiopeia, write *September*. With the wheel turned so that the Dipper is on the left, at the top, write *June*. At the opposite end, write *December*. Fill in the other months in between. You can divide the months into weeks and days. Find the orientation of the northern sky by lining up the desired month with the desired time.

Unlike your other volvelles, the northern sky volvelle will show an accurate sky for any time of day, for any day of the year. As with your other volvelles, remember to take into account standard time and daylight savings. To help you remember, on the horizon portion of volvelle, write *From March through November, add an hour for Daylight Savings.*

*   Turn the wheel so that it aligns with your current month and the time of evening twilight. Observe the northern sky at this time. Does your volvelle agree with your observation? Repeat for midnight and morning twilight, and observe the sky at these times.

*   Use your volvelle to find the orientation of the sky for any night of the year. Compare with your constellation volvelle, and use these two together to become acquainted with the appearance of the sky at different dates and times.

Vega and Capella

Add Vega and Cappella to the movable wheel. On the right side of the perpendicular line that ends at December, draw a star for Capella, about ⅔ of the distance from the center to the edge. On the same side of the perpendicular line, on the opposite side from the center, draw a star for Vega about ¾ of the distance to the edge. Label these stars so you can tell them apart.

* Rotate your volvelle so that Vega and Capella are at the same elevation above the horizon, with Vega in the northeast and Capella in the northwest. Read off your volvelle the time of day for each month when these stars are in this position. Rotate your volvelle so that Vega in the northwest and Capella is in the northeast and read off the time of days when these stars are in this position. Observe these stars during the current month and record your observations.

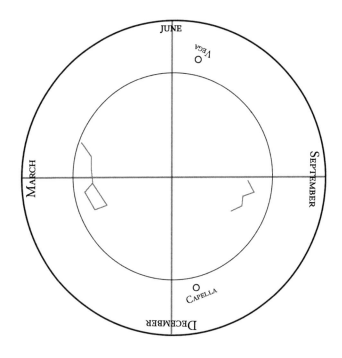

If you like volvelles and would like to make more different types, check out the *Paper Plate Education* Web site – *http://analyzer.depaul.edu/paperplate/*

Field Activities
Chapter 7 - The Wandering Stars

Flat Map Activity

Make some photocopies of your flat map, as you did in previous chapters. For several of the years given in the Appendix, draw the opposition positions and dates of each of the superior planets. Add any positions with dates to the map, especially if you can record the retrograde motion for a planet. On a separate copy, draw the positions among the constellations for the Sun and Venus, indicating the conjunctions and maximum elongations, including dates. Include the positions and dates of any of your own observations. Use more than one copy if your map gets too cluttered.

Solar System Map Activity

Make another copy of your solar system map from Chapter 5. Add circles for the orbits of the superior planets. The orbit of Mars should be 3 inches (about 7.5 cm) in diameter. The orbits of Jupiter and Saturn won't be to scale, so just draw larger circles for these orbits. Make copies of this map. Consulting the table in the Appendix, find the opposition positions for the superior planets for the current year. Draw each planet at that position on its orbital circle, in front of the appropriate constellation. Indicate the orbital position of Earth on those dates and write these dates on the map.

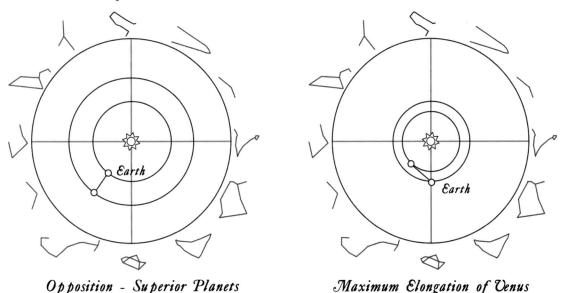

Opposition - Superior Planets   *Maximum Elongation of Venus*

Make another copy of the map to show the cycle of Venus. The orbit of Venus should be 1.5 inches (about 3 cm) in diameter. Make copies of this map. Consult the Appendix for the positions of Venus. Draw these positions of Venus on its orbital circle, indicating the location of Earth at the same time. Be careful with the maximum elongations. First draw where the Earth should be on that date, then draw Venus, as shown in the figure.

Make another copy for each planet. For each superior planet, draw the opposition positions for all the years shown in the Appendix. Label each year. Do the same for Venus, except indicate the positions of one extreme, e.g., inferior conjunction. Note any patterns or recurring cycles that you observe with the orbits of the planets.

Observing Venus

Consult the Appendix to find out whether Venus is currently visible in the morning or the evening. Note how much brighter Venus is than any other stars. It's easy to understand that UFO sightings always increase when Venus is an evening star!

Sketch Venus once a week as it appears in the morning or evening sky. Check Venus in twilight and after night falls. Record the date and time of observations. Note the height of Venus above the horizon and its position with respect to the compass points, along with any ground objects (trees, buildings, utility poles, etc.). Hold your reverse compass to the sky to show whether Venus's elongation is to the east or west of the Sun. If possible, note the constellation that Venus is currently passing through.

Repeat the above at one-week intervals for three months. Referring to the Appendix, determine if Venus is increasing or decreasing in elongation. Note any changes in height above the horizon and distance from the sunset over the weeks and months. Note that Venus may have a large elongation from the Sun but not be high above the horizon. Can you explain why that happens?

Observing the Superior Planets

Consult the Appendix to find the oppositions of the superior planets. If an opposition has already occurred in that season, look for the planets in the evening sky. If any oppositions are yet to come for that season, look for the planet in the morning sky, in or near the constellation of opposition. Sketch the position of the planet amidst its constellation, and record the date and time.

For any superior planets visible in the morning sky, check their positions at least twice a month. Note the movement of the planets against the background stars over the seasonal progression of the constellations. Sketch and record the dates and times of your observations. As the planets approach opposition, note the retrograde motion against the background stars.

Observing the Conjunctions

Moon and Stars – Observe the Moon each month as it passes near one or more of the bright first magnitude stars near the ecliptic – Aldebaran, Regulus, Spica, and Antares. Depending on the season, observe these conjunctions in the evening or morning. Record the date of each. Note whether the Moon is in different phases from month to month during these conjunctions. If possible, observe and note the time when the Moon and star cross the meridian.

Repeat over a period of months. Make a chart for each month's conjunction and record the phase, e.g. *February – Aldebaran – First Quarter*. Note that the phase of the Moon is different from month to month as the Moon passes these stars.

Moon and Planets – As you observe Venus and the superior planets in the previous activities, be sure to note the monthly passages of the Moon. Sketch these appearances in your journal and record the dates and times. Compare the constellations hosting these conjunctions from month to month, and also note any differences in the phase of the Moon.

Stars and Planets – As the planets make their way along the zodiac circle, they can pass very close to the bright stars along the ecliptic. Consult the Appendix to see when a planet will be passing through Taurus, Leo, Virgo or Scorpius. Keep an eye on that part of the sky, and record the date when the star and planet make their closest pass.

Planets and Planets – Conjunctions between two superior planets are less common, but the swifter Mars swings by the slower Jupiter and Saturn with each apparation. Since Jupiter and Saturn move very slowly, these planets come into conjunction with Venus when they are closer to the sunrise or sunset. As you observe the planets, take note if they are drawing near other planets. Sketch and record any planetary conjunctions that you observe, with time and date.

Conjunctions of the Moon, stars and, planets are frequently reported in the Classical Astronomy Update! – www.ClassicalAstronomy.com

Observing the Moon along the Zodiac
Seasonal variations – Observe the thin waxing crescent when it first appears in the evening sky. Using a single panel, sketch the position of the crescent as moves from evening to evening. Is it moving more vertically across the sky each night or it is moving more horizontally? Note the season and determine which constellations the Moon is passing through. Compare this with what you learned of the zodiac in previous chapters.

Observe the rising of the Full Moon and also the waning gibbous Moon for about three or four days thereafter. Note the directions on the horizon where the Moon rises. Note whether the risings of the Moon change from north to south with each night. As the Moon rises higher in the sky, observe the constellations that the Moon is passing through during these nights. Repeat this over a four-month period.

Over the same four-month period, observe the risings of the Full Moon. Using a single panel, sketch the positions of the Moon's rising, showing its direction with respect to due east. Observe the constellations hosting the Full Moon from month to month. Use this to estimate the Sun's position on the ecliptic during these months.

Repeat the moonfinding activity from Chapter 3. Observe the Moon's position at different heights at the meridian over a period of several days. For daytime observations of the Moon, estimate the constellation through which the Moon is passing on that day.

Observing Moon Shadows
Standing in your backyard compass, measure the lengths of the shadows in your backyard compass when the Moon is crossing the meridian. Note the changes from night to night, as the Moon moves from north to south through the constellations.

*   Also, notice the changes of the lengths of the shadows in the same phase from month to month, e.g., from one Full Moon to the next. Compare these shadow lengths with the lengths of shadows from the Sun, when it is in the same constellation, as you measured in Chapter 5.

*   As the Moon approaches the meridian, draw a cardinal line using the Moon's shadows.

Half Moon at Meridian (for advanced observers)
Record the appearance of the half moon at the meridian each month between the solstices. Keep a set of sketches for each month. Note the Moon's terminator: is it vertically straight or is it inclined? (Note the appearances shown on pages 162-165.) Does the tilt of the Moon's terminator change with the seasons? Why would that be? (Hint: compare the constellation of the Moon with the constellation of the Sun, as compared to the celestial equator.)

Constellation Volvelle Activity
On the transparency sheet on which you drew the Sun in Chapter 5, add moons indicating

the phases. Place the Full Moon opposite the Sun, and the First and Last Quarters with their illuminated sides facing the general direction of the Sun. Add 6 moons between each of the quarters to indicate waxing and waning crescents and gibbous moons. By having 28 phases, you'll end up with a cluttered wheel, but it will be more useful for identifying certain celestial events. As with your Sun and Moon volvelle, add a number underneath each phase to indicate the age of the Moon, e.g., 7 days for First Quarter, 14 days for Full Moon, etc.

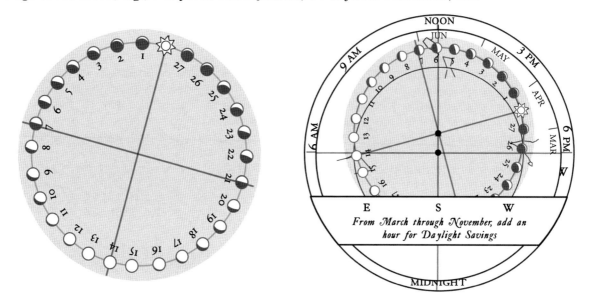

*   As you dial in the Sun for each month, note the constellations in which the Moon's quarters are seen. Confirm this for the current month. Note that in any phase, for any month, the Moon rises, crosses the meridian, and sets with its host constellation. Use your volvelle to confirm the north and south motion of the Moon at each phase, over the course of the seasons. Confirm the observations that you recorded in the above activities, or use your volvelle to predict where the Moon will be in each phase in the coming weeks and months.

*   Use your volvelle to find the approximate dates of conjunctions between the Moon and the stars. Note the places where the Moon passes a bright ecliptic star, and use this as a guide to finding the date. Keep in mind that the motions of the Moon and planets are very complex and can't be perfectly modeled on a flat paper volvelle. But your volvelle, divided into dates, should help you calculate these events to within a day or two. Confirm your volvelle readings with actual observations of the sky.

*   Use removable planet stickers (usually found in craft stores) to indicate the positions of the planets during any month or season indicated in the tables in the Appendix. Your volvelle will help you find the risings, meridian crossings, and settings of any of these planets. The Moon phases drawn on the sheet will also help you find the dates and times of conjunctions between the Moon and planets.

*   Your volvelle can be used as a simple "analog computer" for finding the positions of the Sun, Moon, stars, and planets. Repeat any of the above activities and experiment with your volvelle to estimate interesting celestial events in the coming months and years.

When you're done, keep observing the sky!
There are always new things to learn!

Appendix

Glossary, Biographia of Quoted Authors, and Astronomical Tables of the Bright Stars, Constellations, and Planets

To Assist the Reader in Conducting Celestial Observations

And beside this, giving all diligence, add to your faith virtue; and to virtue knowledge; And to knowledge temperance; and to temperance patience; and to patience godliness; And to godliness brotherly kindness; and to brotherly kindness charity. For if these things be in you, and abound, they make you that ye shall neither be barren nor unfruitful in the knowledge of our Lord Jesus Christ. - 2 Peter 1:5-8

 Signs & Seasons

Gloʃʃary

A Reference for the Principal Terminology Uʃed in Signs & Seaʃons

(Within each entry, terms in italics are croʃs-references to other entries)

A.M. – (from the Latin *ante meridiem*, meaning "before the middle of the day") Traditionally, the morning time of day when the Sun is *east* of the *meridian*, in the "rising" part of the sky. With modern timekeeping, A.M. means any time after 12 midnight until 12 noon, as measured on the clock. (See *Meridian, P.M.*)

Almanack – (possibly from the Teutonic *almaen-achte*, meaning "observations of the months") A resource that includes tables of the Sun's rising and setting for each day of the year, along with tables of the Moon's positions and the positions of planets and other noteworthy celestial objects. The almanack became very popular in Europe after the invention of the printing press and found its greatest expression in colonial America. The colonial almanacks came to include a wide variety of miscellaneous information. Sadly, this is all that is left in many contemporary "almanacs," which have dropped the "k" and also the astronomical information.

"Always Visible" Circle – In the Northern Hemisphere, it is the northern circumpolar circle, centered on Polaris and extending to the northern horizon. These stars never set and are always above the *horizon*, even if they cannot be seen behind the blue daylight sky. (See *Circumpolar Circle*.)

Apparition – (from the Latin *apparare*, meaning "appearance") The cycle of a *planet's* visibility in the sky. For a *superior planet*, its apparition begins with its *heliacal rising*, when it first emerges from the morning glow of the sunrise. It ends with its heliacal setting, when the planet disappears into the evening glow of the sunset. The inferior planets have morning apparitions and evening apparitions.

Armillary Sphere – (from the Latin *armilla*, meaning "bracelet" or "ring") A representation of the *celestial sphere* formed of rings that signify the principal circles in the sky. It was used to simulate the annual motion of the Sun and its rising, setting, and noon positions for any day of the year. An *armillary sundial* adapts this concept to modeling the spherical sky to find the time of day.

Armillary Sundial – (See S*undial, Armillary Sphere*.)

Asterism – (from the Greek *astron* [αστρον] meaning "star.") An informal grouping of stars associated with other constellations. Examples include The Big Dipper, which includes stars from the constellation Ursa Major, and the Summer Triangle, which includes the brightest stars from three other constellations.

Astrology – (from the Greek words *astron* [αστρον] meaning "star" and *logia* [λογια] meaning "teaching," literally "study of the stars") An ancient pseudoscience that teaches that events in the world are directly influenced by the motions of the Sun, Moon, and planets. Placed in its recognizable form by Stoic philosophers in the first century B.C., astrology is based on assigning arbitrary meanings to the Sun, Moon, planets, and the constellations of the *zodiac*. Astrology uses information and terminology from legitimate *Classical Astronomy* (e.g., positions of the celestial bodies in the sky) to derive omens, usually of bad tidings. Astrology is based on the flawed scientific premises of Aristotle, which have been discredited for centuries. Belief in astrology nonetheless persists in the minds of naïve and superstitious persons.

Astronomy – (from the Greek *astron* [αστρον] meaning "star" and *nomos* [νομος] meaning "law," literally "law of the stars") Generally, any study, measurement or purposeful observation of the celestial bodies. **1:** Classical Astronomy is an ancient practice of observing the sky for practical purposes, e.g., to tell time, navigate, or calculate the visible motions of the celestial bodies. It includes spherical astronomy in which geometrical methods are used to measure the sizes and motions of the celestial bodies, traditionally with visual geometrical instruments. **2:** Modern Astronomy is a relatively recent study of the sky, relying on telescopes and employing other instruments such as spectrographs, and in recent decades, the findings of space probes. The field has become very diverse and includes the study of the composition of stars, planets, and a variety of exotic objects not directly observable. As with other modern sciences, broad and far-reaching scientific conclusions are drawn from scanty physical evidence, e.g., negligibly small discrepancies in measured data.

Autumn – (from the Latin *autumnus*) The *season* when the days are growing cool, signifying the end of the growing season when food is harvested and plants begin to die. Traditionally begins on the *autumnal equinox.* (See *Season.*)

Autumnal Equinox – **1:** The point on the *celestial sphere,* currently in the constellation Virgo, where the *ecliptic* crosses the *celestial equator* so that the *Sun, Moon,* and *planets* cross over into the southern hemisphere of the sky. **2:** September 22 or 23, the day when the Sun crosses the *celestial equator* into the southern sky, after which the daylight period is shorter than 12 hours for dwellers north of the equator. Traditionally the first day of autumn. (See *Equinox.*)

Axis – (from the Greek *axon* [αχον], meaning "axle") A geometrical line around which a body rotates. The Earth and all other celestial bodies have an axis of rotation. (See *Pole.*)

Calendar – (from the Latin *kalends,* the first day of the month in the Roman calendar) Any method of reckoning the passage of time, for predicting times of planting and harvest, along with religious feasts, holidays, and other important dates of commemoration. Throughout all the world's cultures, almost all of the various calendars are based on cycles of the Sun, Moon, or other celestial bodies. This fulfills the main purpose for which the celestial bodies were created by God, "for signs and seasons, and days and years (Genesis 1:14)."

Cardinal Points – (from the Latin *cardinalis,* meaning "pivot") The principal points of direction – North, East, West and South, especially as used by mariners for navigation. Also known as the "compass points."

Celestial Equator – (See *Equator.*)

Celestial Pole – (See *Pole.*)

Celestial Sphere – (from the Latin *caelo,* meaning "the sky" or "the heavens") An illusory spherical appearance of the starry sky, resulting from the near-infinite distances to the celestial bodies from the Earth. Though in fact only an illusion, the celestial sphere can still be used to define circles representing the paths and positions of celestial bodies, enabling the mathematical measurement of the sky. The celestial sphere is also called "the vault of the heavens" and "the dome of the firmament."

Circumpolar Circle – A small circle of the celestial sphere, centered on an elevated pole and extending therefrom to touch the horizon. (See *"Always Visible" Circle, "Never Visible" Circle.*)

Classical Astronomy – (See *Astronomy.*)

Compass Points – (See *Cardinal Points.*)

Conjunction – (from the Latin *conjunctus,* meaning "joined together") When two celestial bodies lie along the same line of sight, so that they appear near each other in the sky. Conjunctions can occur between the Moon and a star or planet, between two planets, a star and a planet, or any of these celestial bodies and the Sun.

Constellation – (from the Latin *co,* meaning "together" and *stella,* meaning "star.") Traditional "connect-the-dot" patterns formed in the stars to designate familiar shapes such as animals and persons. Several traditional constellations are associated with the myth and folklore of the Greeks and Romans. Other world cultures have drawn different constellations in the sky related to their own star lore. Forty-eight traditional constellations were recorded in antiquity by Aratus, though eighty-eight constellations are recognized in modern times, including those visible from the Southern Hemisphere which were not seen by ancient Europeans.

Cosmic Rising – (from the Greek *cosmos* [κοσμος], meaning "universe") The invisible rising of a star during daylight, concealed behind the blue daylight sky, so that a star can be seen in the evening sky after sunset.

Crescent – (from the Latin *crescere,* meaning "to grow") A *phase* of the Moon in which less than half of the visible portion is illuminated, appearing as a "fingernail" shape. In a crescent phase, the Moon's *terminator* is curved inwardly toward the illuminated edge. A *waxing* crescent is an increasing crescent, visible in the evening the first week after the *New Moon.* A *waning* crescent is a decreasing crescent, visible in the morning the last week of the month, before the New Moon. (See *Phase.*)

Day – (from the Old English *daeg,* akin to the Latin *dies*) **1:** The most basic unit of measuring time, the period of one rotation of the Sun across the sky, e.g., from one sunrise to the next. **2:** the part of the daily cycle in which it is light, as compared to night.

Dawn – (See *Twilight.*)

Dial – (from the Latin *dialis*, derived from the Latin *dies*, meaning "day") **1:** The "face" of a *sundial*, having markings along the edge to show different *hours* of the *day*. (See *sundial*.) **2:** The "face" of a clock or any other instrument having a circular indicator (such as a rotary telephone), ultimately derived from the traditional sundial design.

Dusk – (See *Twilight*.)

Earth – The world upon which the LORD created human life and upon which occurred the ministry and redemptive sacrifice of Jesus, the Son of God. It is the only place in the universe known to be capable of supporting life. In ancient times, the Earth was considered the center of the universe around which the other celestial bodies revolved. In modern times, this is regarded as an illusion resulting from the daily rotation of the Earth's mass and its annual revolution around the Sun.

Earthshine – A smoky glow seen over the face of the Moon when in the crescent phases. The earthshine is caused by light reflected from the Earth onto the Moon, providing partial illumination to the Moon's surface.

East – (from the Old English *eostre*, meaning "sunrise," akin to the Greek *eos* [ηως], meaning "dawn") **1:** The side of the *horizon* from which the Sun, Moon, and stars rise each day. **2:** One of the *cardinal* or *compass points* used for navigation, in the direction opposite to the *west*.

Easter – (See *Pasch*.)

Ecliptic – (from the Greek *ekleipein* [εχλειπην], meaning to "to be deficient from") A *great circle* of the *celestial sphere* corresponding to the Sun's annual path through the *constellations* of the *zodiac*. An eclipse can occur when the path of the Moon crosses the ecliptic, hence the name. During a *New Moon*, an eclipse of the Sun can occur, in which the Sun is covered by the Moon. During a *Full Moon*, an eclipse of the Moon can occur, in which the Moon passes into the Earth's shadow.

Elongation – (from the Latin word *elongare*, meaning "to be far from") The apparent separation in the sky between the Sun and a planet or the Moon. For an eastern elongation, a planet is east of the Sun and is therefore visible in the evening sky after sunset. For a western elongation, a planet is west of the Sun and is thus visible in the morning sky before sunrise. (See *Maximum Elongation*.)

Equator – (from the Latin *aequus*, meaning "equal") Generally, a *great circle* that divides a sphere at a midpoint between the two poles of rotation. **1:** The terrestrial equator encircles the middle of the Earth between the North and South Poles, and the center of the tropics. At the equator, days are always 12 hours in length. **2:** The celestial equator is a great circle along the middle of the *celestial sphere*, between the *celestial poles*. The celestial equator crosses the *horizon* at due east and due west. The *equinoxes* are the points in the sky where the equator crosses the ecliptic.

Equinox – (from the Latin *aequus*, meaning "equal," and *nox*, meaning "night.") **1:** One of the two points on the *celestial sphere* where the *ecliptic* intersects the *celestial equator*. **2:** One of the two days of the year where the Sun crosses the celestial equator at an equinox point. On these days, the Sun rises due east and sets due west, and the period of daylight is 12 hours, equal to the 12-hour period of nighttime. (See *vernal equinox, autumnal equinox*.)

First Quarter – The point in the Moon's orbit one week past the *New Moon*, where the Moon has completed about one-quarter of its monthly cycle. The First Quarter is a *waxing* half-moon seen in the evening sky, somewhere near the meridian at about 6:00 P.M. (or 7:00 P.M. during daylight savings.)

Fixed Stars – The background stars that form the *constellations*, which rise and set with a regular daily rotation of the sky and do not move about the *zodiac* as do the *planets*.

Full Moon – The phase of the *Moon* in which its entire bright side is turned toward the *Earth*, and so the complete circle of the Moon's face can be seen. The Full Moon occurs at midmonth, about two weeks after the *New Moon*. The Full Moon is at *opposition*, in the opposite place in the sky from the Sun.

Gibbous – (from the Latin *gibbus*, meaning "humped") A phase of the Moon in which more than half of the visible portion is illuminated, giving the Moon a "humped" appearance. In a gibbous phase, the Moon's *terminator* is curved outwardly away from the illuminated edge. A *waxing* gibbous is an increasing humped Moon, visible in the evening the week after the *First Quarter*. A *waning* gibbous is a decreasing humped Moon, visible in the morning the week after the *Full Moon*.

Gnomon – (from the Greek *gignoskein* [γιγνοσκειν], meaning "to know") The pointer of a *sundial*, for casting the Sun's shadow upon a *dial* for finding the *hour* of the *day*. (See *Sundial*.)

Great Circle – A circle that divides a sphere into two equal halves. It is different from a *small circle* that divides a sphere into unequal halves. Great circles of the celestial sphere include the *horizon, the meridian, the celestial equator* and *the ecliptic*.

Gregorian Calendar – A slight modification to the historic *Julian calendar*, implemented by Pope Gregory XIII in A.D. 1582. With the Gregorian calendar, 10 days were dropped from October 1582, and three out of four centennial years were designated not to be leap years, so that the *vernal equinox* would continue to fall on March 21, as it had done in A.D. 325, the era of the Council of Nicaea.

Heliacal Rising – (from the Greek *helios* [ἥλιος], meaning "Sun") The appearance of a star or planet when it emerges from the Sun's glare and is first visible before the sunrise, rising just before the Sun.

High Noon – (See *Meridian, Noon*.)

Horizon – (from the Greek *horizo* [ὁρίζω], meaning "boundary") **1:** The far-off, distant place where the land ends and meets the lower extremity of the sky, in the "horizontal" direction where the eye is level, looking neither up nor down. **2:** A *great circle* of the *celestial sphere*, dividing the visible portion of the sky above from the invisible portion hidden by the Earth. **3:** In navigation, the horizon is the reference for finding direction according to the *cardinal points* or compass points – *north, east, west* and *south*, and for finding any azimuth in between.

Hour – (from the Greek *hora* [ὥρα], meaning "interval") A division of a day, used to measure shorter periods of time within the day. The day has historically been divided into 12 hours of daylight, following a Babylonian custom. Since antiquity, it has been traditional to divide the daily period of the Sun's rotation into 24 hours.

Inferior Conjunction – Occurs when either of the *inferior planets*, Venus or Mercury, is between the Earth and the Sun and along the same line of sight with the Sun, invisibly lost in the Sun's glare. A New Moon is an inferior conjunction of the Moon and the Sun. (See *Conjunction*.)

Inferior Planet – A *planet* as seen from the surface of the Earth to be inside the Earth's *orbit*, between the Earth and the Sun. Inferior planets always remain close to the Sun, drawing away from the Sun in the sky and moving again toward the Sun.

Insolation – (from the Latin word *insolatio*, meaning "to expose to the Sun") The process whereby the Earth slowly gains heat and warms up by absorbing heat from the Sun, over the span of the spring and summer. (See *Lag of the Seasons*.)

Intercalation – (from the Latin word *intercalo*, which means "to call among") The process of regularly adding an extra period of time to a calendar in order to correct a known discrepancy. In our *Gregorian calendar*, an extra intercalary day is added at February 29 in "leap years." In the Hebrew calendar, 7 intercalary months are added at regular periods over a span of 19 years.

Julian Calendar – Based on the solar calendar used for centuries in Egypt and established by Gaius Julius Caesar, dictator of Rome, in 45 B.C. The Julian Calendar is based on a 365-day solar year, with an intercalated day added in "leap years," every fourth year, in order to correct for the inequality of the tropical year. (See *Gregorian Calendar*.)

Lag of the Seasons – During the warm months, when the days are long, the Earth gains heat slowly from the Sun, and so it is hotter in August than in June, when the days are longest. Similarly, during the cold months, when the days are short, the Earth loses heat slowly, and so it is colder in February than in December, when the days are shortest. (See *Insolation*.)

Light Pollution – A dispersal from street lights and other ground lighting onto the night sky, resulting in an artificial orange twilight that perpetually hides the beauty of the unspoiled natural sky from the sight of urban dwellers through which even the brightest stars can barely be seen.

Lower Branch – The portion of the *meridian* that extends below the *celestial poles* and represents the lowest point reached by celestial bodies in the daily rotation of the sky. The stars in the "*Always Visible*" circle cross the lower branch when they are between the elevated *pole* and the *horizon*. The Sun reaches the lower branch, unseen below the horizon, at *midnight*.

Luminaries – (from the Latin *lumen*, meaning "light") A term for generically referring to both the Sun and the Moon, designating them as the celestial bodies created to shine light upon the Earth. They have historically been used for the reckoning of the calendar.

Lunar Calendar – A method of tracking time based on the cycle of the Moon's phases. (See *Calendar*.)

Lunar Month – (See *Month*.)

Magnitude – (from the Latin *magnus*, meaning "great") A scale for ranking the brightnesses of the stars, originally devised by the classical astronomer Claudius Ptolemy. First magnitude stars are the brightest, second magnitude are less bright, and so forth, down to sixth magnitude which are the faintest.

Maximum Elongation – Occurs when either of the *inferior planets*, Venus or Mercury, reaches its extreme separation from the Sun as seen in the skies of Earth, after which they draw again toward the Sun. Maximum eastern elongation is when an inferior planet reaches its greatest distance from the Sun in the evening sky, while Maximum western elongation is when an inferior planet reaches its greatest distance from the Sun in the morning sky. (See *Elongation*.)

Midnight – Traditionally, the time of day when the Sun reaches its lowest place below the horizon. In current times, there is a difference between "astronomical midnight" and "twelve midnight" as read from a clock. **1:** Astronomical midnight occurs when the Sun reaches the *lower branch* of the *meridian*. **2:** 12:00 A.M. may occur earlier or later than astronomical midnight due to standard time and daylight savings.

Meridian – (from the Latin *meridiem*, meaning "middle of the day") An invisible *great circle* of the *celestial sphere* that defines the middle of the sky. At the meridian, the Sun, Moon, and stars reach their highest place in the sky. Each day, the Sun reaches the meridian at *high noon*. Each celestial body has a "noon" of its own when it reaches the meridian.

Milky Way – (the English term for the Greek *galaktos* [γαλαχτος], from *gala* [γαλα] meaning "milk") Our galaxy, a milky band of stars that stretches overhead through the areas of Orion, Cassiopeia, and the Summer Triangle. The Milky Way is only seen from dark skies, far from city lights.

Modern Astronomy – (See *Astronomy*.)

Month – (from the Old English *monath*, from *mona*, which means "moon") A unit of measuring longer periods of time, based on the cycle of the Moon. **1:** A *lunar month* is a complete cycle of the Moon's phases, on average about 29½ days; **2:** A *calendar month* is a convention used to divide the solar year into 12 parts, having either 30 or 31 days, except for February, which has 28 days and 29 in a leap year.

Moon – The Lesser Light that reflects light from the Sun onto the Earth to provide light during the nighttime. The *Moon* circles the Earth each *month* and passes through a cycle of *phases*.

Nadir – (from the Arabic *nazir* [رضن], meaning "opposite") The unseen extreme point below the *horizon*, opposite the *zenith*, in the invisible half of the *celestial sphere*. The *lower branch* of the meridian is defined as passing through the nadir.

"Never Visible" Circle – In the Northern Hemisphere, it is the southern circumpolar circle, centered on the unseen, depressed South Celestial Pole, and extending invisibly to touch the southern *horizon*. Stars within this circle are never seen to rise above the *horizon* and are best seen from the Southern Hemisphere. (See *Circumpolar Circle*.)

New Moon – The phase in the Moon's cycle where it presents no illuminated edge and is generally aligned with the Sun. The New Moon is invisible in the glare of the Sun.

Noon – Traditionally, the time of day when the Sun reaches its highest place in the sky. In current times, there is a difference between the Sun's "high noon" in the sky and "twelve noon" as read from a clock. High noon occurs when the Sun is directly above the southern *horizon*, when the Sun has reached the *meridian*. 12:00 P.M. may occur earlier or later than high noon due to standard time and *daylight savings*.

North – (from the Germanic *nord*, akin to the Greek word *nerteros* [νερτερος], meaning "lower" or "under") **1:** The side of the *horizon* crossed by the *meridian*, over which, in the Northern Hemisphere, the elevated North Celestial Pole defines the pivot point for the *celestial sphere*. **2:** One of the *cardinal* or *compass points* used for navigation, in the direction opposite to the *south*.

Occultation – (from the Latin *occultare*, meaning "to hide") Generally, when the Moon passes in front of a bright star or planet, as seen with the unaided eye. Occultations of the Moon with faint stars are a nearly constant occurrence. Occasionally, a planet can occult a star, and even more rarely, another planet.

Opposition – (from the Latin *ob*, meaning "against," and *ponere*, meaning "to place," literally, "to place against") The point in the sky where a celestial body is opposite the Sun, rising as the Sun sets. The Full Moon is the opposition of the Moon.

Orbit – (from the Latin *orbis*, meaning "circle") A generally circular path of motion of a celestial body that is captured by the gravity of a larger body. For example, the Moon is in orbit around the Earth, and the Earth and other planets are themselves in orbit around the Sun.

Pasch – (from the Greek *pascha* [πασχα], meaning "Passover") A Christian feast in which the resurrection of Jesus is commemorated, derived from the Jewish *Passover.* In the English language, this feast is commonly known as "Easter," after a little-known feast of the pre-Christian Anglo-Saxon pagans.

Passover – (from the Hebrew *pesach* [פסח]) A Jewish feast commemorating Moses's leading of the Israelites out of Egypt, celebrated beginning on the first Full Moon of the Spring.

Phase – (from the Greek *phaseis* [φαισεις], meaning "appearance" or "shine") A changing appearance of the Moon defined by an illuminated portion and a dark portion, as divided by the Moon's *terminator.* The Moon can appear in a *crescent* phase, as a half-moon, a *gibbous* phase, and a *Full Moon.*

Planet – (from the Greek *planetos* [πλανετος], meaning "wanderer") **1:** In ancient times, a planet was considered to be any of the seven "wandering stars" observed to move about through the constellations of the zodiac. (Compare with *fixed stars*.) The Sun and Moon were therefore considered classical planets. **2:** In the modern definition, a planet is considered a body in orbit around the Sun, meeting certain requirements of size, among other things. The Earth is considered a planet by the modern definition, while the Sun and Moon are not. Only eight bodies are considered to be planets. Thousands of smaller objects, including asteroids and dwarf planets, are known to orbit the Sun. In A.D. 2006, Pluto was reclassified as a dwarf planet.

P.M. – (from the Latin words *post meridiem*, meaning "after the middle of the day.") Traditionally, the afternoon time of day when the Sun is *west* of the *meridian*, in the "setting" part of the sky. With modern timekeeping, P.M. means any time after 12 noon until 12 midnight, as measured on the clock. (See *Meridian, A.M.*)

Pole – (from the Greek *polos* [πολος], meaning "pivot.") Generally, an endpoint of an *axis* along a sphere, around which the sphere rotates. **1:** The terrestrial poles are the points where the Earth's axis of rotation crosses the Earth's surface, i.e., The North Pole and The South Pole. **2:** The celestial poles are the points where the Earth's axis is extended up to the sky, and appear as stationary points around which the entire sky appears to rotate. In the Northern Hemisphere, the north celestial pole is elevated above the horizon, and the *North Star, Polaris,* is very near that point.

Precession – (from the Latin *praecedere*, meaning "to go before") A phenomenon where the Earth's axis shifts due to the gravitational pull of the Moon. Over a period of thousands of years, the celestial poles change positions, resulting in a shifting of all the constellations. As a result, different constellations of the zodiac move into the places of the solstices and equinoxes. In classical times, 2000 years ago, the point of the *summer solstice* was in Cancer and the point of the *winter solstice* was in Capricornus. At these times, the Sun was respectively at the zeniths above the *Tropic of Cancer* and the *Tropic of Capricorn.* In our modern times, these solstice points are in Gemini and Sagittarius due to precession.

Quadrature – (from the Latin *quadrans*, meaning "one-quarter") Generally, when the Moon or a planet is one quarter of the way around the zodiac circle from the Sun, meaning that the Sun is in a different quadrant of the sky from the Sun. This is the same idea as the "quarters" of the Moon's phases.

Retrogradation – (from the Latin *retro*, meaning "backwards," and *gradere*, meaning "to move") As a superior planet approaches opposition, it slows down, become stationary, and then reverses direction, moving backwards through the stars toward the west. At the end of its retrogradation, it again resumes its eastward motion.

Season – (from the French *saison*, meaning "to sow.") One of the four seasons – *spring, summer, autumn* or *winter*. **1:** An annual cycle of climatic variations, associated with stages of warming and cooling, upon which depends the growth cycle of plant life, used for growing and harvesting food. **2:** Four divisions of the year, defined as periods between one *solstice* or *equinox* to the next.

Sign – (from the Latin *signus*, meaning "sign") **1:** In the Biblical sense, a position of a celestial object in the the sky that gives an indication of a direction or a time. **2:** An archaic term for divisions of the *celestial sphere*, co-opted by the archaic pseudo-science of *astrology*. **a:** An equal 1/12 division of the *zodiac*, for mathematically simplifying the positions of the celestial bodies; **b:** The image of the object supposedly formed by the constellation pattern.

Skycraft – The traditional arts of observing and understanding the signs in the sky, useful for finding the time during the day and at night and for navigating by positions and movements of the Sun, Moon, and stars.

Small Circle – (See *Great Circle*.)

Solar Calendar – A method of tracking time based on the annual cycle of the Sun and its *seasons*. (See *Calendar*.)

Solar System – The Earth's neighborhood in the universe. Includes all the planets, moons and other celestial bodies in *orbit* around the Sun.

Solstice – (from the Latin *Sol*, meaning "Sun," and *stit*, meaning "stand," literally "the standing of the Sun") **1:** One of the two points on the *celestial sphere* where the *ecliptic* reaches its maximum extent from the *celestial equator*. **2:** One of the two days of the year when the Sun reaches its extreme position to the north or south of the celestial equator at a solstice point. On these days, the period of daylight is either the maximum or minimum for the year. (See *Summer Solstice, Winter Solstice*.)

South – (from the Old English *suth*, from the Old High German *sunna* or "Sun.") **1:** The side of the *horizon* crossed by the *meridian*, over which the Sun, Moon, and stars reach their highest place in the sky each day. **2:** One of the *cardinal points* or "compass points" used for navigation, in the direction opposite to the *north*.

Spring – (from the Old English *springan*, meaning "to shoot") The *season* when the Earth warms and the plants begin to grow. Traditionally begins on the *vernal equinox*. (See *Season*.)

Station – A point in the motion of a *planet* where it stops and becomes "stationary" compared to the background stars, after which its direction is reversed. For an *inferior planet*, a station can result near *maximum elongations*, when the planet's motion is equal and opposite to the apparent motion of the Sun so that they offset. For a *superior planet*, stations occur near the beginning and ending of a *retrogradation*.

Summer – (an Old English word, still used today, for the warm season) The *season* when the days are long and climate is warm, during which the plants grow. Traditionally begins on the *summer solstice*. (See *Season*.)

Summer Solstice – **1:** The point on the *celestial sphere,* currently in the constellation Gemini, where the *ecliptic* reaches its northern extreme from the *celestial equator*. **2:** June 20 or 21, the day when the Sun reaches its northern extreme. The Sun rises and sets farthest to the north and reaches its highest point of the year at the meridian, casting the shortest noon shadows for dwellers of the Northern Hemisphere. It is the longest day of the year, and traditionally the first day of summer. (See *Solstice*.)

Sun – The bright luminary, the Greater Light, that casts daylight and warmth over the Earth and provides illumination to the Moon and all the planets and other bodies in the solar system.

Sundial – An ancient device for learning the hour of the day by the position of a shadow of a *gnomon* or pointer along a *dial*. The gnomon shadow relates to the position of the Sun in the sky. The dial includes markings to represent the hours to which the shadows point in order to indicate the time.

Superior Conjunction – When one of the *inferior* or *superior planets* are on the far side of the Sun as seen from Earth, along the same line of sight with the Sun, lost in the Sun's glare. (See *Conjunction*.)

Superior Planet – A *planet* seen from the surface of the Earth to be beyond the Earth's *orbit*. Superior planets can be in any part of the sky, can be found in *opposition* to the Sun, and display retrogradations in the times before and after opposition.

Synodic Month – The lunar month. (See *Month*.)

Temporal Rising – (from the Latin *tempus*, meaning "time") The visible rising of a star in the night sky, because "astronomical time" was traditionally regarded as beginning after nightfall.

Terminator – (from the Latin *terminus*, meaning "boundary") **1:** Generally speaking, a boundary that encircles a moon or planet that separates the sunlit half from the shadowed half. **2:** On the Earth, the boundary between daylight and the darkness of night. Locations on the Earth cross the terminator during sunrise and sunset.

Tropic – (from the Greek *tropos* [τροπως], meaning "turning") **1:** In Classical Astronomy, it is the Greek equivalent of the Latin *solstice* and is used interchangeably, signifying the extreme northern and southern points of the *ecliptic*. **2:** The tropics commonly refer to the warm climate zone of the Earth, where astronomically, the Sun passes through the *zenith* at least one day a year. The boundaries of the tropics are the Tropic of Cancer and the Tropic of Capricorn, where the Sun passes the *zenith* at *noon* on the *summer solstice* and the *winter solstice* respectively.

Tropical Year – (from the Greek *tropos* [τροπος], meaning "turning") Generally, the period of the year, the annual cycle of the Sun along the *ecliptic*, through the seasons. Specifically, the time between successive passages of the *vernal equinox*, which can change in position among the constellations over a period of centuries due to the subtle effects of *precession*.

Twilight – A light in the sky representing the transition between the blue daytime sky and the starry sky of night, caused by the light of the Sun illuminating the atmosphere overhead when it is below the horizon. Morning twilight is the *dawn* and is seen before the sunrise. Evening twilight is the *dusk* and is seen after the sunset.

Vernal Equinox – (from the Latin *vernalis*, meaning "Spring") **1:** The point on the *celestial sphere*, currently in the constellation Pisces, where the *ecliptic* crosses the *celestial equator* so that the *Sun, Moon,* and *planets* cross over into the Northern Hemisphere of the sky. **2:** March 20 or 21, the day when the Sun crosses the *celestial equator* into the northern sky, after which the daylight period is longer than 12 hours for dwellers north of the equator. Traditionally regarded as the first day of spring, and the beginning of the *tropical year*. (See *Equinox*.)

Volvelle – (from the Latin *volvere*, meaning "to turn") A traditional astronomical calculating instrument, having rotating elements usually formed of paper, for depicting various motions of celestial bodies across the sky.

Waning – (from the Old English *wan*, meaning "deficient," akin to the Latin *vanus*, meaning "empty," i.e., "vanity.") In the second half of the *lunar month*, the time when the *Moon* is visible in the morning sky and decreasing in *phase*. The waning Moon grows a little thinner each morning and draws a little closer to the sunrise.

Waxing – (from the Old English *weaxan*, meaning "to increase") In the first half of the *lunar month*, the time when the *Moon* is visible in the evening sky and increasing in *phase*. The waxing Moon grows a little thicker each evening and draws a little farther away from the sunset.

West – (from the Old German *westar*, akin to the Latin *vesper*, meaning "evening") **1:** The side of the *horizon* from which the Sun, Moon and stars set each day. **2:** One of the *cardinal* or "compass points" used for navigation, in the direction opposite to the *east*.

Winter – (an Old English word, still used today, for the cold season) The *season* when the days are short and the climate is cold, during which plants are dormant. Traditionally begins on the *winter solstice*. (See *Season*.)

Winter Solstice – **1:** The point on the *celestial sphere*, currently in the constellation Sagittarius, where the *ecliptic* reaches its southern extreme from the *celestial equator*. **2:** December 20 or 21, the day when the Sun reaches its southern extreme. The Sun rises and sets farthest to the south and reaches its lowest point of the year at the meridian, casting the longest *noon* shadows for dwellers of the Northern Hemisphere. It is the shortest day of the year, and traditionally the first day of winter. (See *Solstice*.)

Year – (from the Old High German *jar* [pronounced "yar"].) A unit of measuring longer periods of time, based on the cycle of the Sun through the *ecliptic*. Passage of the year is measured by changes in the length of daylight and the resulting changes in climate associated with the *seasons*. The *tropical year*, the period from one *vernal equinox* to the next, is roughly 365¼ days.

Zenith – (from the Arabic *samt* [سمى], meaning "path overhead") The extreme top point in the sky directly overhead, straight up above the observer's place on the ground. The zenith is the opposite point on the *celestial sphere* from the *nadir*. The *meridian* is defined as passing through the zenith.

Zodiac – (from the Greek word *zoe* [ζωη], meaning "life") A band of traditional *constellations* that lie along the plane of the *ecliptic*, i.e., the edge of the *solar system*. The Sun, Moon, and *planets* appear to move among these constellations since they lie along the same line of sight as seen from the *Earth*. It is usually identified with the Hebrew word *Mazzaroth*, found in the book of Job. Though the word zodiac is commonly associated with *astrology*, it simply refers to the stars themselves and should not be confused with this ancient superstition.

Biographia of Quoted Authors

Vignettes of the Lives of the Source Writers,

With Emphafis on Their Relevance to Claffical Aftronomy

HOLY BIBLE – In addition to being the authorized version of the Bible in English, the *King James Version* (A.D. 1611) included a great deal of practical astronomy information, such as an astronomical calendar with sunrise and sunset times for each month, a thirty-nine-year almanack, and instructions for calculating the date of Easter.

AMERICAN ALMANACKS – Following the tradition from England, astronomical almanacks were read by everyone in colonial America and the early republic. In fact, the first publication in America was the Cambridge Almanack, published in 1639, prior to the *Bay Psalm Book*. Initially, the almanacks simply provided sunrise and sunset times, Moon phases, and other useful astronomy information. As time went on, the almanacks became a compendium of sundries and miscellany and an early source of American literature. Many famous and influential men were almanack makers, including Cotton Mather, Nathaniel Ames (father of founding father Fisher Ames), Andrew Ellicott (who surveyed Washington, D.C.), Benjamin Banneker (Ellicott's neighbor and colleague, son of a freed slave, and self-taught astronomer), and, of course, Benjamin Franklin.

ARATUS – *Aratos Solinus* (Αρατος, circa 310-240 B.C.) lived during the height of Greek culture, following the conquests of Alexander the Great. Aratus's famous poem, *Phaenomena,* is our earliest extant source for the traditional constellations and includes a wealth of other astronomy information. Aratus was extremely popular in the Greek and Roman cultures, and it is likely that every educated person in classical times studied his work. Aratus is one of the few pagan authors quoted in the New Testament by the Apostle Paul (Acts 17:28).

ARISTOTLE – (Αριστοτέλης, 384-322 B.C.) Aristotle was one of the greatest Greek philosophers, the student of the great philosopher Plato. Aristotle was the teacher of Alexander the Great, who conquered the entire Persian Empire. Through Aristotle's influence, Greek philosophy and culture flourished from Europe and Egypt to India. Aristotle's logical and scientific works were the standards for 2000 years, until the modern era. Though based on outdated cosmology, Aristotle's great work of astronomy, *de Caelo* or *On the Heavens,* nevertheless includes a wealth of classical astronomy information that is still useful and accurate.

AUGUSTINE – (A.D. 354-430) was one of the greatest scholars and apologists of the early church. His monumental tome, *Civitas Dei – The City of God* – remains a classic of Christian scholarship, an exhaustive refutation of Greco-Roman paganism and affirmation of Christian doctrine. As with the majority of classical and early Christian writings, Augustine's works include numerous references to astronomy.

BASIL – *Basil the Great, Bishop of Caesarea* (circa A.D. 330-379) was a great teacher in the early church and remains a prominent figure in Eastern Orthodoxy. Basil's great work, the *Hexaemeron,* is a series of teachings on the six days of creation and includes considerable useful information on the natural sciences, including astronomy.

BEDE – *The Venerable Bede* (A.D. 672-735) was a bright, shining light during the darkest days of the so-called Dark Ages. Bede wrote the first history of England, which remains an important source for early Anglo-Saxon Britain. Bede is also remembered for writing *de Temporum Ratione* or *On the Reckoning of Time*, which became the standard medieval work on *computus* or calendar-making. Bede also wrote a great number of commentaries on many of the books of the Bible.

BYRHTFERTH – (circa A.D. 990– circa 1015) Byrhtferth was a medieval English monk who wrote several important works of *computus*, following the tradition established by the Venerable Bede. *Byrhtferth's Manual* includes astronomical tables and useful information for keeping a Christian church calendar. *Byrhtferth's Manual* is regarded as a predecessor to the modern almanack.

CALVIN – *John Calvin* (Jean Chauvin, A.D. 1509-1564), the great Reformer, was a prolific writer. His works include *Institutes of the Christian Religion* and numerous commentaries on most of the books in the Bible. Calvin's theology was deeply influenced by the fourth-century church father Augustine. As was true of every scholar of centuries past, Calvin was well versed in Classical Astronomy, and his writings include several astronomical references.

CHAUCER – While *Geoffrey Chaucer* (circa A.D. 1343-1400) is best remembered for *The Canterbury Tales*, he is also the author of two notable works of Classical Astronomy. He wrote *Treatise on the Astrolabe* for his son, Little Lewis. Though this work describes the functions of the astrolabe, an astronomical instrument, it also includes a wealth of general astronomy information. Chaucer also wrote *Equatorie of the Planets*, describing the construction and operation of another astronomical instrument.

CICERO – *Marcus Tullius Cicero* (106-43 B.C.) is remembered as a great Roman orator and statesman and widely regarded as the greatest Latin rhetorician. A contemporary of Julius Caesar, Cicero was an active participant in the turbulent period at the end of the Roman republic. As a student of the great Stoic astronomer Posidonius, Cicero's writings reveal a deep understanding of Classical Astronomy. Cicero's poem *The Dream of Scipio* combines the traditional Earth-centered astronomy with Roman theology. In this allegory, the spirit of the Roman general Scipio ascends into "heaven" among the spheres of the planets. Cicero's poem was a source for later works by Macrobius and Dante.

DANTE – *Dante Aligheri* (A.D. 1265-1321) wrote *The Divine Comedy*, an allegorical tour of the afterlife considered to be the greatest work of medieval European literature. Dante's work interweaves elements of Christian theology and classical culture, incorporating the framework of classical Earth-centered cosmology. Heaven is presented as a hierarchy of levels above the Earth, corresponding to the spheres of the Sun, Moon, and other classical planets. In this, Dante borrows elements from Cicero's *Dream of Scipio* and also the astronomical commentary on the same by Macrobius.

DECREE OF CANOPUS – (238 B.C.) This decree was issued by Ptolemy III Euergetes of Egypt and his wife Queen Bernice. While a 365-day solar year had been long-known in Egypt, this decree first established the intercalary "leap year" every four years. Ptolemy III was the third in the line of Greek kings of Egypt, which began with Ptolemy I Soter, a general of Alexander the Great, who became ruler of Egypt after Alexander's death. The line of the Ptolemies ran until 30 B.C. when Egypt under Ptolemy XV and his mother Cleopatra was conquered by the Romans under Octavian, who later became Caesar Augustus.

EMPEDOCLES – (Ἐμπεδοκλῆς, circa 490-435 B.C.) was a Pre-Socratic Greek philosopher whose opinions were very influential on later Greek philosophy. He was the first to propose that all matter was made of the four elements – earth, air, fire and water. This later became the basis for Aristotle's science, which endured until the modern era. Aristotle also names him as the inventor of rhetoric. Empedocles was the first to conclude that the Moon shines by reflected light from the Sun.

EUCLID – (Ευκλείδης, circa 325-265 B.C.) lived and worked at the great Museum of Alexandria and is considered to be the father of geometry. Borrowing from many sources and compiling all known geometrical knowledge, Euclid wrote the *XIII Books of the Elements,* which remains the standard work on geometry, over 2300 years later. In addition to the latter famous work, Euclid also wrote *Phaenomena,* the seminal work of astronomical spherical geometry, a mathematical treatment of the celestial sphere and its circles, great and small.

FRANCIS - *Francis of Assisi* (A.D. 1182-1226) was born into a wealthy family but embraced poverty and a simple life after devoting his life to Jesus. He took up the life of an itinerate street evangelist in medieval Italy, and started a religious order called "The Little Brothers of Jesus." Though a Roman Catholic saint, he is popular to this day among Christians of many denominations. Francis is especially remembered for his love of animals and beautiful prayers and poems about God's creation, especially *Canticle to Brother Sun.*

GALILEO – *Galileo Galilei* (A.D. 1564-1642.) distinguished himself at an early age as a scientific experimenter. His studies proved to him first hand that the "science" of Aristotle was merely "armchair science" – derived from logic alone with no actual method of observing nature. He became an early proponent of Kopernikanism in Roman Catholic Europe, and corresponded with Kopernikan scientists in Protestant countries. The first to point a telescope to the sky, Galileo's observations of Jupiter, the Sun, and the Moon proved the falsehood of certain teachings in Aristotle's *de Caelo.* Galileo kept silent with his provocative views for 20 years at the command of the church. He got into trouble again upon publishing his *Dialogue of the Two Chief World Systems* in which he was believed to have mocked the Pope. While under house arrest he was visited by the young John Milton, who later wrote the famous poem *Paradise Lost.* Galileo died the same year his successor Isaac Newton was born.

GEMINUS – *Geminus of Rhodes* (circa 100– circa 40 B.C.) was the author of *Introduction to Astronomy,* one of the most comprehensive works on the subject up to that time. Geminus was a contemporary of Marcus Tullius Cicero, and like Cicero, studied under the great Stoic philosopher Posidonius. Little is known of the life of Geminus, and it is not known whether he personally knew Cicero or any of the other famous persons of that turbulent period.

GREGORY XIII – *Pope Gregory XIII* (1502-1585 A.D.) instituted and established the Gregorian calendar. Based on the astronomical groundwork laid by the astronomer Christopher Clavius, this calendar reform effort corrected an error in the Julian calendar, which did not conform precisely to the Sun's annual cycle. Today, the Gregorian calendar is the basis for the civil calendar for the world.

HERODOTUS – (Ηρόδοτος, circa 400 B.C.) Herodotus wrote *Histories,* the first definitive work of history. In fact, the term "history" was first coined for the title and body of this work. Herodotus's work was primarily devoted to the ongoing war between the Greeks and the Persians. It is a valuable secular source for King Cyrus and other personages known from Scripture. In addition, Herodotus gave descriptions and histories of other places in the old world including Egypt.

HIPPARCHUS – (Ιππαρχος, circa 190– circa 120 B.C.) Hipparchus was perhaps the greatest Greek astronomer of antiquity. Having obtained centuries of Babylonian astronomical records, Hipparchus discovered precession, in which the constellations of the zodiac slip through the equinoxes and solstices over a period of centuries. He is credited with inventing the epicycle, a mathematical technique for simulating the varying motions of the planets using rotating circles. A prolific writer, ironically most of Hipparchus's works are lost except for a commentary on Aratus's *Phaenomena.* Hipparchus is best known today through the works of Claudius Ptolemy, who quoted his writings and built upon his work.

HOMER – (Ὅμηρος, 8ᵗʰ or 7ᵗʰ centuries B.C.) Homer lived at the grey dawn of Greek culture, before writing was introduced into the Greek world. If there ever was a real poet named Homer, his stories probably survived in oral tradition for centuries before being written down. Homer's two great poems – the *Iliad* and the *Odyssey* – present a highly mythologized account of the legendary Trojan War, circa 1100 B.C. In the poems of Homer, one can see the hopelessness of Greek paganism, in which humans are used as mere pawns in contests between aloof, capricious, unmerciful gods. Homer's works remain a cornerstone of secular western literature.

ISIDORE – *Isidore, Bishop of Seville* (circa A.D. 560-636) was one of the rare lights of the Dark Ages. He is credited with helping to convert the Visigothic conquerors of Spain to orthodox Christianity. With classical culture in ruins throughout Europe, Isidore compiled an encyclopedia – *the Etymologies* – of all available knowledge, with a Christian commentary. The language of Isidore's writing is fascinating to philology in that it represents a transitional state between Latin and Spanish, incorporating distinguishing elements of both.

JOSEPHUS – *Flavius Josephus* (circa A.D. 37-100), the great first-century Jewish historian, wrote many works on Jewish history and culture. These valuable works are our greatest non-Biblical sources for ancient Jewish customs and traditions. Josephus's *Antiquities of the Jews* provides non-canonical insights into the events and persons of the Old Testament. His *Jewish War* describes the destruction of Jerusalem by the Romans. Significantly for Christians, Josephus is an important contemporary secular source for the life and ministry of Jesus.

KOPERNIK – *Mikolaj Kopernik* (A.D. 1473-1543), a native of Poland, is best known by his pen name *Copernicus*, even though he only signed his name that way six times in his last year of life at the age of 70. Inspired by the calendar reform movement that resulted in the Gregorian calendar, Kopernik developed a radical hypothesis – that the apparent motions of the Sun could be attributed to motions of the Earth. In his *On the Revolutions*, published in A.D. 1543, Kopernik showed that the daily motion of the sky could be the result of the Earth, not the celestial sphere, rotating along its axis. The annual motion of the Sun along the ecliptic could be caused by the Earth revolving around the Sun in a planetary orbit. Kopernik's notions challenged certain Roman Catholic doctrines based on the philosophy of Aristotle, and so the Kopernikan theory originally became popular in Protestant Germany and England during the Reformation period. Kopernik's Sun-centered mathematical scheme was greatly simplified compared to the Earth-centered mathematics used up to that time, and it improved the calculations of almanacks. As almanacks became popular in the seventeenth and eighteenth centuries, they were a primary vehicle for promoting the Kopernikan theory among the common people.

LEONARDO – *Leonardo da Vinci* (A.D. 1452-1519) was the definitive "Renaissance Man," and his remarkable works spanned a wide range of human achievement. A renowned painter and sculptor, Leonardo was also an engineer and inventor. His notebooks included, among many other things, plans for a crude helicopter. He was also a student of the medical sciences and made detailed anatomical sketches from cadavers he personally dissected. In astronomy, his explanation of the earthshine went against the conventional wisdom of the time but has been vindicated by modern science.

LUCRETIUS – *Titus Lucretius Carus* (circa 95– circa 50 B.C.) was a Roman philosopher and poet of the Epicurean tradition. His work *de Rerum Natura* included numerous colorful references to Classical Astronomy, and to the seasonal cycles and the related arts of agriculture, which depend on the annual cycle of the Sun.

LUTHER – *Martin Luther* (A.D. 1483-1546), the great German reformer, was a younger contemporary of the astronomer Mikolaj Kopernik. Luther's works reveal an understanding and appreciation of Classical Astronomy, as would be expected from an educated person of that period. Luther is reported to have made critical remarks of Kopernik and the Sun-centered theory, arguing that it would contradict the Biblical account of the stopping of the Sun by Joshua. Nonetheless, Kopernik's theory first became popular in Luther's own community at Wittenberg, under Philip Melanchthon, Luther's successor. Kopernikanism flourished in Reformation Germany, while it languished under prohibition in Catholic countries.

MACROBIUS – *Ambrosius Theodosius Macrobius* (flourished circa A.D. 400) may have been a latter-day pagan, but he more likely was a Christian writing in the traditional classical style, as was common in late antiquity. Macrobius's *Commentary on Cicero's Dream of Scipio,* in addition to commenting on Cicero's poem, provides a considerable amount of astronomical background information. Macrobius's work was an invaluable source of Classical Astronomy in the early medieval period, and influenced Dante in his *Divine Comedy.* It remains today a clear, easy-to-understand reference for many key astronomical concepts. Macrobius also wrote the *Saturnalia,* which provides much detail about the Roman calendar and traditional Roman feasts.

MANILIUS – *Marcus Manilius* (flourished first century A.D.), a Latin poet, was the author of *Astronomicon.* He lived in the early Roman empire, perhaps while Jesus walked the Earth, and his poem was an early and influential work of astrology that was then becoming very popular among the Roman upper class. *Astronomicon* nevertheless includes much useful astronomy information and many colorful descriptions. This illustrates the utter dependence of the ancient pseudo-science on the legitimate science of astronomy.

COUNCIL OF NICAEA – (A.D. 325) was the first universal gathering of Christian bishops, who, in that period, presided over independent local churches with no central authority. The main purpose of the Nicene Council was to condemn the heretic Arius, who taught that Jesus was just a man adopted by the Father as His Son. In response, the Council formulated the doctrine of the Trinity, which is still affirmed by Christians today. Among other issues, the Council of Nicaea established a common Sunday celebration of the Pasch for all churches and included rules for the reckoning the time of this feast, so that all Christian churches would celebrate the LORD's Resurrection on the same day.

PLINY THE ELDER – *Gaius Plinius Secundus* (A.D. 23-79) was a keen observer of nature and a compiler of all knowledge available in the Roman world of his time. His *Natural History,* which is regarded as the first encyclopedia, encompassed legitimate science as well as fanciful folklore. For example, Pliny's Book II is dedicated to Classical Astronomy. Other portions of *Natural History* discuss mythological beasts such as griffins and minotaurs, as though they were actual creatures! Pliny's nephew – Pliny the Younger – was a Roman official who wrote one of the earliest secular accounts of Christianity and described the early Christians in a very positive light. Pliny the Elder died in A.D. 79 during a rescue operation at the eruption of Mt. Vesuvius, which also buried the Roman city of Pompeii.

PLUTARCH – *Mestrius Plutarchus* (Πλούταρχος, circa A.D. 46-127), a Greek writer in the early Roman Empire, wrote on a wide variety of subjects. Plutarch is best remembered for *Parallel Lives,* a lengthy collection of short biographies. Down through history, until the late, lamented twentieth century, *Parallel Live*s was a standard work studied by children to learn of the great men of ancient Greece and Rome. Benjamin Franklin praised the work, and Charlotte Mason recommended it. Plutarch also wrote on scientific matters, and his *Face on the Moon* is remarkable for questioning Aristotle's Earth-centered cosmology, foreshadowing the rise of Kopernikanism centuries later.

PTOLEMY – *Claudius Ptolemy* (Πτολεμαῖος, circa A.D. 90-168) was the author of important works of astronomy, geography, and geometrical optics, in addition to a work on astrology. Ptolemy's magnum opus, *Syntaxis,* was so popular that Arab astronomers called it *Al-magest*, meaning "the greatest." Ptolemy compiled all known astronomy knowledge of his time, based on the Earth-centered cosmology of Aristotle. The Almagest was the definitive work of mathematical astronomy for 1500 years, until the rise of modern science. Though his geocentric premises and mathematical technique are discredited, much of Ptolemy's astronomy is still useful today.

SACROBOSCO – *John Sacrobosco* (circa A.D. 1195– circa 1235) was the author of *Treatise on the Sphere*, a definitive work of medieval astronomy. Unlike the computistic work of Bede, which was simply based on the arithmetic of the solar and lunar cycles, Sacrobosco's *Treatise* developed the geometrical principles of spherical astronomy. Though based on geocentric premises, Sacrobosco's work is still useful today for understanding the geometry of the celestial sphere and its circles.

SHAKESPEARE – *William Shakespeare* (A.D. 1564-1616), ever-popular English poet and playwright, wrote numerous plays based on English kings and other historical figures. His works included numerous astronomical references. The passage quoted in *Signs & Seasons* is from Shakespeare's *Julius Caesar*.

SHEPHERDES KALENDER – (A.D. 1506) This was an early printed astronomical work from the English Renaissance, following the invention of the printing press. It was originally published in France in 1493, and nothing is known of the original compiler. *The Shepherdes Kalender* includes a wealth of astronomical almanack information. It is lavishly illustrated with two-color woodcuts on astronomical and theological subjects.

SIMPLICIUS – *Simplicius of Cilicia* (flourished A.D. 500) was "The Last Pagan." Simplicius was a Neoplatonist working well into the period of the Christian Roman empire. He wrote numerous commentaries on the works of Aristotle, including *de Caelo*. Simplicius taught Greek philosophy at Athens until A.D. 529, when the Christian emperor Justinian closed the pagan schools of learning and banned the practice of pagan religion. Simplicius relocated to the Persian empire, but returned two years later. It is believed he founded or influenced a school of pagan philosophy at Harran, which later became a center of Arab science.

STRABO – (Στράβων, 64 B.C. –A.D. 24) Strabo was the author of *Geographica*, a veritable travelogue of the ancient world, including colorful descriptions of notable features such as the Seven Wonders of the World. As was true of all geographical works of antiquity, Strabo's *Geography* describes notable astronomical features visible from those locations, such as the height and orientation of the Sun and visibility of certain stars from various locales.

SUETONIUS – *Gaius Suetonius Tranquillus* (circa A.D. 70-130) wrote *The Twelve Caesars*, a primary source for the lives and careers of the first Roman emperors. Suetonius is one of our main sources for Julius Caesar's adoption of the Egyptian solar calendar as the official calendar of Rome.

VIRGIL – *Publius Vergilius Maro* (70-19 B.C.) was a celebrated Roman poet. His great poem *The Aeneid* details the adventures of the legendary Aeneas, who escaped the fall of Troy to the Greeks in 1100 B.C. After many adventures, Aeneas settled in Italy, becoming the ancestor of the Roman people. Virgil's other works include *Georgics*, a poem about agriculture that included many astronomical themes. Virgil is a main character in Dante's *Divine Comedy*, the "virtuous heathen" who guides Dante through the *Inferno* and the *Purgatorio*.

WATTS – *Isaac Watts* (A.D. 1674-1748) is perhaps the most famous and prolific writer of hymns in church history. Many of his 750 hymns are still widely sung in churches today, including "O God Our Help in Ages Past" and the beloved Christmas carol "Joy to the World." Isaac Watts was also quite a scholar and an avid astronomer. He wrote several books on logic, and also *The First Principles of Astronomy and Geography* in A.D. 1726.

Astronomical Tables – For Finding the Stars and Planets

Table I – Finding Orion

(Note: Orion's annual cycle begins with its heliacal rising in August, as explained in Chapter 6.)

Month	Rising	Southing	Setting	Best Time to View	Where to Look
January	4:00 PM (day)	10:00 PM	4:00 AM	Before Midnight	(At Meridian)
February	2:00 PM (day)	8:00 PM	2:00 AM	Evening	(At Meridian)
March	12:00 PM (day)	6:00 PM (day)	12:00 AM	Evening	(West of the Meridian)
April	11:00 AM (day)	5:00 PM (day)	11:00 PM	Evening	(Western Sky)
May	9:00 AM (day)	3:00 PM (day)	9:00 PM	Not Visible	
June	7:00 AM (day)	1:00 PM (day)	7:00 PM (day)	Not Visible	
July	5:00 AM	11:00 AM (day)	5:00 PM (day)	Not Visible	
August	3:00 AM	9:00 AM (day)	3:00 PM (day)	Before Sunrise	(Rising)
September	1:00 AM	7:00 AM (day)	1:00 PM (day)	Before Sunrise	(Eastern Sky)
October	11:00 PM	5:00 AM	11:00 AM (day)	Early Morning	(At Meridian)
November	8:00 PM	2:00 AM	8:00 AM (day)	After Midnight	(At Meridian)
December	6:00 PM	12:00 AM	6:00 AM (day)	Midnight	(At Meridian)

Table II – Finding the Big Dipper (and Cassiopeia – across Polaris opposite the Big Dipper)

(Note: The constellations will appear near these places for about one hour before and after the indicated times.)

Month	East of the Pole	Meridian	West of the Pole	Lower Meridian	Early Evening
January	10:00 PM	4:00 AM	10:00 AM (day)	4:00 PM (day)	Dipper Rising in the East
February	8:00 PM	2:00 AM	8:00 AM (day)	2:00 PM (day)	Dipper East of Polaris
March	6:00 PM (day)	12:00 AM	6:00 AM (day)	12:00 PM (day)	Dipper High to the East
April	5:00 PM (day)	11:00 PM	5:00 AM	11:00 AM (day)	Dipper East of the Meridian
May	3:00 PM (day)	9:00 PM (day)	3:00 AM	9:00 AM (day)	Dipper at the Meridian
June	1:00 PM (day)	7:00 PM (day)	1:00 AM	7:00 AM (day)	Dipper West of the Meridian
July	11:00 AM (day)	5:00 PM (day)	11:00 PM	5:00 AM	Dipper West of Polaris
August	9:00 AM (day)	3:00 PM (day)	9:00 PM	3:00 AM	Cassiopeia Rising in the East
September	7:00 AM (day)	1:00 PM (day)	7:00 PM (day)	1:00 AM	Cassiopeia East of Polaris
October	5:00 AM	11:00 AM (day)	5:00 PM (day)	11:00 PM	Cassiopeia High to the East
November	2:00 AM	8:00 AM (day)	2:00 PM (day)	8:00 PM	Cassiopeia at the Meridian
December	12:00 AM	6:00 AM	12:00 PM (day)	6:00 PM	Cassiopeia West of Meridian

Table III – Finding the Zodiac Constellations

Find the hour at the meridian for each constellation in each month
(Note: The constellations will appear near the meridian for about one hour before and after the indicated times.)

(* = Daylight Savings Time)

	January	February	March	April *	May *	June *
Pisces	4:00 PM	2:00 PM	12:00 PM	11:00 AM	9:00 AM	7:00 AM
Aries	6:00 PM	4:00 PM	2:00 PM	1:00 PM	11:00 AM	9:00 AM
Taurus	8:00 PM	6:00 PM	4:00 PM	3:00 PM	1:00 PM	11:00 AM
Gemini	10:00 PM	8:00 PM	6:00 PM	5:00 PM	3:00 PM	1:00 PM
Cancer	12:00 AM	10:00 PM	8:00 PM	7:00 PM	5:00 PM	3:00 PM
Leo	2:00 AM	12:00 AM	10:00 PM	9:00 PM	7:00 PM	5:00 PM
Virgo	4:00 AM	2:00 AM	12:00 AM	11:00 PM	9:00 PM	7:00 PM
Libra	6:00 AM	4:00 AM	2:00 AM	1:00 AM	11:00 PM	9:00 PM
Scorpius	8:00 AM	6:00 AM	4:00 AM	3:00 AM	1:00 AM	11:00 PM
Sagittarius	10:00 AM	8:00 AM	6:00 AM	5:00 AM	3:00 AM	1:00 AM
Capricornus	12:00 PM	10:00 AM	8:00 AM	7:00 AM	5:00 AM	3:00 AM
Aquarius	2:00 PM	12:00 PM	10:00 AM	9:00 AM	7:00 AM	5:00 AM

	July *	August *	September *	October *	November	December
Pisces	5:00 AM	3:00 AM	1:00 AM	11:00 PM	8:00 PM	6:00 PM
Aries	7:00 AM	5:00 AM	3:00 AM	1:00 AM	10:00 PM	8:00 PM
Taurus	9:00 AM	7:00 AM	5:00 AM	3:00 AM	12:00 AM	10:00 PM
Gemini	11:00 AM	9:00 AM	7:00 AM	5:00 AM	2:00 AM	12:00 AM
Cancer	1:00 PM	11:00 AM	9:00 AM	7:00 AM	4:00 AM	2:00 AM
Leo	3:00 PM	1:00 PM	11:00 AM	9:00 AM	6:00 AM	4:00 AM
Virgo	5:00 PM	3:00 PM	1:00 PM	11:00 AM	8:00 AM	6:00 AM
Libra	7:00 PM	5:00 PM	3:00 PM	1:00 PM	10:00 AM	8:00 AM
Scorpius	9:00 PM	7:00 PM	5:00 PM	3:00 PM	12:00 PM	10:00 AM
Sagittarius	11:00 PM	9:00 PM	7:00 PM	5:00 PM	2:00 PM	12:00 PM
Capricornus	1:00 AM	11:00 PM	9:00 PM	7:00 PM	4:00 PM	2:00 PM
Aquarius	3:00 AM	1:00 AM	11:00 PM	9:00 PM	6:00 PM	4:00 PM

Table IV – First Magnitude Stars

(Note: As seen from the midtemperate latitudes of the Northern Hemisphere.)

Star Name	Magnitude (modern)	Constellation	Evening Visibility:	Name Known From:
SIRIUS	-1.46	Canis Major	Winter	Aratus
ARCTURUS	-0.04	Boötes	Spring	Aratus
VEGA	0.03	Lyra	Summer	Arabic
CAPELLA	0.08	Auriga	Winter	Ptolemy
RIGEL	0.12	Orion	Winter	Arabic
PROCYON	0.38	Canis Minor	Winter	Aratus
BETELGEUSE	0.5	Orion	Winter	Arabic
ALTAIR	0.77	Aquila	Summer	Arabic
ALDEBARAN	0.85	Taurus	Winter	Arabic
ANTARES	0.96	Scorpius	Summer	Ptolemy
SPICA	0.98	Virgo	Spring	Latin
POLLUX	1.14	Gemini	Winter	Latin
FOMALHAUT	1.16	Piscis Austrinis	Autumn	Arabic
DENEB	1.25	Cygnus	Summer	Arabic
REGULUS	1.35	Leo	Spring	Latin

Other Prominent Stars

CASTOR	1.58	Gemini	Winter	Latin
BELLATRIX	1.64	Orion	Winter	Latin
POLARIS	2.02	Ursa Minor	Always	Latin
KOCHAB	2.08	Ursa Major	Always	Arabic
ALGOL	2.12	Perseus	Autumn	Arabic
DENEBOLA	2.14	Leo	Spring	Arabic
MIZAR	2.27	Ursa Major	Always	Arabic

Table V – The Constellations of Signs & Seasons

Of the 88 Modern Constellations, 48 of Which Were Known to Aratus, 35 Are Taught Herein (Zodiac Constellations Shown in Bold)

Name	Meaning	Evening Visible	Bright Stars	Neighboring Constellations	Distinguishing Features
Andromeda	(proper name)	Autumn		Cassiopeia, Perseus, Pegasus	Andromeda Galaxy (M31)
Aries	The Ram	Autumn		Pegasus, Andromeda	Vernal Equinox – 200 B.C.
Aquarius	The Water Bearer	Autumn		Pegasus, Capricornus	The Water Jar (asterism)
Aquila	The Eagle	Summer	Altair	Sagitta, Delphinus, Ophiuchus	Part of Summer Triangle
Auriga	The Charioteer	Winter	Capella	Taurus, Perseus, Gemini	Hexagon of brighter stars
Boötes	The Herdsman	Spring	Arcturus	Ursa Major, Virgo, Leo	Shaped like a skinny kite
Cancer	The Crab	Winter		Gemini, Leo	Summer Solstice – 200 B.C.
Canis Major	The Big Dog	Winter	Sirius	Orion, Canis Minor	Sirius = Brightest Star
Canis Minor	The Little Dog	Winter	Procyon	Gemini, Orion, Canis Major	Near Milky Way, Celestial Equator
Capricornus	The Goat	Summer		Aquarius, Piscis Austrinus	Winter Solstice – 200 B.C.
Cassiopeia	The Queen	Always		Ursa Minor, Perseus	Shaped Like a "W" or a "3"
Corona Borealis	The Northern Crown	Summer		Hercules, Boötes	A tight arc of stars
Corvus	The Crow	Spring		Leo, Virgo, Crater	Fairly square-shaped
Crater	The Cup	Spring		Leo, Corvus	Actually looks like a cup
Cygnus	The Swan	Summer	Deneb	Lyra, Cassiopeia	Northern Cross (asterism)
Delphinus	The Dolphin	Summer		Sagitta, Aquila, Pegasus	Diamond pattern with "tail"
Gemini	The Twins	Winter	Castor, Pollux	Orion, Auriga, Taurus	Summer Solstice – Today
Hercules	(proper name)	Summer		Corona Borealis, Lyra	The Keystone (asterism)
Leo	The Lion	Spring	Regulus	Ursa Major, Virgo, Boötes	Trapezoid of brighter stars
Libra	The Balance	Spring		Virgo, Scorpius	Autumnal Equinox – 200 B.C.
Lyra	The Lyre	Summer	Vega	Hercules, Cygnus	Part of Summer Triangle
Ophiuchus	The Serpent Handler	Summer		Scorpius, Hercules, Aquila	Big constellation!
Orion	The Hunter	Winter	Rigel, Betelguese	Taurus, Gemini, Canis Major	Orion's Belt (asterism)
Pegasus	The Horse	Autumn	(2d mag.)	Cygnus, Cassiopeia	Great Square (asterism)
Perseus	(proper name)	Autumn	Algol	Cassiopeia, Auriga, Taurus	Algol = Eclipsing Binary
Pisces	The Fishes	Autumn		Pegasus, Aries, Aquarius	The Circlet (asterism)
Piscis Austrinus	The Southern Fish	Autumn	Fomalhaut	Aquarius, Capricornus	Low to the southern horizon
Sagitta	The Arrow	Summer		Aquila, Delphinus	Looks like an arrowhead
Sagittarius	The Archer	Summer		Scorpius, Capricornus	The Teapot (asterism)
Scorpius	The Scorpion	Summer	Antares	Sagittarius, Ophiuchus	Scorpion's Head (asterism)
Serpens Caput	The Serpent's Head	Summer		Corona Borealis, Ophiuchus	Includes a triangle of stars
Taurus	The Bull	Winter	Aldebaran	Orion, Auriga, Aries	The Pleiades (star cluster)
Ursa Major	The Great Bear	Always	(2d mag.)	Ursa Minor, Leo	The Big Dipper (asterism)
Ursa Minor	The Small Bear	Always	Polaris	Ursa Major, Cassiopeia	Polaris = the North Star
Virgo	The Maiden	Spring	Spica	Leo, Libra, Boötes	Autumnal Equinox – today

Table VI – Oppositions of the Superior Planets, A.D. 2005-2020

(including host constellation)

	2005	2006	2007	2008	2009	2010	2011	2012
Mars	Oct 30 *Aries*		Dec 18 *Gemini*			Jan 27 *Cancer*		Mar 5 *Leo*
Jupiter	Apr 4 *Virgo*	May 5 *Libra*	June 7 *Scorpius*	Jul 10 *Sagittarius*	Aug 15 *Capricornus*	Sep 20 *Pisces*	Oct 27 *Aries*	Dec 1 *Taurus*
Saturn	Jan 13 *Gemini*	Jan 27 *Cancer*	Feb 10 *Cancer*	Feb 24 *Leo*	Mar 8 *Leo*	Mar 21 *Virgo*	Apr 3 *Virgo*	Apr 15 *Virgo*

	2013	2014	2015	2016	2017	2018	2019	2020
Mars		Apr 14 *Virgo*		May 30 *Libra*		Jul 31 *Capricornus*		Oct 13 *Pisces*
Jupiter		Jan 4 *Gemini*	Feb 6 *Cancer*	Mar 8 *Leo*	Apr 8 *Virgo*	May 10 *Libra*	Jun 12 *Scorpius*	Jul 15 *Sagittarius*
Saturn	Apr 28 *Libra*	May 10 *Libra*	May 23 *Scorpius*	Jun 3 *Scorpius*	Jun 15 *Sagittarius*	Jun 27 *Sagittarius*	Jul 9 *Sagittarius*	Jul 21 *Capricornus*

Table VII – Cycles of Venus, A.D. 2005-2020

(including host constellation)

	2005	2006	2007	2008	2009	2010	2011	2012
Superior Conjunction	Mar 31 *Pisces*			Jun 9 *Taurus*		Jan 11 *Sagittarius*		
Max. Eastern Elongation	Nov 3 *Sagittarius*		Jun 9 *Cancer*		Jan 14 *Aquarius*	Aug 20 *Virgo*		Mar 27 *Aries*
Inferior Conjunction		Jan 13 *Sagittarius*	Aug 18 *Leo*		Mar 27 *Pisces*	Oct 29 *Virgo*		Jun 6 *Taurus*
Max. Western Elongation		Mar 25 *Capricornus*	Oct 28 *Leo*		Jun 5 *Pisces*		Jan 8 *Libra*	Aug 15 *Gemini*
Superior Conjunction		Oct 27 *Virgo*					Aug 16 *Leo*	

	2013	2014	2015	2016	2017	2018	2019	2020
Superior Conjunction	Mar 28 *Pisces*			Jun 6 *Taurus*		Jan 9 *Sagittarius*		
Max. Eastern Elongation	Nov 1 *Sagittarius*		Jun 6 *Cancer*		Jan 12 *Aquarius*	Aug 17 *Gemini*		Mar 24 *Aries*
Inferior Conjunction		Jan 11 *Sagittarius*	Aug 15 *Leo*		Mar 25 *Pisces*	Oct 26 *Virgo*		Jun 3 *Taurus*
Max. Western Elongation		Mar 22 *Capricornus*	Oct 26 *Leo*		Jun 3 *Pisces*		Jan 6 *Libra*	Aug 13 *Gemini*
Superior Conjunction		Oct 25 *Virgo*					Aug 14 *Leo*	

For Further Reading

Thefe additional refources will help you learn more about aftronomy and the night fky.

Sky & Telescope
The Essential Magazine of Astronomy
www.SkyTonight.com

Since 1941, *Sky & Telescope* has been the gold standard of amateur astronomy publications. The web site features highlights of celestial sights in the night sky and helps you find astronomy clubs, observatories and planetariums in your area.

The Old Farmer's Almanac
www.Almanac.com

The oldest continuous publication in the United States, *The Old Farmer's Almanac* has been around since 1792, one of the few surviving early American almanacks, (though updated for the 21st century). It is still a very valuable resource of astronomy information, and readily available at most groceries and pharmacies. Look for the new annual issue every year in the fall.

Local Planetariums, Astronomy Clubs and Observatories

There are over 1000 planetariums and hundreds of astronomy clubs in the United States. At each, you will find knowledgeable astronomy enthusiasts who would be very eager to assist you in discovering the night sky. Perhaps you can start a Christian homeschool astronomy club of your own?

Exploring Creation With Astronomy
By Jeannie Fulbright
www.JeannieFulbright.com

Take a journey through space with your young Christian homeschool students! Mrs. Fulbright has written an elementary introduction to astronomy, with many hands-on activities, all presented from a Biblical, creationist perspective. Be sure to have your young homescholars study elementary science with all the books in Jeannie's wonderful series from Apologia Press.

Astronomy and the Bible
By Donald B. DeYoung

In this fun little book, this prominent creationist astronomer answers all your astronomy questions from a Biblical perspective. Check out the other books in Dr. DeYoung's *Science and the Bible* series, along with the rest of his 15 books spanning many areas of science.

The Astronomy of the Bible
E.W. Maunder

This work is for the serious Christian astronomer ready to take the next step. Written in 1907 by the distinguished solar astronomer, famous for discovering the Maunder Minimum of the Sun's cycle, this book brilliantly weaves scientific and Biblical scholarship. This book clearly demonstrates that, in years past, many accomplished mainstream scientists were devoted Christians.

The Classical Astronomy Update
www.ClassicalAstronomy.com

The author's free email newsletter, created especially for Christian homeschoolers (though everyone is welcome!) The Update will keep you posted on happenings in the night sky, and will answer your astronomy questions, all from a Biblical point of view.

Selected Bibliography

The following Selected Bibliography lifts various fources confulted by the author. Except where fpecifically indicated, all quotations are believed to be from public domain fources or within the fcope of "Fair Ufe" in accordance with 17 U.S.C. § 107.

The Reader is encouraged to read thefe fources, and otherwife make it a practice to ftudy primary fources of knowledge, fince it is a truly edifying manner of learning a fubject.

It is efpecially recommended that the Reader obtain "Ancient Hiftory from Primary Sources" by Harvey & Laurie Bluedorn, which includes the Brainfly CDs with the texts of many fources.

Primary Sources

American Almanacks

Ames' Almanack - 1786; *Benjamin Banneker's Almanack* - 1793; *The Boston Ephemeris* - 1683 *(a.k.a Cotton Mather's Almanack)*; *The Connecticut Almanack* - 1780; *Samuel Danforth's Almanack* - 1647; *Daniel Leeds Almanack* - 1694; *The North-American Almanack* - 1787; *Pocket Almanack* - 1779; *Weatherwise's Town and Country Almanack* - 1782. *Early American Imprints, Series 1, Evans* (microfiche). In the collection of the Cleveland Public Library, http://www.cpl.org.

Aratus

A Literal Translation of the Astronomy and Meteorology of Aratus (C. Leeson Prince, translator), Farncombe and Co., Printers. 1895.

Callimachus, Lycophron, Aratus (G.R. Mair, translator), Loeb Classical Library. Harvard University Press, Cambridge, Massachusetts, 1921 (1955).

Sky Signs: Aratus' Phaenomena (Stanley Lombardo, translator). North Atlantic Books, Berkeley, California, 1983.

Aristotle

On The Heavens (J.L. Stocks, translator), *On Generation and Corruption* (H.H. Joachim, translator), *The Complete Works of Aristotle*. Princeton University Press, Princeton, New Jersey, 1984. These texts are also available on the Brainfly CD set that accompanies *Ancient History from Primary Sources* by Harvey & Laurie Bluedorn.

Augustine

Confessions, On Christian Doctrine, and *City of God* in *Select Library of the Christian Church – Nicene and Post-Nicene Fathers* (Philip Schaff, editor). Hendrickson Publishers, Peabody, Massachusetts (originally published in 1886). Also available at the Christian Classics Ethereal Library, http://www.ccel.org. *Confessions* and *City of God* included on the Brainfly CD set that accompanies *Ancient History from Primary Sources* by Harvey & Laurie Bluedorn.

Basil of Caesarea

The Hexaemeron, Select Library of the Christian Church – Nicene and Post-Nicene Fathers, Second Series (Philip Schaff and Henry Wace, editors). Hendrickson Publishers, Peabody, Massachusetts (originally published in 1895). Also available at the Christian Classics Ethereal Library, http://www.ccel.org.

Bede

De Temporvm Ratione Liber, Corpvs Christianorvm, Series Latina (translated by the present author). Brepols Turnholt, (Belgium) 1977.

The Reckoning of Time (Faith Wallis, translator) in *Translated Texts for Historians, Vol. 29.* Liverpool University Press, Liverpool, England, 1999.

John Calvin

Institutes of the Christian Religion (Henry Beveridge, translator). One-volume edition, Wm. B. Eerdmans Publishing Co., Grand Rapids, Michigan, 1989. Also available at the Christian Classics Ethereal Library, http://www.ccel.org.

Geoffrey Chaucer

The Complete Poetry and Prose of Geoffrey Chaucer (John H. Fisher, editor). Harcourt Brace College Publishers, 1989. (Dragged into contemporary English by the present author).

Cicero
On the Nature of the Gods (C.D. Yonge, translator). Harper & Brothers, Publishers, New York, 1877. PDF facsimile text on the Brainfly CD set that accompanies *Ancient History from Primary Sources* by Harvey & Laurie Bluedorn.
On the Nature of the Gods (Horace C.P. McGregor, translator). Penguin Classics, Penguin Books, New York, New York, 1972.

Dante
The Divine Comedy: Inferno and Paradiso (Charles Eliot Norton, translator). Project Gutenberg, http://www.Gutenberg.org.
The Divine Comedy (Allen Mandelbaum, translator). Everyman's Library, Alfred A. Knof, New York, Toronto, 1980, 1982, 1984.

Decree of Canopus
An Egyptian Hieroglyphic Reading Book for Beginners, by E.A. Wallis Budge (translation by the present author). Dover Publications, Inc., Mineola, New York, 1993 (originally published 1896).
Ancient Egyptian Science, Volume II: Calendars, Clocks, Astronomy, by Marshall Clagett. American Philosophical Society, Philadelphia, Pennsylvania, 1995.

Empedocles
Selections from Early Greek Philosophy, by Milton C. Nahm. Meredith Publishing Company, New York, New York, 1964.

Euclid
Euclid's Phaenomena (J.L. Berggren and R.S.D. Thomas, translators). Garland Publishing, New York, New York, 1996.

Francis of Assisi
Canticle of Brother Sun, public domain text at http://prayerfoundation.org/canticle_of_brother_sun.htm.

Benjamin Franklin (Richard Saunders, pseudonym)
The Complete Poor Richard Almanacks, Vols. I and II (facsimile edition). Imprint Society, Barre, Massachusetts, 1970.

Geminus
Greek Astronomy, by Sir Thomas L. Heath. Dover Publications, Inc., Mineola, New York, 1991 (originally published 1932).
Geminos's Introduction to the Phenomena (James Evans and J. Lennart Berggren, translators.) Princeton University Press, Princeton, New Jersey, 2006.

Gregory XIII
Inter Gravissimas -1582 A.D. (translation by the present author). http://www.thelatinlibrary.com/gravissimas.html

Asaph Hall
"On the Teaching of Astronomy in the United States." *Science,* Vol. XII, No. 288, July 6 1900. The American Association for the Advancement of Science (AAAS). Available for download at http://www.sciencemag.org/.

Homer
The Odyssey (Samuel Butler, translator). Project Gutenberg, http://www.Gutenberg.org.
The Odyssey (E.V. Rieu, translator). Penguin Classics, Penguin Books, New York, New York, 1946.

Herodotus
The History of Herodotus (George Campbell Macaulay, translator). Project Gutenberg, http://www.Gutenberg.org.
The Histories (Aubrey de Selincourt, A.R. Burn, translators). Penguin Classics, Penguin Books, New York, New York, 1972.

Holy Bible
Authorized King James Version. Harwin Press Ltd., London, 1976.
1611 Edition, King James Version. Hendrickson Publishers, Inc., Peabody, Massachusetts, 2003.
Young's Analytical Concordance to the Bible, Robert Young, Wm. B. Eerdmans Publishing Company, Grand Rapids, Michigan, 1978 printing.

Isidore of Seville
An Encyclopedist of the Dark Ages, Studies in History, Economics and Public Law, Vol. XLVIII, Number 1, Ernest Brehaut. Columbia University, New York, New York, 1912.

Josephus
   The Works of Flavius Josephus (William Whitson, A.M., translator). Baker Book House, Grand Rapids, Michigan, October 1990 printing. Also available on the Brainfly CD set that accompanies *Ancient History from Primary Sources* by Harvey & Laurie Bluedorn.

Mikolaj Kopernik (Nicholas Copernicus, pseudonym)
   Source Book in Astronomy by Harlow Shapley and Helen Howarth. McGraw-Hill Book Company, New York, New York, 1929.
   On the Revolutions of the Heavenly Spheres (Charles Glenn Wallis, translator), in *Great Books of the Western World, Vol. 15: Ptolemy, Copernicus, Kepler.* Encyclopedia Britannica, Chicago, Illinois. Reprinted with permission from Great Books of the Western World ©1952, 1990 Encyclopaedia Britannica, Inc.

Leonardo da Vinci
   The Notebooks of Leondardo da Vinci (Edward MacCurdy, translator). Konecky & Konecky, Old Saybrook, Connecticut.

Lucretius
   On the Nature of Things (William Ellery Leonard, translator). Project Gutenberg, http://www.Gutenberg.org. Also available on the Brainfly CD set that accompanies *Ancient History from Primary Sources* by Harvey & Laurie Bluedorn.
   Re Rerum Natura (W.H.D. Rouse, translator). Loeb Classical Library. Harvard University Press, Cambridge, Massachusetts, 1924 (1982).

Martin Luther
   Table Talk (William Hazlit, translator). Christian Classics Ethereal Library, http://www.ccel.org/ccel/luther/tabletalk.html.

Macrobius
   Commentary on the Dream of Scipio by Macrobius (William Harris Stahl, translator). Copyright © 1952, 1990 Columbia University Press. Reprinted with permission of the publisher.
   Macrobius, the Saturnalia, (Percival Vaughan Davies, translator). Columbia University Press, New York, New York, 1969.

Manilius
   Astronomicon, Liber Primus, (translation by the present author). http://www.thelatinlibrary.com/manilius1.html.
   Astronomica (G.P. Goold, translator). Loeb Classical Library. Harvard University Press, Cambridge, Massachusetts, 1977 (1992).

Pliny the Elder
   C. Plinius Secundus The Historie of the World, Book II, (Philemon Holland, translator). http://penelope.uchicago.edu/holland/pliny2.html. Also available on the Brainfly CD set that accompanies *Ancient History from Primary Sources* by Harvey & Laurie Bluedorn.
   Pliny's "Natural History" In Philemon Holland's Translation (selected by Paul Turner). Centaur Press Ltd., London, 1962.
   Pliny the Elder, Natural History (John Bostock, H.T. Riley, translators). Taylor & Francis, London, 1855. http://www.perseus.tufts.edu/cgi-bin/ptext?lookup=Plin.+Nat.+toc.
   Natural History, Books II and XVIII, (H. Rackham, translator). *Loeb Classical Library*. Harvard University Press, Cambridge, Massachusetts, 1950.

Plutarch
   On the Face Appearing Within the Orb of the Moon, Plutarch's Morals, Vol. 5, (William W. Goodwin, translator). Little, Brown and Company, New York, New York., 1870. Available on the Brainfly CD set that accompanies *Ancient History from Primary Sources* by Harvey & Laurie Bluedorn.
   Concerning the Face Which Appears In the Orb of the Moon, Plutarch's Moralia XII, (Harold Chernis and William C. Helmbold, translators), Loeb Classical Library. Harvard University Press, Cambridge, Massachusetts, 1957.

Ptolemy
   The Almagest, (R. Catesby Taliaferro, translator), *Great Books of the Western World, Vol. 15: Ptolemy, Copernicus, Kepler.* Encyclopedia Britannica, Chicago, Illinois. Reprinted with permission from Great Books of the Western World ©1952, 1990 Encyclopaedia Britannica, Inc.

Council of Nicaea
   "The Synodical Letter of the Nicene Council," *The Life of Constantine, Chapter XVIII* by Eusebius of Caesarea, in *Select Library of the Christian Church: Nicene and Post-Nicene Fathers, Second Series* (Philip Schaff and Henry Wace, editors). Hendrickson Publishers, Peabody, Massachusetts (originally published in 1895). Also available at the Christian Classics Ethereal Library, http://www.ccel.org. Also available on the Brainfly CD set that accompanies *Ancient History from Primary Sources* by Harvey & Laurie Bluedorn.

John Sacrobosco

The Sphere of Sacrobosco and Its Commentators, (Lynn Thorndike, translator). The University of Chicago Press, Chicago, Illinois, 1949. Used in accordance with University of Chicago Press Guidelines for Fair Use.

William Shakespeare

The Tragedy of Julius Caesar. Project Gutenberg, http://www.Gutenberg.org.

Shepherdes Kalender

The Kalender of Shepherdes (Facsimile, R. Pyson's Edition of London 1506), by H. Oskar Sommer. Kegan Paul, Trench, Trübner & Co., Ltd., London, 1892. (18 of 300 copies.)

Strabo

The Geography of Strabo, (H.C. Hamilton and W. Falconer, translators). Henry G. Bohn, London, 1854. Available on the Brainfly CD set that accompanies *Ancient History from Primary Sources* by Harvey & Laurie Bluedorn.
Geography (Horace Leonard Jones, translator), Loeb Classical Library. Harvard University Press, Cambridge, Massachusetts, 1917.

Suetonius

Suetonius: The Lives of the Twelve Caesars, text reproduced from the Loeb Classical Library, 1913. http://penelope.uchicago.edu/Thayer/E/Roman/Texts/Suetonius/12Caesars/home.html
The Twelve Caesars (Robert Graves, translator). Penguin Classics, Penguin Books, New York, New York, 1957.

Virgil

Georgics, (H. Rushton Fairclough and G.P. Goold, translators), Loeb Classical Library. Harvard University Press, Cambridge, Massachusetts, 1916 (1999). Also available on the Brainfly CD set that accompanies *Ancient History from Primary Sources* by Harvey & Laurie Bluedorn.

Isaac Watts

The Knowledge of the Heavens and the Earth made easy, etc. by Isaac Watts, J. Clark and R. Hett, London, 1726. University Microfilms. In the collection of the Cleveland Public Library, http://www.cpl.org.

Other Sources (Including Illustrations)

An Astronomical Description of the Comet by John Bainbridge, (London, 1619). *The English Experience No. 710.* Walter J. Johnson, Norwood, New Jersey, 1975.

The Complete Woodcuts of Albrecht Dürer by Dr. Willi Kurth. Dover Pictorial Archive Series. Dover Publications, Inc., Mineola, New York, 1963.

The Dore' Bible Illustrations: 241 Illustrations by Gustave Dore'. Dover Pictorial Archive Series. Dover Publications, Inc., Mineola, New York, 1974.

The Schoole of Skil, Thomas Hill (London, 1599). *The English Experience No. 607.* Theatrvm Orbis Terrarvm, Amsterdam & De Capo Press Inc., New York, 1973.

Lore and Lure of Outer Space by Ernst and Johanna Lehner. Tudor Publishing Company, 1964. Reprinted as *Astrology and Astronomy: A Pictorial Archive of Signs and Symbols.* Dover Publications, Inc., Mineola, New York, 2005.

Symbols, Signs & Signets by Ernst Lehner. Dover Publications, Inc, New York, New York, 1969.

Webster's Third New International Dictionary of the English Language, Unabridged. G. & C. Merriam & Co., Springfield, Massachusetts, 1961.

Wikipedia - The Free Encyclopedia. http://www.wikipedia.org/

Selected Index

Star and Constellation Names are Indicated in Boldface, Books of Scripture are Indicated in Italics

A

Abraham 6, 77, 79
Acts, Book of 35, 85, 177, 237
Adam 77
Ahaz, Dial of 12
Alaska 104, 115, 198
Aldebaran 84, 88, 120, 132, 155, 158, 224, 246
Alexander the Great 131, 147, 237, 238
Algol 130, 246
almanack 7, 8, 35, 211, 229, 237, 238, 242
Altair 120, 128, 246
Andromeda 129, 130, 219, 246
Antares 88, 126, 155, 158, 224, 246
Aphrodite 147, 150 *(See Venus)*
apparition 153, 159, 229
April 99, 123, 138, 175, 211, 212, 216, 243, 244
Aquarius 91, 129, 207, 214, 244, 246, 248
Aquila 128, 245, 246
Aratus 29, 33, 34, 35, 45, 51, 58, 69, 83, 84, 86, 87, 88, 90, 91, 121, 122, 125, 127, 129, 130, 132, 143, 169, 230, 237, 245, 246, 251
Archer 90, 113, 114, 128, 138, 139, 140, 246 *(See Sagittarius)*
Arcturus 125, 126, 127, 141, 143, 246
Ares 126, 147 *(See Mars)*
Aristotle 6, 27, 37, 61, 71, 73, 229, 237, 238, 239, 240, 241, 242, 251
armillary 38, 53, 81, 110, 229
Arrow 128, 246 *(See Sagitta)*
Astarte 177
asterism 31, 32, 86, 128, 139, 246
astrology 35, 77, 75, 76, 147, 229, 234, 236, 241
atmosphere 17, 201, 236
atomic time 8, 182, 183
August 106, 107, 128, 171, 174, 232, 243, 244
Augustine 4, 10, 238, 251
Augustus 88, 174, 238
Auriga 123, 245, 246
Austria 177
autumn 95, 112, 134, 142, 161, 164, 195, 214, 230, 234

autumnal equinox 86, 87, 108, 133, 137, 141, 162, 164, 174, 206, 211, 230, 231
axis 43, 80, 94, 192, 196, 214, 230, 234, 240

B

Babel, Tower of 78
Babylon 6, 78, 131, 147
Babylonians 169
backyard compass 189, 190, 191, 192, 195, 196, 197, 198, 199, 201, 203, 207, 212, 213, 216, 225
Balance 87, 88, 109, 125, 139, 246 *(See Libra)*
Banneker's Almanack 36, 251
Basil, Bishop of Caesarea 15, 18, 24, 59, 63, 67, 98, 159, 237, 251
Bede, the Venerable 177, 178, 179, 237, 238, 242, 251
Bernice 171, 238
Betelgeuse 122
Bible vii, xi, 4, 6, 7, 12, 34, 35, 75, 76, 78, 125, 132, 170, 177, 237, 238, 249, 252, 254
Bull 33, 35, 84, 85, 100, 102, 123, 132, 136, 138, 140, 142, 246 *(See Taurus)*
Byrhtferth's Manual 176, 238
Byzantine empire 131

C

Caesar 5, 6, 88, 173, 174, 176, 179, 232, 238, 242, 254
calendar xi, 5, 6, 7, 33, 56, 57, 70, 122, 143, 167, 168, 169, 170, 172, 173, 174, 175, 176, 177, 178, 179, 180, 181, 182, 201, 202, 230, 232, 233, 237, 238, 239, 240, 241, 242
calendar reform 173, 180, 239, 240
Calvin, John 2, 79, 238, 251
Canada 104, 198
Cancer 86, 104, 105, 114, 124, 133, 234,

236, 244, 246, 247, 248
Canis Major 33, 122, 218, 245, 246
Canopus, Decree of 171, 172, 252
Capella 120, 123, 130, 137, 141, 218, 221, 246
Capricornus 90, 115, 129, 217, 234, 244, 246, 247, 248
cardinal 19, 24, 189, 190, 196, 207, 225, 231, 232, 233, 235, 236
Cassiopeia 32, 42, 44, 45, 46, 119, 123, 129, 130, 137, 140, 141, 142, 195, 196, 197, 198, 207, 218, 220, 233, 243, 246
Castor 85, 122, 138, 139, 246
Cepheus 129
Chaldeans 6, 77
Charioteer 123, 246
Chaucer, Geoffrey xi, 76, 98, 101, 112, 238, 251
Chelae 88 *(See Libra)*
Chicago 102, 198, 253, 254
Christ 202, 227
Christian 7, 147, 176, 177, 178, 179, 181, 234, 237, 238, 240, 241, 242, 249, 251, 253
Christmas 176, 179, 182, 242
Chronicles, Second Book of 57
Cicero, Marcus Tullius xi, 6, 7, 14, 31, 92, 95, 145, 146, 155, 161, 238, 239, 252
Circlet 83, 207, 214, 246
circumpolar 45, 46, 196, 197, 198, 229, 233
civil calendar 100, 170, 176, 178, 181, 239
Claws 88, 112 *(See Libra)*
Cleopatra 173, 238
Cleveland xii, 102, 198, 213, 251, 254
compass 17, 20, 21, 22, 23, 50, 189, 190, 191, 192, 193, 195, 196, 197, 198, 199, 201, 203, 206, 207, 212, 213, 216, 218, 224, 225, 230, 231, 232, 233, 235, 236
conjunctions 157, 158, 159, 160, 223, 224, 225, 226
constellations 3, 31, 33, 39, 42, 46, 51, 52, 71, 73, 75, 76, 82, 84, 88, 91, 92, 93, 94, 96, 101, 120, 121, 123, 124, 125, 129, 130, 132, 133, 136, 139, 145, 146, 148, 156, 160, 162, 187, 195, 196, 197, 205, 206, 207, 208, 209, 211, 214, 215, 216, 217, 218, 219, 223, 224, 225, 226, 229, 230, 231, 234, 236, 237, 239, 243, 244
Corinthians, First Letter to 37, 119
Corona Borealis 127, 246
Corvus 124, 246
cosmic 8, 134, 135
Crab 86, 89, 105, 106, 124, 246 *(See Cancer)*

Crater 124, 246
crescent 5, 55, 58, 59, 61, 62, 65, 70, 158, 201, 202, 203, 204, 225, 230, 231, 234
Cross, Southern 46
Cross, Northern 128, 246
Crow 124, 246 *(See Corvus)*
Crown, Northern 127, 246 *(See Corona Borealis)*
Cup 124, 246 *(See Crater)*
Cygnus 128, 245, 246
Cyrus 131, 239

D

Daniel 5, 131, 184
Dante 115, 116, 120, 238, 241, 242, 252, xi
dawn 3, 9, 10, 18, 31, 34, 69, 74, 117, 143, 168, 231, 236, 240
day vii, ix, x, xi, xii, 1, 2, 3, 4, 5, 7, 9, 10, 12, 13, 14, 16, 17, 18, 19, 20, 21, 24, 26, 27, 29, 33, 41, 48, 49, 51, 55, 56, 63, 64, 65, 68, 70, 71, 72, 73, 89, 90, 93, 97, 98, 100, 101, 102, 103, 105, 106, 107, 108, 111, 112, 113, 114, 115, 116, 117, 119, 121, 131, 134, 136, 137, 141, 142, 143, 147, 154, 161, 168, 169, 170, 171, 172, 173, 174, 175, 176, 178, 179, 180, 181, 182, 183, 189, 190, 191, 192, 194, 197, 198, 199, 201, 202, 203, 204, 211, 212, 219, 220, 221, 225, 226, 229, 230, 231, 232, 233, 234, 235, 236, 238, 239, 241, 243
daylight ix, 5, 10, 13, 16, 59, 64, 68, 87, 93, 95, 97, 99, 100, 102, 103, 105, 106, 109, 111, 112, 117, 134, 135, 140, 163, 164, 165, 190, 191, 192, 204, 211, 212, 213, 219, 220, 229, 230, 231, 232, 233, 235, 236
December 107, 113, 115, 116, 129, 174, 182, 211, 215, 220, 221, 232, 236, 243, 244
Delphinus 128, 246
Deneb 120, 128, 246
depressed 45, 46, 95, 113, 233
Deuteronomy 78, 175
dial 12, 13, 110, 204, 220, 226, 231, 235
Dipper 20, 31, 32, 33, 34, 35, 42, 44, 45, 52, 84, 88, 119, 123, 124, 125, 126, 137, 140, 141, 142, 143, 195, 196, 197, 198, 207, 217, 218, 219, 220, 229, 243, 246
directions 10, 19, 20, 21, 24, 53, 187, 189, 190, 191, 195, 198, 212, 217, 218, 225

Dog Star 33, 122, 246 *(See Sirius)*
Dog Days 170, 171
Dolphin 128, 246 *(See Delphinus)*
Dore', Gustave 176, 254
Durer, Albrecht 2, 6
dusk 16, 236
dwarf planet 75

E

Eagle 128, 246 *(See Aquila)*
Earth viii, 1, 4, 5, 6, 7, 8, 16, 17, 18, 23, 27,
        36, 37, 38, 39, 40, 41, 42, 43, 44, 45,
        50, 51, 55, 56, 57, 58, 59, 60, 61, 62,
        63, 64, 65, 71, 73, 74, 75, 79, 80, 94,
        95, 98, 99, 102, 103, 104, 106, 107,
        113, 115, 116, 117, 119, 124, 145, 148,
        150, 151, 152, 153, 154, 155, 156, 170,
        182, 183, 191, 192, 201, 203, 211, 212,
        214, 219, 223, 230, 231, 232, 233, 234,
        235, 236, 238, 240, 241, 254
earthshine 59, 201, 231, 240
east 8, 17, 18, 21, 22, 41, 44, 50, 52, 58, 61,
        62, 64, 65, 66, 67, 73, 83, 84, 86, 87,
        90, 91, 92, 94, 96, 98, 101, 108, 112,
        114, 116, 121, 122, 123, 127, 128, 129,
        133, 134, 140, 142, 143, 145, 151, 155,
        177, 190, 192, 195, 196, 197, 198, 199,
        206, 207, 212, 213, 216, 218, 220, 224,
        225, 229, 231, 232, 236
Easter 174, 176, 177, 178, 179, 181, 202,
        231, 234, 237
Ecclesiastes, Book of 17
eclipse 18, 72, 96, 231
ecliptic 72, 73, 74, 75, 76, 80, 81, 82, 83,
        84, 85, 86, 87, 88, 89, 90, 91, 94, 95,
        96, 97, 102, 103, 104, 113, 114, 117,
        121, 127, 137, 146, 150, 155, 158, 160,
        206, 208, 209, 211, 212, 215, 217, 224,
        225, 226, 230, 231, 232, 235, 236, 240
Egypt 6, 23, 63, 77, 131, 133, 170, 171, 173,
        174, 175, 176, 232, 234, 237, 238, 239
Egyptians 6, 122, 170, 171, 172
elevated pole 42, 45, 95, 110, 230, 232, 233,
        234
elongation 151, 152, 153, 156, 224, 231,
        233
Empedocles 56, 238, 252
England 181, 198, 237, 240, 251
Eostre 177
equator 51, 52, 53, 73, 80, 81, 83, 86, 87,
        91, 92, 94, 95, 97, 98, 104, 108, 112,

115, 117, 122, 161, 164, 196, 198, 199,
        206, 207, 208, 225, 230, 231, 232, 235,
        236
equinoctial 51, 81, 97, 101, 108, 112, 164
equinox 83, 86, 87, 91, 97, 98, 101, 102,
        105, 108, 115, 133, 135, 137, 141, 142,
        161, 162, 163, 164, 167, 174, 176, 178,
        179, 180, 182, 206, 211, 212, 214, 216,
        230, 231, 232, 234, 235, 236
Esther 175
Euclid 40, 239, 252
Europe 7, 19, 104, 181, 229, 237, 239, 240
Evening Star 146, 150, 206, 236, 243, 245,
        246
Exodus, Book of 63, 175, 174
Ezra 131, 175

F

fall 5, 20, 81, 101, 108, 109, 112, 117, 164,
        169, 190, 199, 214, 232, 242, 249
February 107, 116, 122, 132, 180, 181, 224,
        232, 233, 243, 244
Fishes 83, 98, 129, 136, 142, 246 *(See
        Pisces)*
Fomalhaut 120, 129, 142, 246
Francis of Assisi 9, 239, 252, 253
Franklin, Benjamin 97, 181, 237, 241, 252

G

galaxy 233
Gemini 85, 86, 105, 122, 133, 136, 139,
        142, 161, 162, 163, 164, 165, 206, 207,
        208, 209, 211, 214, 215, 218, 234, 235,
        244, 245, 246, 247, 248
Geminus 38, 89, 93, 103, 108, 113, 114,
        149, 150, 151, 168, 169
Genesis 1, 3, 4, 230
geocentric 6, 10, 17, 27, 192, 219, 242
Gethsemane, Garden of 63, 176, 202
gibbous 61, 62, 66, 67, 68, 158, 201, 202,
        203, 225, 226, 231, 234
globe 17, 39, 43, 66, 95, 103, 109, 117, 187,
        192, 196, 198, 203, 208, 214, 215, 217,
        219
gnomon 11, 12, 110, 235
Goat 90, 91, 114, 115, 129, 138, 142, 246
        (See Capricornus)
God ix, xii, 1, 4, 9, 10, 17, 29, 30, 34, 39, 46,

49, 53, 57, 63, 71, 76, 77, 78, 79, 111, 131, 166, 175, 183, 185, 205, 230, 231, 237, 242, 251

Great Square 129, 140, 141, 142, 246

Greece 12, 20, 131, 172, 241

Greeks 3, 6, 7, 76, 82, 83, 88, 146, 169, 172, 230, 239, 242

Gregorian calendar 180, 181, 182, 232, 239, 240

Gregory XIII 180, 181, 232, 239, 252

H

Hall, Asaph xii, 187, 252

heathen 77, 78, 242

Hebrew 34, 76, 77, 79, 125, 169, 175, 176, 177, 232, 234, 236

heliacal 133, 135, 153, 156, 171, 229, 243

heliocentric 7, 155, 192

Hercules 127, 139, 219, 246

Hermes 147 *(See Mercury)*

Herodotus 239, 252

Hesperos 146, 147, 150

Hipparchus 179, 180, 239

horizon 4, 9, 18, 20, 23, 32, 36, 40, 42, 45, 46, 47, 48, 49, 52, 53, 60, 61, 63, 65, 70, 71, 87, 95, 98, 101, 103, 104, 112, 113, 115, 116, 121, 126, 128, 134, 136, 137, 138, 139, 140, 141, 161, 190, 191, 192, 193, 194, 195, 197, 199, 201, 202, 204, 207, 212, 215, 216, 217, 218, 220, 221, 224, 225, 229, 230, 231, 232, 233, 234, 235, 236, 246

hours 13, 14, 41, 42, 44, 65, 66, 67, 69, 70, 97, 98, 100, 102, 114, 123, 132, 134, 135, 136, 140, 143, 154, 158, 163, 167, 168, 179, 182, 187, 194, 195, 196, 202, 203, 206, 211, 215, 216, 217, 219, 220, 230, 231, 232, 235, 236

Hyades 84, 132

I

Iceland 115

inclination 80

India 131, 237

inferior 148, 151, 152, 157, 223, 229, 232, 233, 235

insolation 107

intercalary 168, 169, 174, 175, 180, 232,

238

Iran 131

Iraq 131

Isaiah 11, 34, 70, 167

Ishtar 177

Isidore of Seville 17, 34, 41, 43, 146, 147, 155, 240, 252

Israel 29, 63, 174, 175

Israelites 56, 57, 63, 168, 174, 176, 234

J

January 97, 112, 115, 132, 181, 182, 243, 244

Jeremiah, Book of 78

Jesus vii, 5, 63, 176, 177, 178, 202, 231, 234, 239, 240, 241

Job, Book of 33, 39, 76, 84, 125, 132, 236

John, Gospel of 76

Josephus, Flavius 77, 175

Julian calendar 6, 173, 174, 178, 180, 181, 182, 232, 239

July 105, 106, 126, 133, 170, 171, 174, 243, 244, 252

June 102, 106, 107, 126, 174, 211, 215, 220, 232, 235, 243, 244, 247

Jupiter 75, 146, 147, 149, 150, 158, 159, 223, 225, 239, 247

K

Keystone 127, 219, 246 *(See Hercules)*

Kopernik, Mikolaj 23, 42, 73, 180, 240, 253

Kronos 147 *(See Saturn)*

L

lag of the seasons 107, 116

leap year 139, 174, 178, 179, 180, 181, 183, 232, 233, 238

Leo 86, 123, 124, 136, 137, 142, 143, 207, 219, 224, 244, 245, 246, 247, 248

Leonardo da Vinci 59, 240, 253

Libra 87, 88, 98, 112, 125, 244, 246, 247, 248

Lion 35, 86, 89, 106, 108, 123, 124, 139, 246 *(See Leo)*

LORD ix, 1, 2, 12, 16, 26, 33, 34, 35, 36, 53, 56, 57, 63, 70, 77, 78, 79, 84, 93, 97, 160, 167, 168, 174, 175, 181, 231
Lucretius 19, 41, 168, 171, 240, 253
luminaries 1, 3, 5, 8
Luther, Martin 79, 240, 253
Lyra 127, 245, 246
Lyre 127, 246 *(See Lyra)*

M

Macedonia 131
Macrobius 5, 6, 12, 19, 46, 55, 61, 72, 96, 138, 139, 158, 238, 241, 253
magnitude 119, 120, 122, 123, 124, 125, 126, 127, 128, 129, 130, 132, 137, 145, 149, 150, 151, 155, 157, 180, 217, 218, 219, 224, 233
Maiden 87, 108, 124, 246 *(See Virgo)*
Manilius 20, 34, 87, 91, 241, 253
March 97, 99, 115, 117, 122, 135, 174, 175, 178, 179, 180, 182, 190, 204, 211, 213, 215, 216, 220, 232, 236, 243, 244
Mars 75, 126, 146, 147, 150, 154, 158, 159, 223, 225, 247
Mather, Cotton 35, 237
May 100, 106, 123, 135, 138, 211, 212, 243, 244, 247
Mediterranean 131
Medusa 130
Mercury 74, 75, 146, 147, 151, 152, 159, 232, 233
meridian 14, 16, 19, 47, 48, 49, 50, 52, 53, 60, 64, 65, 66, 67, 70, 82, 85, 92, 100, 102, 109, 110, 123, 125, 126, 128, 132, 134, 135, 136, 137, 141, 142, 152, 153, 161, 163, 164, 165, 194, 196, 197, 198, 199, 202, 203, 204, 206, 207, 209, 211, 213, 216, 217, 218, 219, 220, 224, 225, 226, 229, 231, 232, 233, 234, 235, 236, 244
Mesopotamia 6, 34, 168, 172
Meton 169
midnight 48, 55, 66, 67, 69, 132, 133, 134, 135, 136, 137, 140, 141, 142, 153, 154, 165, 195, 198, 199, 202, 206, 207, 215, 217, 219, 220, 229, 232, 233, 234
Milky Way 29, 30, 33, 51, 85, 90, 122, 123, 128, 140, 217, 218, 233, 246
Mohammed 131
month ix, x, 2, 5, 55, 56, 57, 58, 62, 63, 64, 66, 67, 69, 70, 72, 85, 88, 89, 92, 94,

100, 106, 107, 109, 138, 139, 149, 150, 154, 156, 157, 161, 167, 168, 169, 171, 172, 173, 174, 175, 176, 177, 178, 180, 182, 197, 202, 203, 206, 211, 215, 216, 217, 218, 219, 220, 221, 224, 225, 226, 230, 233, 235, 236, 237, 244
Moon vii, viii, ix, x, xi, 1, 2, 3, 4, 5, 6, 7, 8, 17, 18, 24, 25, 27, 29, 41, 49, 53, 55, 56, 57, 58, 59, 60, 61, 62, 63, 64, 65, 66, 67, 68, 69, 70, 71, 72, 73, 74, 75, 76, 77, 78, 79, 81, 82, 88, 89, 92, 94, 96, 119, 143, 146, 149, 150, 151, 154, 156, 157, 158, 159, 160, 161, 162, 163, 164, 165, 166, 168, 169, 174, 175, 176, 178, 180, 182, 183, 187, 190, 194, 201, 202, 203, 204, 205, 211, 215, 224, 225, 226, 229, 230, 231, 232, 233, 234, 235, 236, 237, 238, 239, 241, 253
Morning Star 18, 150, 207, 236, 243
Moses 5, 168, 169, 174, 175, 176

N

nadir 48, 233, 236
Nebuchadnezzar 5
Neptune 75
Nicaea, Council of 178, 179, 180, 182, 232, 241, 253
Nile 6, 170, 171
Nimrod 78
Nisan 175, 178
noon 14, 19, 47, 64, 65, 66, 69, 100, 101, 103, 105, 106, 109, 110, 111, 112, 113, 115, 116, 117, 133, 135, 136, 161, 189, 190, 191, 192, 194, 211, 213, 214, 215, 229, 233, 234, 235, 236
north 8, 17, 18, 21, 22, 32, 43, 45, 49, 71, 73, 81, 83, 84, 89, 90, 92, 95, 97, 99, 100, 101, 102, 103, 104, 105, 106, 108, 114, 115, 116, 122, 124, 130, 140, 141, 146, 161, 189, 190, 192, 195, 196, 197, 198, 206, 207, 208, 212, 213, 216, 218, 225, 226, 230, 232, 235, 236
November 111, 112, 129, 134, 204, 213, 215, 220, 243, 244
Numa Pompillus 173

O

occultation 158

October 109, 129, 180, 181, 232, 243, 244, 253
Odyssey 52, 240, 252
Ophiuchus 88, 90, 127, 246
opposition 154, 155, 156, 158, 159, 162, 164, 223, 224, 231, 234, 235
orbit 55, 57, 58, 59, 62, 64, 65, 74, 80, 92, 95, 102, 106, 148, 152, 153, 155, 156, 180, 182, 183, 201, 203, 212, 223, 231, 232, 234, 235, 240
Orion 33, 34, 35, 51, 52, 53, 83, 84, 85, 87, 88, 119, 122, 123, 132, 133, 134, 135, 136, 138, 139, 142, 143, 164, 169, 171, 195, 196, 199, 206, 207, 208, 215, 218, 219, 220, 233, 243, 245, 246, iii, iv

P

pagan xi, 35, 77, 78, 131, 147, 167, 177, 237, 241, 242
Pasch 177, 178, 182, 231, 234, 241
Passover 63, 169, 174, 175, 176, 177, 178, 202, 234
Pegasus 129, 130, 141, 142, 246
Pentecost 176
Perseus 129, 130, 131, 132, 245, 246
Persians 131, 237, 242
pesach 177, 234
Phaethon 146
Phainon 146, 147, 149
phase 55, 57, 58, 59, 60, 61, 62, 64, 157, 162, 201, 202, 204, 224, 225, 226, 230, 231, 233, 234, 236
Phosphoros 146, 150
Pisces 83, 86, 91, 105, 129, 138, 139, 140, 141, 161, 162, 163, 164, 165, 207, 208, 211, 212, 214, 215, 217, 236, 244, 246, 247, 248
Piscis Austrinus 129, 245, 246
planetarium vii, 38, 187
Pleiades 33, 84, 132, 140, 219, 246
Pliny xi, 2, 6, 20, 21, 37, 57, 58, 68, 170, 174, 189, 241, 253
Plutarch 62, 241, 253
Pluto (useless iceball, former planet) 75, 234
Pointers 32
Polaris 32, 43, 44, 46, 80, 94, 113, 119, 124, 126, 140, 141, 195, 196, 197, 198, 199, 207, 229, 234, 243, 246
Pollux 85, 120, 122, 138, 139, 246
precession 83, 105, 114, 208, 234, 236, 239
Procyon 120, 122, 246

Proverbs, Book of 1, 53
Protestant 181, 239, 240
Psalms, Book of 9, 14, 27, 49, 55, 71, 166, 237
pseudoscience 75, 229
Ptolemy, Claudius 6, 23, 73, 119, 120, 128, 179, 180, 233, 239, 241, 245, 253
Ptolemy III Euregetes 171, 238
Pyrois 146, 147, 150

Q

quadrature 153, 154, 156, 164
Quadrivium viii

R

Ram 83, 84, 91, 99, 100, 132, 136, 138, 140, 246 *(See Aries)*
Regulus 86, 87, 88, 123, 155, 158, 224, 246
retrogradation 155, 234, 235
Revelation, Book of 183
Rigel 120, 122, 246
Romans 6, 14, 88, 104, 147, 176, 230, 238, 240
Rome 6, 78, 85, 131, 172, 173, 176, 178, 232, 241, 242
Romulus 172, 173
Rosh Hashana 169
rotation , 27, 42, 44, 64, 71, 73, 80, 82, 95, 182, 183, 192, 195, 196, 197, 199, 215, 230, 231, 232, 234

S

Sacrobosco, John 13, 40, 41, 42, 51, 81, 104, 133, 134, 242, 254
Sagitta 128, 246
Sagittarius 90, 128, 136, 140, 141, 161, 162, 163, 164, 207, 208, 209, 211, 214, 215, 234, 236, 244, 246, 247, 248
Saturn 75, 146, 147, 149, 150, 159, 223, 225, 247
Scandinavia 115
Schiller, Julius 35
Scorpion 35, 87, 88, 89, 90, 112, 113, 126, 127, 246 *(See Scorpius)*

- 260 -

Scorpius 88, 90, 126, 127, 207, 224, 244, 245, 246, 247

Scripture 17, 34, 77, 89, 169, 239

seasons 3, 5, 8, 13, 56, 71, 73, 76, 81, 92, 93, 94, 95, 107, 109, 110, 111, 116, 117, 121, 123, 132, 143, 162, 163, 165, 166, 167, 168, 169, 173, 174, 181, 182, 184, 199, 206, 211, 212, 213, 214, 216, 225, 226, 230, 234, 235, 236

second 4, 8, 73, 108, 119, 122, 123, 125, 126, 129, 130, 150, 178, 182, 183, 206, 233, 236

September 108, 109, 128, 133, 142, 174, 181, 190, 211, 215, 220, 230, 243, 244

Seth 77

shadow 9, 12, 13, 17, 18, 20, 21, 29, 56, 60, 95, 101, 102, 103, 108, 161, 189, 190, 192, 212, 214, 225, 231, 235

Shakespeare, William 43, 242, 254

Shepherdes Kalendar 5, 30, 48, 93, 167, 242, 254

signs 1, 8, 17, 26, 30, 53, 89, 93, 98, 106, 109, 111, 132, 143, 166, 167, 189, 214, 219, 230, 235

Simplicius 107, 242

Sirius 33, 122, 133, 145, 149, 150, 151, 170, 171, 246

skycraft 7, 8, 184

solar 6, 22, 39, 56, 74, 76, 80, 96, 107, 122, 143, 149, 155, 160, 167, 168, 169, 170, 172, 173, 174, 176, 179, 211, 217, 223, 232, 233, 235, 236, 238, 242, 249

solstice 85, 86, 90, 102, 103, 104, 105, 113, 114, 115, 124, 134, 136, 138, 139, 140, 141, 161, 163, 165, 174, 206, 211, 212, 214, 234, 235, 236

Sosigenes 173

south 8, 17, 21, 49, 51, 71, 81, 83, 85, 86, 87, 92, 97, 99, 101, 104, 106, 109, 112, 114, 115, 122, 124, 125, 126, 129, 142, 146, 161, 189, 190, 195, 196, 198, 199, 206, 207, 208, 212, 216, 218, 219, 225, 226, 232, 233, 235, 236

sphere 37, 38, 39, 40, 41, 42, 43, 45, 47, 48, 50, 51, 53, 61, 71, 72, 73, 74, 81, 86, 97, 101, 110, 148, 199, 208, 229, 230, 231, 232, 233, 234, 235, 236, 239, 240, 242

Sphinx 24

Spica 87, 88, 120, 124, 126, 155, 158, 224, 246

spring 95, 98, 99, 100, 101, 102, 104, 105, 106, 109, 112, 115, 125, 133, 135, 136, 138, 139, 143, 161, 162, 175, 176, 190,

195, 199, 212, 219, 232, 234, 236

station 152, 235

Stilbon 146, 147, 151

Strabo 21, 45, 242, 254

Suetonius 174, 242, 254

summer 85, 86, 95, 101, 102, 103, 104, 105, 106, 107, 108, 109, 113, 114, 116, 124, 125, 126, 128, 133, 136, 137, 139, 140, 142, 161, 163, 165, 170, 171, 174, 195, 206, 211, 212, 214, 218, 232, 234, 235, 236

Sun vii, viii, ix, xi, 1, 2, 3, 4, 5, 6, 7, 8, 9, 10, 12, 13, 14, 16, 17, 18, 19, 20, 21, 22, 24, 25, 26, 27, 39, 41, 47, 48, 49, 53, 56, 57, 58, 59, 60, 61, 62, 63, 64, 65, 66, 67, 68, 69, 70, 71, 72, 73, 74, 75, 76, 77, 78, 79, 80, 81, 82, 86, 88, 89, 91, 92, 93, 94, 95, 96, 97, 98, 99, 100, 101, 102, 103, 104, 105, 106, 107, 108, 109, 110, 111, 112, 113, 114, 115, 116, 117, 119, 121, 133, 134, 135, 136, 137, 138, 139, 140, 141, 142, 143, 146, 148, 149, 150, 151, 152, 153, 154, 155, 156, 157, 159, 160, 161, 162, 163, 164, 165, 166, 168, 169, 170, 171, 172, 174, 175, 176, 179, 180, 182, 183, 187, 189, 190, 191, 192, 193, 194, 196, 202, 203, 204, 205, 211, 212, 213, 214, 215, 216, 217, 219, 220, 223, 224, 225, 226, 229, 230, 231, 232, 233, 234, 235, 236, 238, 239, 240, 241, 242, 252,

sundial 4, 12, 13, 100, 110, 183, 213, 229, 231

sunrise 9, 10, 13, 17, 18, 19, 21, 48, 64, 65, 66, 67, 68, 69, 70, 73, 96, 101, 103, 104, 109, 111, 115, 121, 132, 133, 134, 135, 136, 138, 139, 142, 146, 150, 151, 152, 153, 154, 159, 163, 171, 190, 192, 195, 197, 201, 202, 206, 207, 211, 212, 217, 219, 225, 229, 230, 231, 232, 235, 236, 237

sunset 4, 16, 17, 18, 19, 21, 58, 59, 60, 61, 63, 64, 65, 66, 67, 68, 70, 73, 96, 103, 104, 111, 115, 121, 123, 132, 134, 135, 136, 138, 139, 141, 142, 146, 150, 151, 152, 154, 156, 159, 165, 170, 190, 191, 192, 195, 201, 202, 211, 212, 217, 219, 224, 225, 229, 230, 231, 235, 236, 237

superior 148, 149, 150, 151, 152, 153, 154, 155, 156, 157, 159, 223, 224, 229, 234, 235

Swan 128, 246 *(See Cygnus)*

synodic month 168

Syria 131

T

tabernacle 9, 71, 72, 82, 92
Taurus 33, 84, 122, 132, 133, 135, 139,
    206, 211, 224, 244, 245, 246, 247, 248
teapot 90, 107, 139, 141
telescope 72, 75, 120, 149, 150, 151, 154,
    159, 187, 219, 239
temporal rising 134
Tep Renpit 171
terminator 15, 16, 56, 60, 61, 67, 103, 192,
    201, 203, 214, 219, 225, 230, 231, 234,
    235
tide 78, 79
trigonometry 6
Trinity 178, 241
trio 160
Trivium viii
tropic 102, 104, 105, 114
tropical 97, 167, 171, 174, 179, 182, 232,
    236
twilight ix, 9, 16, 29, 65, 66, 70, 96, 104,
    109, 115, 133, 134, 135, 139, 141, 158,
    159, 191, 201, 202, 217, 219, 220, 224,
    232, 236
Twins 85, 102, 105, 124, 246 *(See Gemini)*

U

Uranus 75
Ursa Major 31, 32, 229, 245, 246

V

Vega 120, 127, 128, 137, 141, 218, 221, 246
Venus 75, 146, 147, 149, 150, 151, 152,
    158, 159, 223, 224, 225, 232, 233, 248
vernal equinox 83, 86, 91, 97, 98, 101, 102,
    105, 135, 137, 142, 162, 163, 164, 167,
    174, 176, 178, 179, 180, 182, 206, 211,
    212, 216, 231, 232, 235, 236
Virgil 42, 88, 242, 254
Virgo 87, 101, 124, 125, 136, 137, 141, 143,
    161, 162, 163, 165, 207, 208, 211, 214,
    215, 224, 230, 244, 245, 246, 247, 248
volvelle 193, 194, 196, 197, 199, 203, 204,
    208, 209, 215, 216, 218, 219, 220, 221,
    226

W

waning 67, 68, 70, 162, 164, 165, 201, 205,
    225, 226, 230, 231, 236
Washington, D.C. 24, 25, 102, 237
Waterbearer 91, 116, 129, 138, 142 *(See
    Aquarius)*
Watts, Isaac 12, 137, 242, 254
waxing 58, 59, 60, 65, 66, 67, 68, 69, 70,
    165, 201, 202, 203, 204, 205, 225, 226,
    230, 231, 236
west 8, 17, 23, 41, 50, 52, 62, 66, 70, 73,
    87, 92, 94, 96, 98, 101, 108, 112, 114,
    116, 123, 125, 126, 128, 134, 135, 140,
    141, 143, 145, 152, 155, 156, 165, 190,
    192, 195, 196, 197, 198, 199, 206, 207,
    212, 213, 216, 218, 224, 231, 232, 234
winter 90, 95, 100, 112, 113, 114, 115, 116,
    121, 122, 132, 134, 135, 136, 137, 138,
    141, 142, 143, 161, 165, 174, 195, 199,
    206, 211, 214, 218, 234, 236

Y

year xi, 1, 3, 4, 5, 7, 14, 24, 35, 56, 60, 66,
    71, 73, 77, 79, 89, 93, 94, 95, 97, 100,
    102, 103, 104, 106, 110, 111, 113, 115,
    116, 117, 120, 121, 122, 123, 131, 142,
    143, 149, 150, 152, 154, 161, 163, 167,
    168, 169, 170, 171, 172, 173, 174, 175,
    176, 179, 180, 181, 182, 183, 187, 197,
    205, 211, 212, 216, 219, 220, 223, 229,
    231, 232, 233, 234, 235, 236, 237, 238,
    239, 240, 249

Z

zenith 47, 48, 85, 105, 107, 114, 126, 143,
    195, 197, 198, 218, 233, 236
Zeus 147 *(See Jupiter)*
zodiac 75, 76, 78, 79, 80, 81, 82, 83, 84,
    85, 87, 88, 89, 92, 93, 94, 95, 96, 101,
    104, 106, 112, 113, 121, 124, 127, 129,
    136, 139, 143, 145, 146, 148, 149, 150,
    152, 153, 155, 156, 157, 158, 160, 161,
    162, 170, 205, 206, 207, 208, 211, 214,
    215, 216, 217, 218, 219, 224, 225, 229,
    231, 234, 236

Notes

Notes

Notes

Notes

Notes